KT-403-684

# NEEDLECRAFTS

*Master new sewing skills with these simple-to-make projects*

MILOSAVLJEVICH, GUERRIER, HALL, MORE

CHARTWELL BOOKS, INC.

A QUINTET BOOK

Published by Chartwell Books
A Division of Book Sales, Inc.
114 Northfield Avenue
Edison, New Jersey 08837

This edition produced for sale in the U.S.A., its
territories and dependencies only.



ISBN 0-7858-0596-6

This book was designed and produced by
Quintet Publishing Limited
6 Blundell Street
London N7 9BH

Creative Director: Richard Dewing
Designer: Isobel Gillan
Project Editors: Anna Briffa, Diana Steedman
Editors: Lydia Darbyshire, Samantha Gray
Photographer: Andrew Sydenham
Illustrators: Terry Evans, Elsa Godfrey, Nicola Gregory

Typeset in Great Britain by
Central Southern Typesetters, Eastbourne
Manufactured by Eray Scan Pte. Ltd., Singapore
Printed by Star Standard Industries (Pte.) Ltd., Singapore

# Contents

# APPLIQUÉ

*Simple yet decorative effects to create wall hangings, clothes, or soft furnishings, using a variety of applique techniques*

# INTRODUCTION

Appliqué, in simplest terms, is the stitching of different fabrics to a background to create a decorative effect. The versatility of appliqué means that it can be suitable for wall-hangings and pictures, clothing and soft-furnishings of all types. The projects in this book will give you a sound basis for various appliqué techniques using hand and machine stitching with suggestions for equipment and materials, finishing techniques and how to design your own work. The projects range from the simple Pot Holder to the more complex Rainbow Trout Wall-hanging and are designed to extend your knowledge and improve your technique. They have been chosen to present as many different styles, methods, and items as possible.

## Basic Materials

### *Fabric*

Many different types and weights of fabric can be used for appliqué, although it is a good idea to choose compatible weights for both appliqué and background in any one project. Cotton fabrics have been used for the projects in this book, and are highly recommendable since they are easy to cut and stitch, adhere well with bonding and are easy to launder. It is always advisable to wash all chosen fabrics before use to check for shrinkage and color fastness.

### *Wadding*

This is a fibrous material used as a filling between layers of fabric. It is available in polyester, silk, and cotton, and is generally sold by weight per square yard. It is usually washable and requires no special treatment, although some cotton wadding or batting may need washing before use – always check the manufacturer's instructions. 2oz polyester wadding or batting is recommended as good, general, all-purpose wadding, since it is light and easy to stitch. Do not iron items once the wadding or batting is in place, since it will lose its "springy" quality.

### *Interfacing*

Fusible interfacing has been used for these projects. It has a double-sided adhesive web, bonded on one side to a paper backing. This allows accurately drawn motifs to be pressed onto fabrics before stitching by hand or machine. It is not necessary to leave a seam allowance since the bonding prevents the fabric from fraying.

To use, trace your motif onto the paper backing, remembering that the resulting image will be reversed. Press the non-paper side of the interfacing onto the wrong side of your fabric and cut out the motif, using the drawn outline as a guide. Carefully remove the paper backing from the motif, position the motif on your background fabric and iron into place.

### *Freezer paper*

The use of freezer paper as an aid to appliqué is quite recent. It has a waxy surface on one side and plain paper on the other. Primarily it is used to ensure that the appliqué motif is kept as flat as possible while being hand stitched to the background fabric. To use, transfer your motif to the plain side of the freezer paper, remembering the resulting image will be reversed. Cut the motif out, and iron the paper, waxy side down to your fabric. Cut round this with a ¼–½ inch seam allowance, which is then clipped and pressed over the paper shape before stitching it to the background fabric. The paper can be removed through a gap left, and there is no sticky residue.

Freezer paper can also be used to prevent puckering and wrinkling when a motif is sewn to a background fabric by machine and satin stitch is used. Simply iron the waxy side of a suitably sized piece of freezer paper to the underside of the background fabric to correspond with the position of the motif. Then peel off once the piece is stitched in place.

A large part of the fun of appliqué lies in choosing matching and contrasting fabrics from the vast selections available.

## Basic Equipment

### *Sewing kit*

A sewing kit with good quality tools is essential for all types of appliqué work. Equip yourself with the basics initially, and then add to your kit as you develop your skills and designs.

A basic sewing kit needs to consist of: dressmaking scissors, sharp-pointed embroidery scissors, general-purpose scissors, needles, pins, a wide range of threads, suitable for hand and machine stitching, fabric marker, thimble, tape measure, and unpicker/seam ripper.

Other items that you may wish to add are pinking shears for decorative edges, beeswax to strengthen the thread for hand quilting, and a rotary cutter which offers greater accuracy when cutting fabric.

Your basic sewing kit need not be expensive, and is essential in order to produce professional-looking work.

### *Frames*

Small appliqué projects do not generally require the use of a frame. However, using an embroidery frame can result in a better finish, since the fabric is kept taut, and allows for more accurate stitching. An embroidery frame can also be used for machine appliqué if the presser foot is removed and the feed dog dropped to allow for free-style embroidery. Practice is essential for good results.

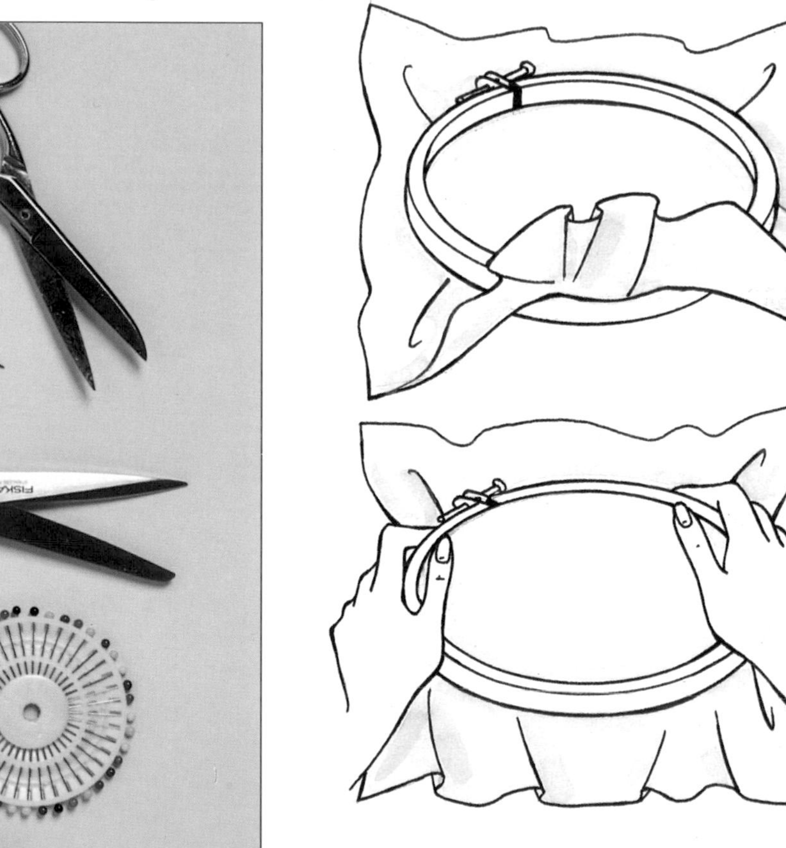

Hoops come in a wide range of sizes, and all work on the same principle as the one above.

Quilting frames can be bought in many shapes and sizes, generally larger than hand-held embroidery frames, and often free-standing, leaving both hands free for stitching.

## BASIC TECHNIQUES

### *Hand stitching*

The Turned Edge Method is always used when applying motifs by hand. Once your motif is in position on the background fabric, it can be pinned and basted. Then it can be stitched neatly in place with small stitches, always ensuring that the seam allowance is turned under with your fingers or the needle as you go.

### *Machine stitching*

Generally motifs are applied by machine using satin stitch. This is a very dense zigzag stitch, usually used for buttonholes. You will need to set the right length and width of stitch before starting, and you may wish to practice on scrap material first.

It may help to keep your motif in place using interfacing or freezer paper (see page 7).

Begin stitching at the edge of the motif and continue slowly and smoothly around the shape. Keep the needle in the fabric when changing direction, and finish off by leaving long threads which you then pull through to the wrong side and fasten off by tying together.

### *Bias strips*

The true bias of any fabric is always at a 45 degree angle to the selvedge.

To make bias strips from a square of material using the selvedge as a guide, you need to fold the material diagonally and press the fold. Mark strips of an equal width parallel to the fold, open the fabric and cut these strips. (Remember to leave a seam allowance on both edges of the strip.)

If you have no selvedge to act as a guide, you will need to establish the grain of the fabric, then measure and cut a square. Then you can proceed as before.

If the strips need to be joined, place one strip on top of another at right angles to each other with the right sides together, and stitch across the diagonal join.

### *Bias tubes*

They are used quite often in appliqué and can be made quite easily. Firstly you need to measure and cut a strip of binding which is twice the required width, plus ¼inch seam allowance on both edges. Fold the strip in half lengthwise, right sides together and stitch. It is not necessary to turn the tube to the right side, but it can be pressed with the seam in the center, hiding the raw edges.

It may help to have a press bar for this purpose. This is a precut length of heat resistant plastic which can be bought in varying widths. It is inserted into the tube and ensures that the seam is centered accurately.

## Templates

Accuracy is important when making templates in order to achieve good shapes for appliqué work.

When it comes to cutting the template out, use a craft knife or good quality paper-cutting scissors. You should never use dressmaking scissors for cutting card or paper.

### *To make templates*

1 Trace the motif using a sharp pencil and either tracing paper or template plastic. The templates need to be very accurate and have no seam allowance added. Template plastic is useful as its transparency allows the selective placement of the template onto patterned fabric.

2 The motif may need to be enlarged. Use graph paper or a photocopier and follow the scale given.

3 Cut out the motif and, if using tracing paper, glue to firm card, remembering to reverse the image if required to for the project.

4 Write any particular instructions on the template – direction of grain, number of motifs to be cut, etc.

5 Place the template onto the right side of the fabric, aligning the grain of the fabric with your line on the template. The grain of your motif should run the same way as on the background fabric.

6 Draw around the template with a marker pen or pencil and cut out with a seam allowance of ¼ inch.

A sharp pencil and good ruler are essential for template-making. Graph paper can be used to enlarge or reduce the sizes of a template, and template plastic is useful for the more accurate placing of motifs on fabrics.

## Appliqué Techniques

### *Persian appliqué*

This technique involves cutting out motifs from patterned fabrics, which are then reassembled into a new design. Motifs from several different fabrics can be used, generally on a plain background for a more striking effect.

*Shadow appliqué*

Transparent layers of fabric such as muslin, voile, and organza can be overlaid on bright colors, to produce a more subdued effect. The appliqué motifs are arranged on the background, before being covered. Careful stitching around the motif, usually by hand, ensures that it is firmly held between the layers. Embroidery on the transparent fabric can be added if extra embellishment is required.

*Padded appliqué*

Appliqué shapes can be padded in order to give the illusion of being larger and more rounded. Wadding or toy stuffing is used, and can be inserted either through a gap left in the stitching before the shape is completely applied, or by making a cut in the wrong side of the fabric, behind the applied shape, which is then overstitched after stuffing.

*Hawaiian appliqué*

Originating in Hawaii, this technique traditionally involves just one single motif being applied to a background fabric. The motif is initially cut from a piece of paper that has been folded into quarters and then eighths, and which is then attached to fabric folded in exactly the same way. This is then cut out, and the result is a symmetrical shape with 4 or 8 points. This is then applied, by hand, using the turned edge method. Striking two-color combinations are particularly effective using this method.

*Ribbon appliqué*

This is an effective and decorative way of applying fabrics to a background, and the variety of ribbons, lace, braids, and broderie anglaise available is extensive. They can be applied either flat or preformed as bows and rosettes, or can be used to form decorative patterns or highlight specific areas of design.

*Designing your own work*

Designing something that will be enjoyable to create and which will give pleasure once finished can involve a lot of planning and preparation. It is advisable to keep a design simple when aiming to create an effective example of the technique chosen, and to avoid being too ambitious, aiming to complete your work within a reasonable timescale. Color, shape, and texture are of primary importance for your design, and inspirations may come from a great many sources – items at home, holiday souvenirs, pictures from books, and magazines to name but a few.

Always look for strong, well-defined shapes which will translate easily into a flat design. Plan your ideas on paper using a geometry set if you have one. Trace shapes from pictures, and simplify them if necessary. Look at fabrics available and be inspired by the patterns, shapes, and colors.

Once you have decided on the technique and size of your finished item, draw your design to actual size, making templates for it if required, and calculate the amount of material you will need. Then you can cut out your shapes and arrange them on a background fabric, until you have an arrangement that you are happy with.

# HAWAIIAN APPLIQUÉ CUSHION

*Finished size: 18 x 18 inches*

*This cushion, which is made from medium weight cotton fabric, is decorated with a striking motif that is cut from a single piece of fabric and applied to the background fabric by hand. The vivid greens look bright and summery, and the cushion would be perfect in a conservatory, porch or sunny breakfast room.*

YOU WILL NEED

- card for template
- patterned fabric: 11 x 11 inches
- cream fabric: 1 piece 14 x 14 inches; 2 pieces, each 20 x 12 inches
- needles, sewing thread to match, scissors, pins
- plain green fabric: 2 pieces, each 14 x 3 inches; 2 pieces, each 20 x 3 inches
- muslin or cheesecloth: 20 x 20 inches
- lightweight polyester wadding or batting: 20 x 20 inches
- quilting thread

Copy the template (see page 45) and transfer it to the card. The outline given represents one-quarter of the finished shape.

1 Fold the square of patterned fabric in half, then in half again. Press with an iron and pin to hold the layers together. Place the template on the fabric, matching the edges of the template with the folds of the fabric. Hold it firmly and draw around the template. Remove the template and cut out the motif through all four layers of fabric. Remove the pins, open out the motif, and press it lightly.

2 Take the square of cream fabric and fold it diagonally into quarters. Press it lightly with an iron and open it out.

3 Place the motif on the cream fabric, using the creases to position the motif symmetrically. Pin the motif in place then baste it so that the line of stitches is about ⅜ inches from the edge of the motif.

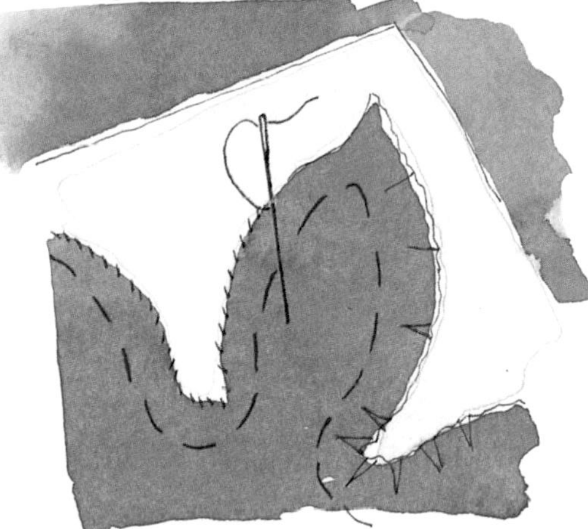

4 Use matching thread to slip stitch the motif to the cream fabric, turning under the raw edge with your needle as you work. Clip the concave curves so that they lie smoothly, and remove the basting.

5 With right sides facing, pin and baste the two short strips of plain green to opposite sides of the cream square. Stitch, leaving a seam allowance of ¼ inch. Press the seams together and outward.

6 Repeat with the two longer strips on the two remaining sides, stitching across the ends of the shorter strips as well as across the cream square. Remove pins and basting.

7 Place the muslin, wadding and cushion top on your work surface.

8 Beginning in the center and working outward in all directions, pin and baste the layers together.

9 Use quilting thread and a small running stitch to quilt a line all around the motif, about ¼ inch from the edge of the patterned fabric. If you wish, add more quilting lines. Remove pins and basting.

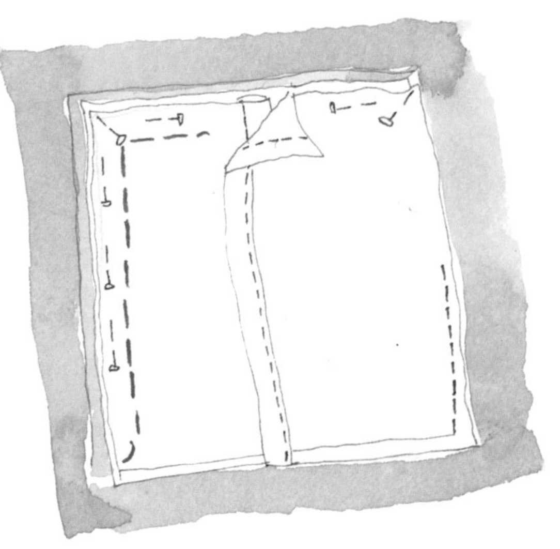

10 Take the two cream rectangles and turn in a hem of about ½ inch on one of the long edges of each piece. Lay the two pieces, right sides facing, over the cushion front. The pieces will overlap in the center. Pin and baste, then stitch around all four edges. Clip the corners, remove pins and basting and turn to the right side before inserting a cushion pad.

# STAR POT HOLDER

*Finished size: 7 x 7 inches*

*The simple four-pointed star is pieced together from diamonds made with a paper base. The star is then applied by hand to the front of the pot holder, and a layer of wadding between the back and front provides protection from hot handles and dishes. Medium weight cotton fabric is used throughout.*

YOU WILL NEED

- card and brown paper for templates
- small pieces of patterned fabric, at least 4 x 4 inches
- needles, sewing thread to match, scissors, pins
- plain fabric: 2 squares, each 7 x 7 inches
- fabric for edging, 2½ inches wide: 2 pieces, each 7 inches long; 1 piece 8 inches long; 1 piece 11½ inches long
- lightweight polyester wadding or batting: 7 x 7 inches

Trace the diamonds (see page 45) and make templates for the paper and fabric. Use the smaller diamond to cut four diamonds from the brown paper. Use the larger shape for the card template, which includes a seam allowance of ¼ inch on all sides, to draw diamonds on the patterned fabrics.

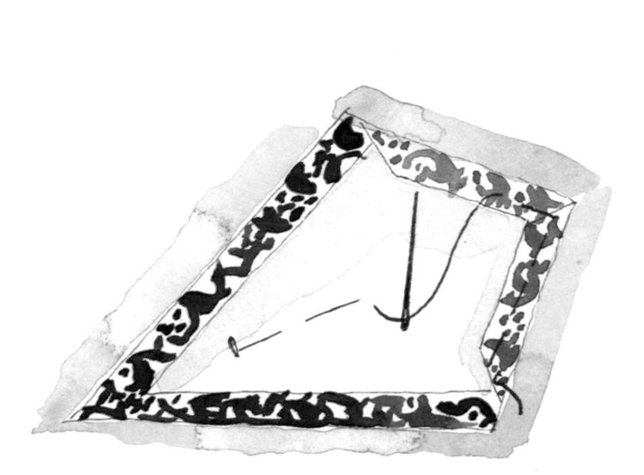

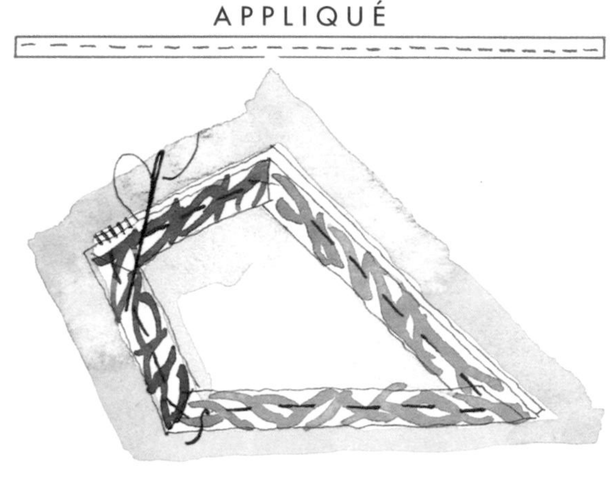

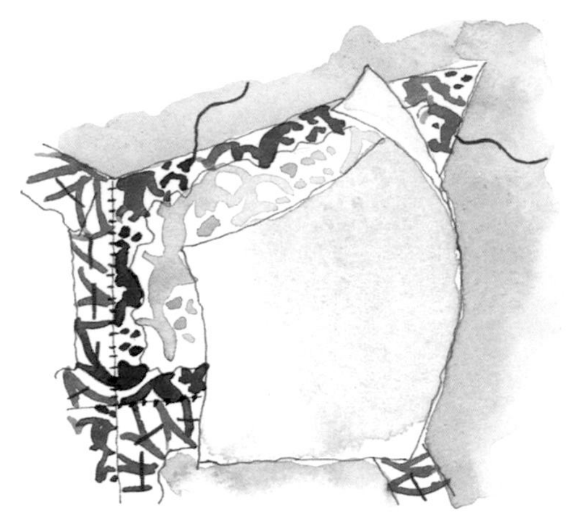

1 Cut out the four diamonds from the fabric. Place a paper diamond on the wrong side of each fabric diamond and pin it in place.

Fold the seam allowance firmly down over the paper, starting at the bottom of the diamond. Tie a knot in a length of basting thread and baste the paper and fabric together. Stitch right around each diamond, taking especial care at the points to miter the fold so that the fabric forms a neat angle.

2 Press each diamond under a hot iron and then place them on a flat surface so that they form a star.

3 Take two adjacent diamonds and, right sides facing, carefully overstitch along one short edge. Take care to match the center points and try not to stitch through the paper. Repeat with the two remaining diamonds.

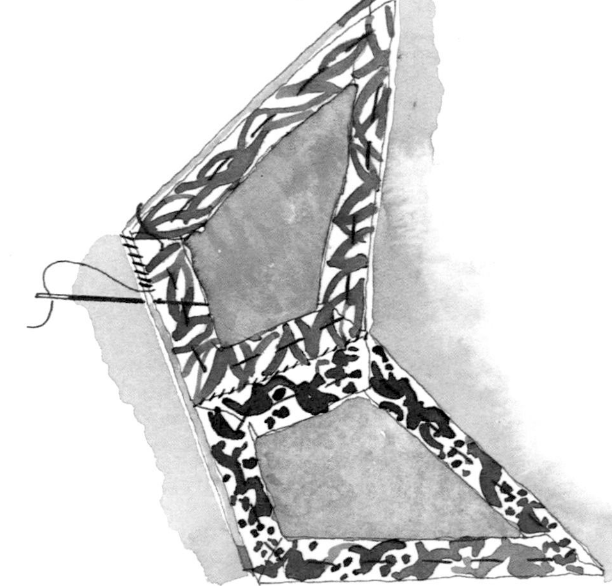

4 Complete the star shape by placing the diamonds together, right sides facing, and overstitching along the center line. Take great care to align the center point.

5 Carefully remove the basting thread from around each diamond and ease out the paper. Press and baste the free edges down again.

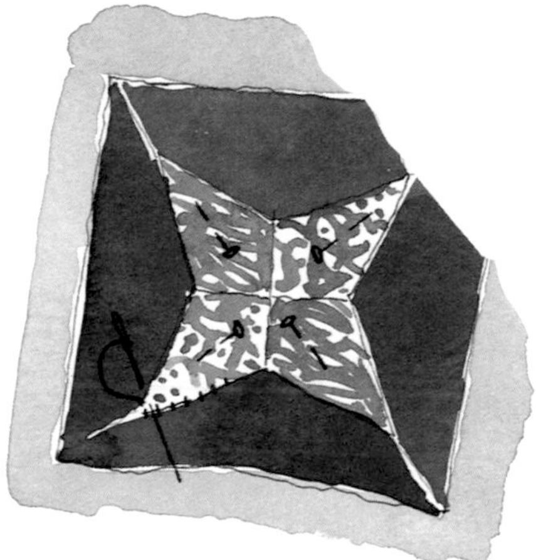

6 Take one of the large squares and fold it in half diagonally, then again into quarters. Press it and unfold it. Place the star shape on top, right side up, and align the points of the star with the creases, making sure that the star is equidistant from the corners.

Pin and baste the star in position. Using matching thread, carefully overstitch around the edge of the star, finishing off on the wrong side. Remove all pins and basting stitches, then press.

## STAR POT HOLDER

7 Sandwich the wadding between the two squares of fabric. Pin and baste together. Take the strips of edging fabric and fold each in half lengthwise with wrong sides together, ironing them in place. Place one of the short strips, raw edges together, along one edge of the fabric and wadding. Pin and baste, then stitch down, leaving a seam allowance of ¼ inch.

8 Fold over the strip to the back of the square and hem down. Repeat on the opposite side.

Take the folded edging strip that is 8 inches long and place it, raw edges together, along the front edge of one of the remaining sides. Allow ½ inch overlap on each end of strip. Pin, baste and stitch in place. Turn over the strip to the back, turn in the ends at the corners and overstitch them neatly before hemming the edge of the back.

9 Place the remaining strip along the fourth side so that it overlaps by about ½ inch at one end and 4 inches at the other. Pin, baste and stitch in place along the front edge of the square. Turn in the short end and overstitch to form a neat corner. Turn over the strip to the back of the square and hem it in place, overstitching the edges of the unattached length together and turning in the end to neaten.

10 Make a loop by stitching the free end of the binding strip securely to the back of the edging. Remove all pins and basting stitches.

If you wish, quilt by stitching along the outside shape of the star.

# Table Mat

*Finished size: 11½ x 14½ inches*

*The machine quilted gingham table mat looks fresh and bright with its large appliqué apple. The apple, which is stitched by hand, is shaped on freezer paper, which gives a smooth, wrinkle-free finish. Cotton wadding is used to give a firm base for the quilting, and medium weight cotton fabric is used for the mat and for the apple.*

YOU WILL NEED

- card for templates
- freezer paper
- red cotton: 6 x 6 inches
- green cotton: 6 x 6 inches
- cotton wadding or batting: 11½ x 14½ inches
- gingham fabric: 1 piece 11½ x 14½ inches; 1 piece 13 x 16 inches
- needles, sewing thread to match, scissors, pins

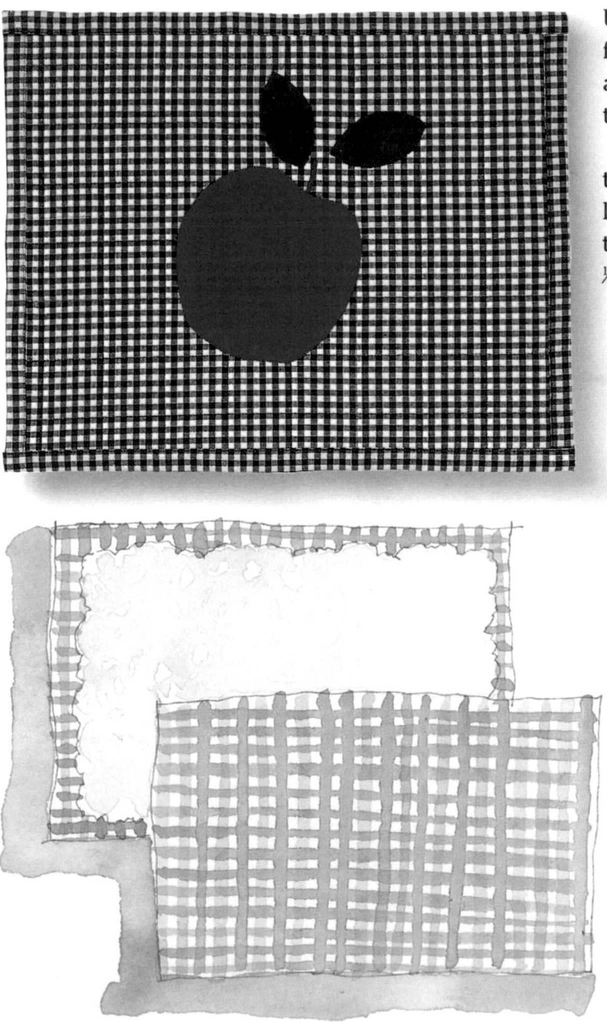

Use the outlines on page 45 to make templates for the apple and leaves. Reverse the templates and draw around them onto the paper side (not the waxy side) of the freezer paper.

Cut out the shapes and iron the waxy side of the apple to the reverse of the red fabric, and the leaves to the reverse of the green fabric. Cut out the apple and the leaves, leaving an allowance of ½ inch all round each shape.

1 Place the wadding centrally on the larger piece of gingham, and lay the smaller piece of gingham so that it exactly covers the wadding. Pin and baste the layers together, making sure that they are held by vertical and horizontal rows of stitches at intervals of 4 inches.

2 Using the gingham squares as a guide, quilt the mat by machine stitching vertical and horizontal lines, spaced at intervals of 10 squares or 1½ inches. Remove pins and basting.

3 Use sharp scissors to make a series of snips, about ½ inch apart, around the shape, taking care not to cut too close to the freezer paper. Press the allowance over the paper to form a smooth, neat edge.

4 Position the apple on the mat, pinning and basting it in place. Slip stitch around the apple, leaving a gap of about 1½ inches.

Remove the pins and basting stitches and ease the paper through the gap. Fold the edge under to keep the apple in shape and close the gap. Repeat the process with the leaves. Use a sewing-machine to satin stitch the stem or embroider it by hand. Press lightly if necessary.

5 Turn in the side edges of the bottom layer of gingham, folding them over twice to create a hem about ½ inch deep that covers the raw edges of the wadding and the top layer of gingham. Pin and baste in place, then machine stitch along the edge of each hem.

Repeat the process along the two long edges, making sure that the corners are square. Remove all pins and basting stitches.

# CAFETIÈRE COVER

*Finished size: 13 inches*

*Keep your coffee hot with this stylish cafetière cover. The striped medium weight cotton is firmly machine quilted so that it will withstand frequent laundering and so that it does not puff out between the letters, which are formed from bias strips and applied by hand.*

YOU WILL NEED

- striped fabric: 1 piece 13½ x 20½ inches; 1 bias strip 1½ x 20 inches (join 2 pieces if necessary)
- card for template
- needles, sewing thread to match, scissors, pins
- lining fabric: 13½ x 20½ inches
- lightweight polyester wadding or batting: 13½ x 20½ inches
- contrasting fabric: about 9 x 36 inches for bias strips; 1 x 4 inches (not on bias)

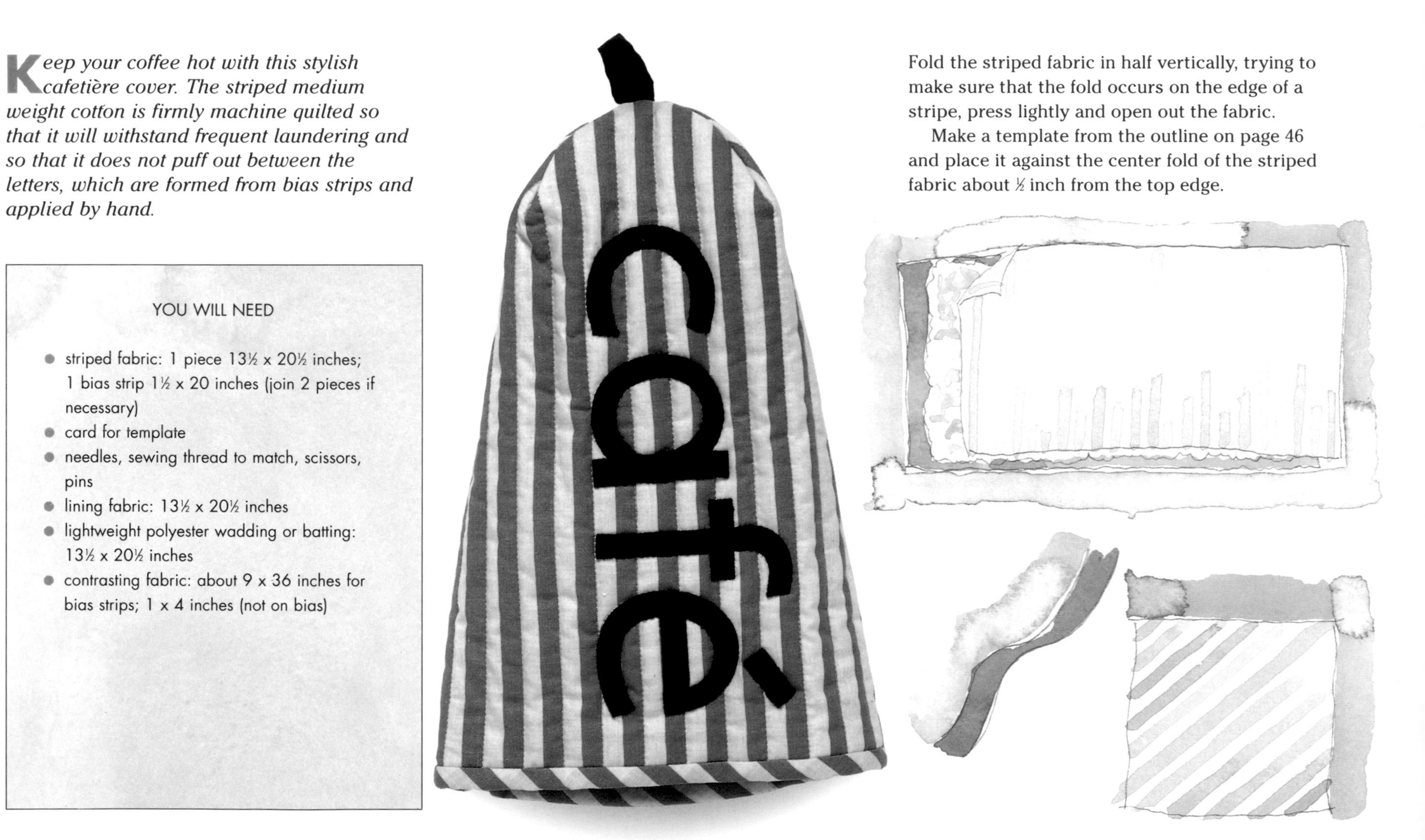


Fold the striped fabric in half vertically, trying to make sure that the fold occurs on the edge of a stripe, press lightly and open out the fabric.

Make a template from the outline on page 46 and place it against the center fold of the striped fabric about ½ inch from the top edge.

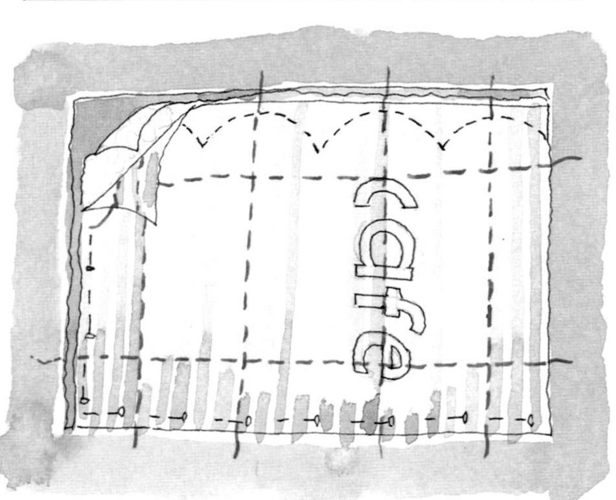

1 Draw around the outline with a pencil or marker pen. Use a contrasting color of cotton to baste a vertical line of stitches from the apex of the arch to the bottom edge of the fabric and baste a second, horizontal row, across the lowest points of the curve. These lines are to help you position the lettering.

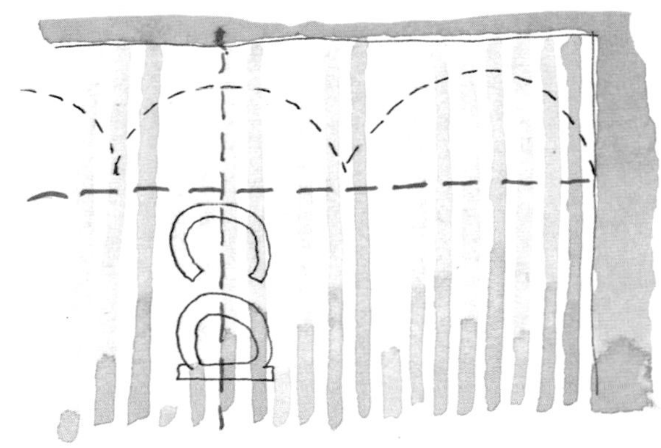

2 Draw around the template three more times across the fabric and stay stitch around the top curves. Trace the letters for 'café' (see page 46) and transfer them to the fabric, positioning them sideways and using the basting stitches as a guide so that the curve of the 'c' just touches the horizontal line and the vertical line passes through the centers of the letters.

3 Lay the lining material, wrong side up, on your working surface, place the wadding on top of it and place the striped fabric, right side up, on the wadding. Pin and baste the layers together, with both horizontal and vertical lines of stitches, which should be about 4 inches apart.

Use your sewing-machine to quilt the layered fabric, stitching in vertical lines and using the stripes as a guide. The quilting lines should be no more than ¾ inch apart. Take out the pins and basting stitches.

4 Prepare bias strips 1¼ inches wide, for the letters (see page 8) and, with wrong sides together, fold each in half lengthwise. Stitch ¼ inch in from the raw edges and trim the raw edge carefully. Press the tube so that the seam is central when the tube is flattened and begin to apply the letters, starting with the 'c.'

Baste both sides of each letter in place before slip stitching it down firmly. The raw ends of all the letters should be turned under to give a neat finish, but the ends of the curved section of the 'a' and the straight cross piece of the 'e' can be left because they will be covered by the other pieces of the letters.

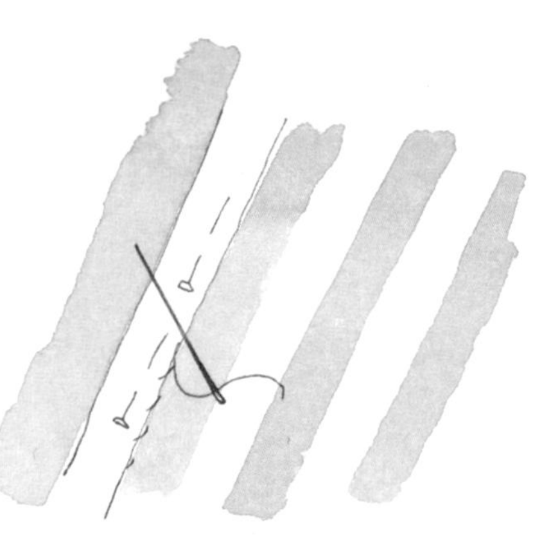

5 Cut around the arch shapes, about ¼ inch from the stay stitches, then, with right sides together and the curves matching, pin and baste the short edges together to form a tube. Leave a generous allowance and stitch the seam. Remove the pins and basting stitches, then carefully trim one side of the lining, wadding and striped fabric to about ¼ inch from the seam and the striped fabric and wadding of the other side. Fold the remaining lining over the trimmed edges, turn in the raw edge and baste then slip stitch the turned edge to the lining.

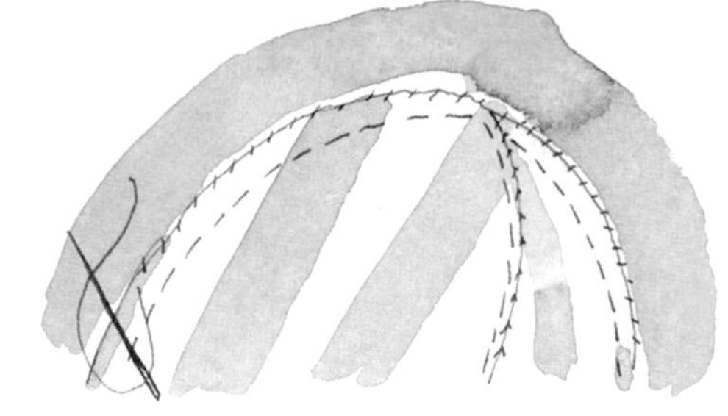

6 With right sides facing and working clockwise, match adjacent curves, pinning and basting before stitching from the base of each curve to the center top, with a seam allowance of about ¼ inch. Neaten the seams by overstitching and fasten off securely in the center.

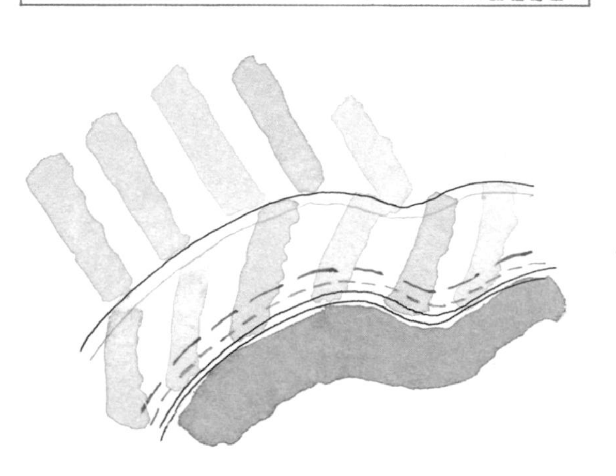

7 Turn to the right side and, with right sides facing, place the bias strip of striped fabric around the bottom of the cover, beginning at the side seam and allowing about ½ inch turn-in. Baste and stitch in place. Remove the basting stitches and turn the strip up to the inside of the cover. Turn in the raw edge by about ¼ inch and slip stitch into place.

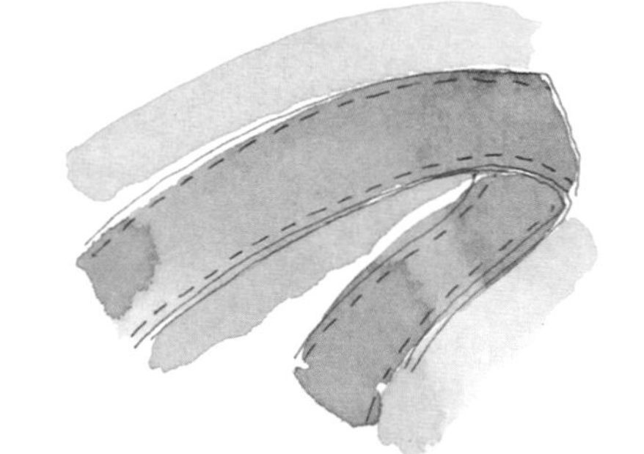

8 Take the small piece of contrasting fabric and stitch it, with right sides facing, to form a tube. Turn to the right side and fold in the ends by about ¼ inch to neaten. Join the ends to form a loop and attach it securely to the center top of the cover.

# GARDENING APRON

*Finished size: 16½ x 16½ inches*

*This useful apron is ideal for gardening – the deep pockets are large enough for packages of seeds and balls of twine and all those other small items that seem to go missing just when you need them. The apron is made from hard-wearing and practical gabardine, and the long ties make it easy to fasten. The motifs are applied to the front with a sewing-machine.*

YOU WILL NEED

- card for templates
- fusible interfacing
- gabardine: 1 piece 18 x 26 inches; 1 piece 60 x 5 inches (join 2 pieces together if necessary)
- needles, sewing thread to match, scissors, pins
- medium weight cotton for motifs: 2 pieces, each about 8 x 8 inches
- contrasting thread for appliqué

Copy the template (see page 46) and cut two pieces of iron-on interfacing, each about 8 x 8 inches. Draw the outline on the back of the interfacing, remembering to reverse the motif as necessary. Iron the interfacing to the back of the material for the motifs and cut out the shapes neatly.

1 Take the large rectangle of gabardine and fold it in half lengthwise. Press and run a line of basting stitches along the crease. Open out the material. Turn over one of the short edges by about ¼ inch, then turn this amount over again to create a hem. Pin and baste, press it, then top stitch with a medium length machine stitch.

Measure 10 inches from the hemmed edge, with the stitched edge outward, and fold the fabric back. Press along this fold, which will become the bottom of the apron, and mark the fold with a line of basting stitches.

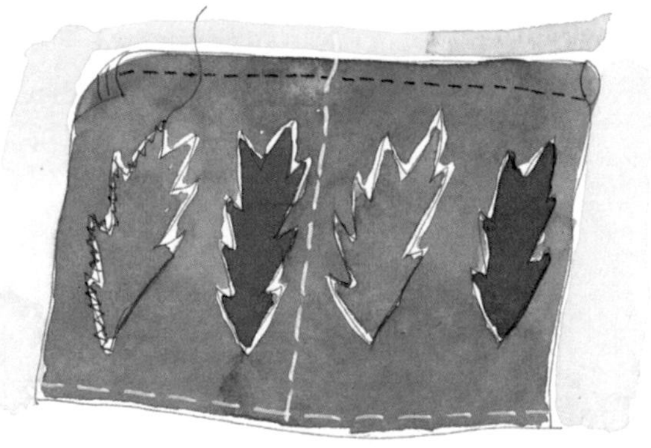

2 Remove the backing paper from one motif and place it on the front section of the apron – that is, with the hemmed edge facing – about 1½ inches in from one side and 1 inch up from what will be the bottom edge. Iron the motif in place then use the satin stitch setting on your machine and a suitable thread to stitch around the motif (see page 8). Make sure that the stitches cover all raw edges.

Apply the second motif – we alternated the colors – making sure it aligns with the first. Apply the third and fourth motifs, aligning them at the base and spacing them evenly across the gabardine so that the fourth one is about 1½ inches in from the other side. Press.

3 Fold the apron along the line of basting stitches at the bottom of the apron so that the motifs are facing outward. Pin and baste the side edges together and pin and baste the central line along the basting stitches made in step 1. Turn in the side edges by ½ inch and then by the same amount again to form a neat hem. Pin, baste, then, with a medium setting, machine stitch along both sides.

Machine stitch down the center of the apron front to form the two pockets, finishing off with a triangle of stitches at the center top to strengthen the stitching line. Remove all pins and basting stitches and press.

4 Make the waistband and ties by finding the center of the strip of gabardine. Mark this point. Fold the strip in half lengthwise and, with right sides together and matching the center points, place the strip along the top edge of the apron front. Insert a pin at the edges of the apron and snip or mark the tie at these points.

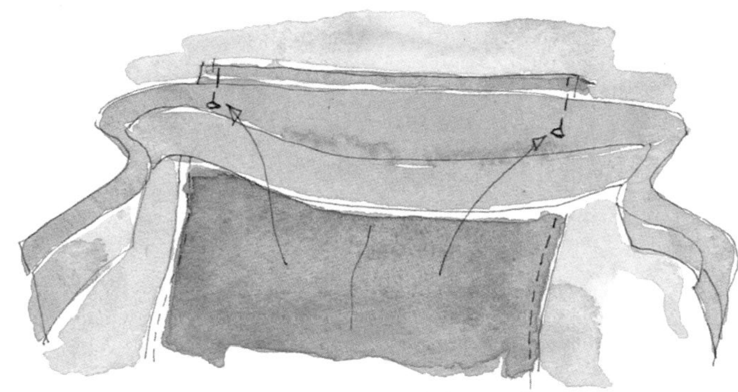

Remove the pins and fold the tie lengthwise, right sides together. Pin and baste, then, beginning at one of the short ends, machine stitch the tie together, turning at the corner and continuing up to the mark. Repeat at the other end.

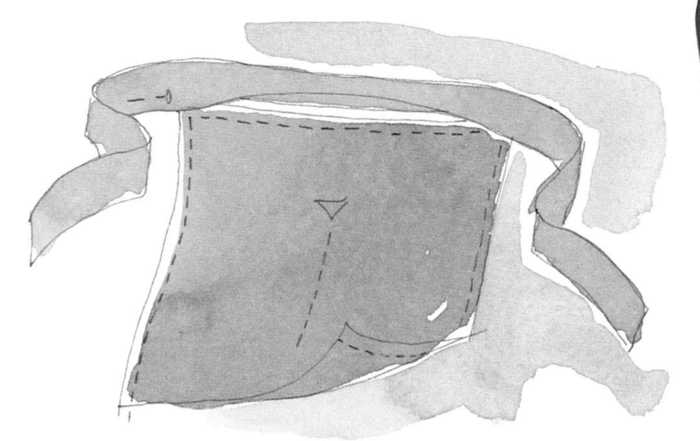

**5** Clip the corners and turn the tie to the right side. Place it, right sides facing and matching centers, on the front of the apron so that the raw edges align. Pin and baste one side of the tie to the apron, then machine stitch in place. Remove pins and basting stitches and turn the tie to the back. Fold in the seam allowance and pin and baste in position before slip stitching to the back of the apron. Press before using your sewing-machine to top stitch the ties and waistband all round about ¼ inch from all edges.

# SHELF EDGING

*Finished size: 5¼ x 23 inches*

*This shelf edging is made entirely of felt and it has a scalloped edge and appliquéd leaf shapes. Since felt is non-woven it is ideal for appliqué because crisply cut shapes will not fray. This pretty blue and white design would be ideal in many situations.*

YOU WILL NEED

- card for templates
- white felt: 9 x 72 inches
- blue felt: 9 x 72 inches
- needles, sewing thread, scissors, pins
- medium weight interfacing
- pinking shears

Cut templates for the scallop and leaf shapes (see page 47). From the white felt cut two pieces, each 6 x 23 inches. From the blue felt cut one piece 6 x 23 inches and 16 leaf shapes.

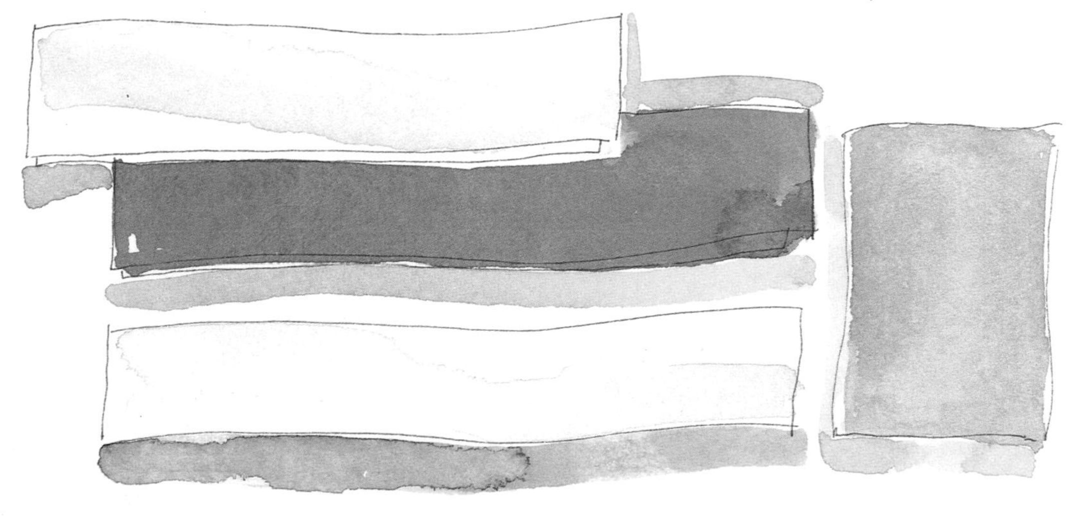

# SHELF EDGING

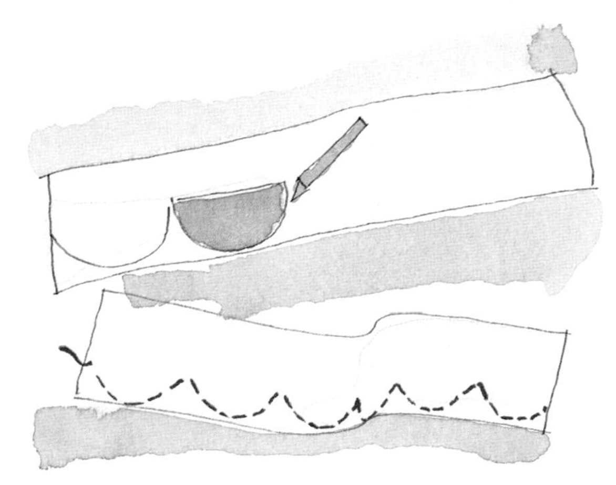

1 Place the scallop template about ½ inch from the bottom edge of one of the strips of white felt. Draw lightly around the template to make six shapes. Baste along this line.

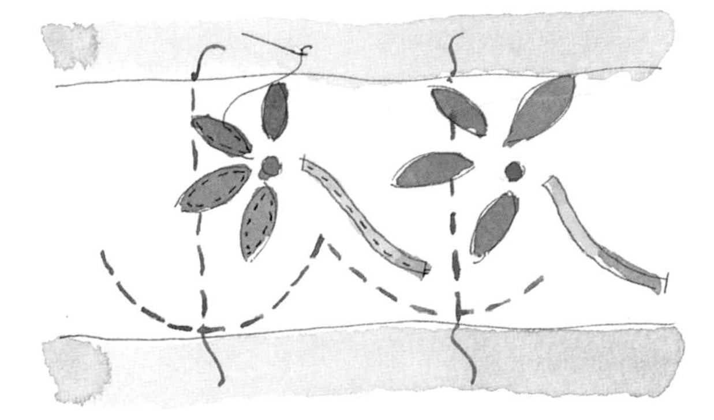

2 Mark and baste a vertical line through the center of each shape. Using these lines as a guide, pin and tack the leaves to the white felt. Stitch in position with small running stitches. Cut narrow strips of blue felt, each ⅜ x 4 inches, for the stems and carefully stitch them in position.

Cut small circles of blue felt and place them in the center of each group of leaves. Stitch them in position. Remove the vertical lines of basting stitches.

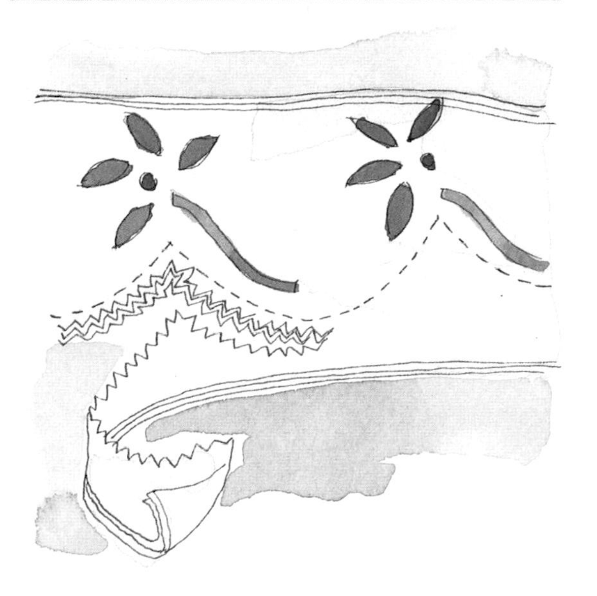

3 Place the decorated felt strip on top of the second strip of white felt. Cut a strip of interfacing to fit and place it beneath the white felt. Pin, baste and stitch the three layers together on all edges, carefully stitching around the scallops on the drawn and basted lines. Remove the basting stitches.

Use pinking shears to cut carefully around the scallops, keeping ¼ inch from the stitched line.

4 Place the white felt on top of the blue felt, matching the scalloped edge to the bottom edge of the blue felt. Pin, baste and stitch around all the sides. Then carefully stitch around the scallops through all the layers. Trim the top edge if necessary before removing all tacking stitches.

# Bolster Cushion

*Finished size: about 22 inches*

*The floral design has been applied to both ends of the bolster cushion using a technique known as* appliqué perse *or Persian appliqué. This involves cutting out motifs from patterned fabric then reassembling them into a new design. We used a medium weight cotton fabric and machine stitched around each motif, but the cut-out shapes could be hand stitched in place, using a turned edge method throughout.*

YOU WILL NEED

- card for template
- background fabric: 1 piece 18 x 23 inches; 2 pieces, each 10 x 10 inches
- needles, sewing thread to match, scissors, pins
- 'stitch and tear' interfacing
- floral fabric (select a piece from which several motifs can be cut)
- zipper: 10 inches (optional)
- bolster cushion pad

Make a circular template, 7 inches in diameter, and draw around the template on one of the squares of background fabric. Baste around the drawn line. Repeat on the other square.

1 Cut two squares of interfacing, each about 10 x 10 inches, and pin and baste them to the squares of background fabric.

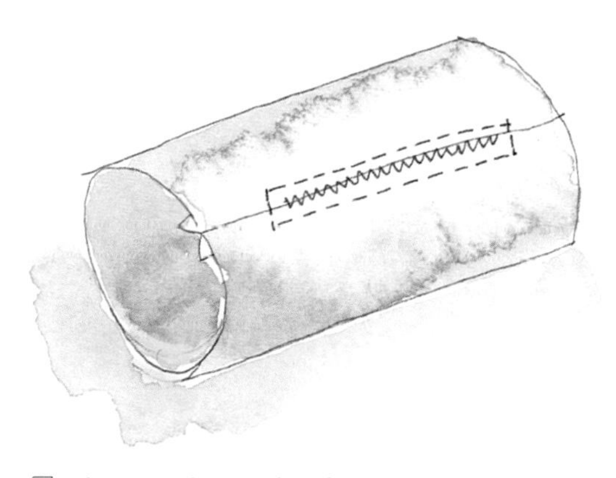

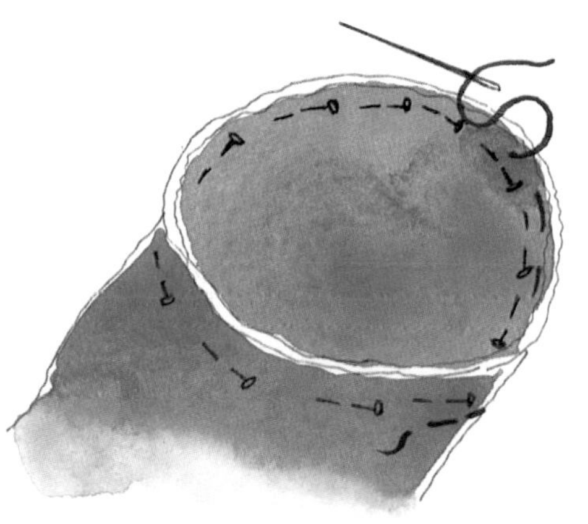

2 Cut out the chosen motifs from the patterned fabric, leaving a seam allowance of ¼ inch all round if they are to be attached by hand but slightly less than this if you are using a sewing-machine.

Arrange the motifs within the circles to make a pleasing pattern. If they are to be hand stitched, carefully clip around the edges of the motifs before turning them under so that they will lie flat. Pin, then baste them in position. Stitch around each motif. Press, remove the basting stitches and press again if necessary.

3 If a sewing-machine is used, pin and baste the motifs in position, then, with an even, dense satin stitch in a contrasting cotton, follow the outline of each shape. Remove the basting stitches and press.

4 Cut out the circles, leaving a seam allowance of ½ inch.

Take the rectangle of backing fabric and pin and baste the long sides together. Stitch, leaving a gap of 10 inches in the center of the seam. Remove the basting stitches and press. Insert a zipper if wished.

5 With right sides facing, pin, baste and stitch the circles to the short ends of the tube. Clip around the seam and turn to the right side before pressing. Insert the cushion pad and close the gap in the long seam if a zipper has not been used.

# TOY BAG

*Finished size: 15 x 30 inches*

*We have used bright blue and red medium weight cotton, and matching plaid fabric, for this useful draw-string bag, which is decorated with black squirrels. The pieces are machine stitched, and the appliqué shapes are also machined on. The bag is lined, and the quilted base provides a firm foundation for a host of toys.*

YOU WILL NEED

- card for templates
- fusible interfacing: 9 x 36 inches
- red fabric: 1 piece 5 x 30 inches; 1 piece 18 x 30 inches; 2 pieces, each 3 x 14 inches; 2 circles, each with a diameter of 9½ inches
- blue fabric: 1 piece 5 x 30 inches
- needles, sewing thread, scissors, pins
- plaid fabric: 1 piece 8 x 30 inches; 1 piece 1½ x 30 inches, cut on the bias (join 2 shorter pieces if necessary)
- black fabric: 9 x 36 inches
- freezer paper
- lightweight polyester wadding or batting: 1 circle 9½ inches in diameter
- cord: 80 inches

Trace the outline of the squirrels (see page 47) onto the interfacing, remembering that you need two pairs, facing in opposite directions. Do not remove the backing paper at this stage.

**1** With right sides facing, pin and baste the red piece measuring 5 x 30 inches, and the blue piece measuring 5½ x 30 inches together. Stitch along one long edge, leaving a seam allowance of ½ inch. Remove the pins and basting stitches and press open the seam.

**2** Cut roughly around the squirrels and iron the interfacing to the back of the black fabric. Carefully cut out the squirrels and place them, in pairs, on a flat surface.

Remove the backing paper from one squirrel and position it so that it covers the seam between the red and blue pieces and is approximately 2 inches from the side edge. Iron the squirrel in place.

To keep the background smooth and wrinkle free while the motif is stitched in place, cut out a piece of freezer paper measuring about 8 x 8 inches and iron it onto the reverse side of the red and blue fabric, behind the squirrel.

Select a matching thread – we used black – and use your sewing-machine to satin stitch around the edge of the squirrel (see page 8). The stitches should be even and dense and completely cover all the raw edges. Fasten off on the reverse of the fabric and remove the freezer paper.

**3** Position the second motif so that it faces the first and aligns along the bottom edge. Leave a gap of about 1 inch between the front legs of the squirrels. Stitch the squirrel in position as before.

Cut out a nut shape from a piece of black fabric, bonded with interfacing, and stitch it between the two squirrels.

Position and stitch the remaining two squirrels on the red and blue fabric, placing the last one about 2 inches from the side edge.

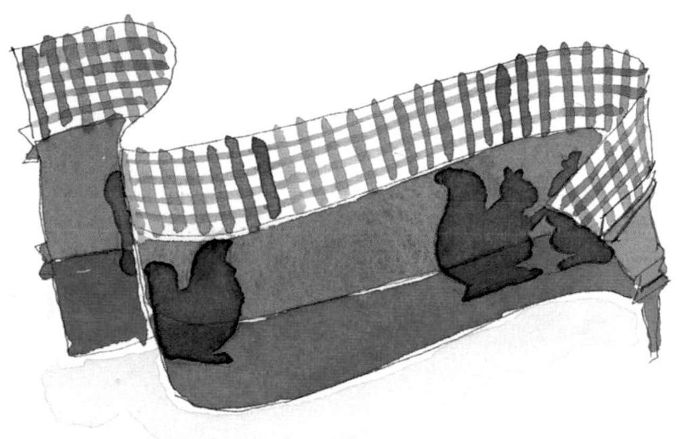

**4** With the right sides together, pin and baste the plaid material to the top edge of the blue fabric. Stitch the pieces together, with a seam allowance of ½ inch. Remove the pins and basting stitches and press open the seam.

**5** Take the large piece of red fabric. This will be the lining of the bag so trim it to size if necessary. With right sides facing, pin and tack the long top edges together. Stitch, leaving a seam allowance of ½ inch, remove the pins and basting stitches and press the seam to one side.

6 With the right sides facing, pin and baste the long side seam together to form one long tube. Stitch the seam, leaving an allowance of ½ inch, remove the pins and basting stitches and press open the seam.

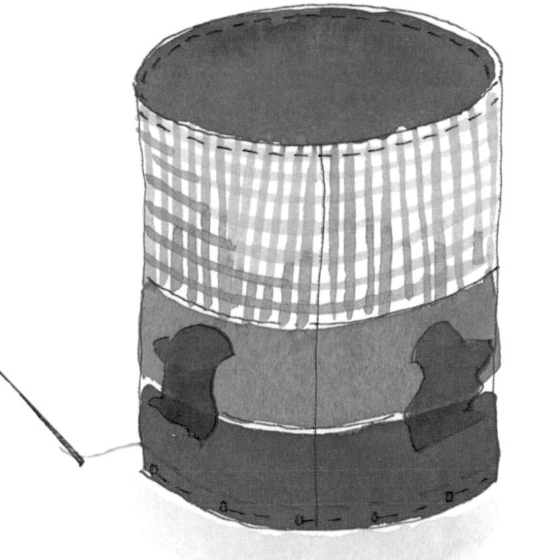

7 Turn the bag the right way out and fold it along the seamed top edge. Align the side seams and pin and baste the bottom edges together. Top stitch around the top edge of the bag.

8 Take the two strips of red fabric and fold each in half lengthwise. Stitch them to form a tube with a ¼ inch seam allowance. Press each tube so that the seam is in the center. Turn in the ends and pin and baste each one to the top of the bag, about 1½ inch down from the top edge and with about 1½ inch between the strips. Top stitch along the top and bottom edges of the strips, leaving the ends open.

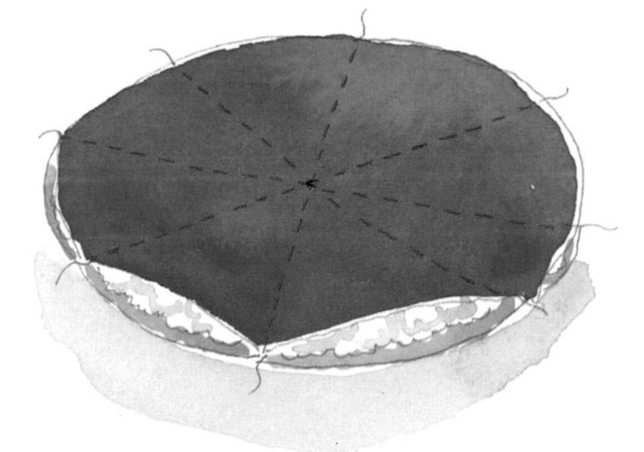

9 Use compasses to draw a circular template with a diameter of 9½ inches. Cut two red circles and one circle from the wadding. Fold one of the red circles into eighths and press it. Open out the circle and make a sandwich with the wadding in the center. Pin and baste the three layers together. Stitch along the pressed creases to quilt the fabric. Remove all pins and basting stitches.

10 With the right sides facing, pin and baste the base to the bottom edge of the bag. Stitch around the bag so that the seam is on the outside. Remove the pins and basting stitches.

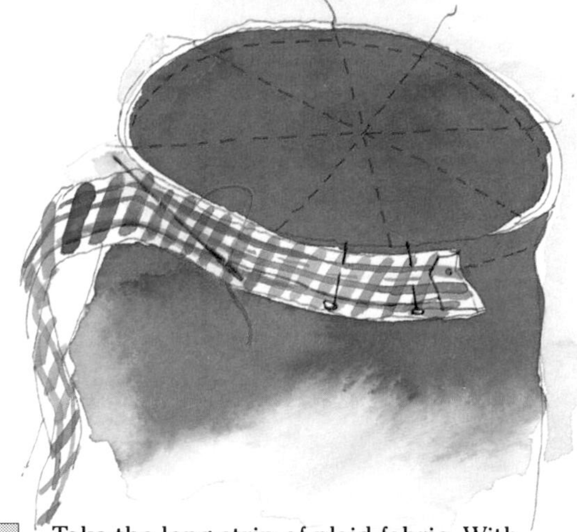

11 Take the long strip of plaid fabric. With right sides together and starting at the side seam, pin the bias strip to the bottom edge of the bag, leaving about ½ inch overlap at each end of the strip to be turned under to neaten. Stitch the bias strip to the base of the bag and remove all pins and basting stitches. Turn under about ¼ inch of the bias strip to neaten the raw edge and slip stitch it to the base of the bag.

**12** Cut the cord into two equal lengths and thread each through the channels at the top of the bag in opposite directions. Knot the ends firmly together to stop the cord from fraying.

# WALL-HANGING

*Finished size: about 16 x 16 inches*

*This rainbow colored fish is an appealing image for children of all ages, and it could be used as an aid to learning about colors. The fish is pieced together from strips of fabric, applied to the background material by the freezer paper technique, and it has been slightly padded to give a more rounded shape. The hanging is framed with a border of triangles, and the edges have been bound with a dark patterned fabric. Medium weight fabric has been used throughout.*

YOU WILL NEED

- card for template
- red, orange, yellow, green, blue, indigo, violet, and lavender fabrics: about 9 x 45 inches of each color
- needles, sewing thread, scissors, pins
- freezer paper
- background fabric: 18 x 45 inches
- button toy eye or small circle of felt
- small amount of polyester toy stuffing
- calico or muslin: 18 x 45 inches
- lightweight polyester wadding or batting
- binding fabric: 9 x 45 inches
- ½ inch dowel, 18 inches long

Make a template for the fish's body (see page 48). From both the lavender and violet fabrics cut a piece measuring 4 x 7 inches. From each of the other colored fabrics cut one piece measuring 1½ x 7 inches.

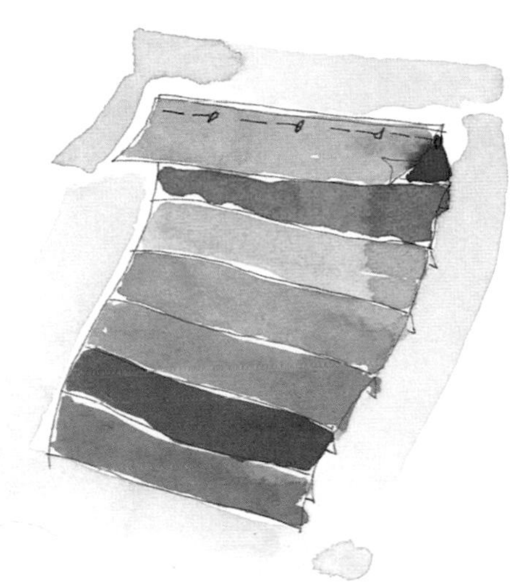

1 With seam allowances of ¼ inch on all pieces, stitch the rectangles together in the following order: lavender, red, orange, yellow, green, blue, indigo, and violet. Press all seams to one side.

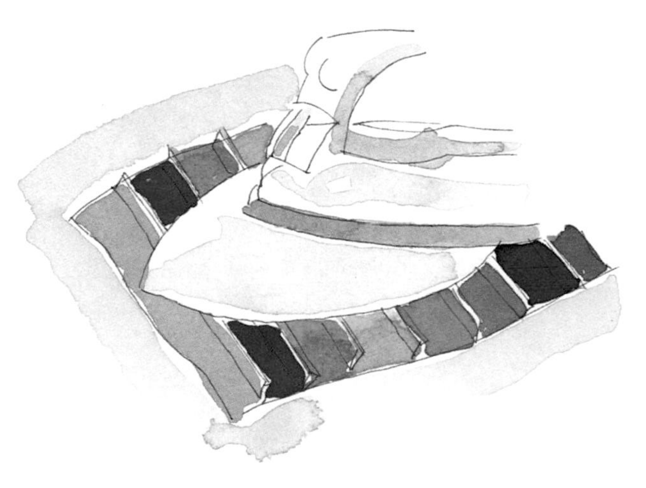

2 Reverse the fish template and draw around the outline on the paper side of the freezer paper. Cut out the shape and iron it to the wrong side of the colored fabrics. Cut out around the fish shape, allowing ½ inch all round, and clip into the curves by about ¼ inch. Press the seam allowance down over the freezer paper.

3 Cut a square of background fabric measuring 12½ x 12½ inches and position the fish on the square. Pin and baste. Slip stitch around the fish shape, leaving a gap of about 2 inches in the center of the top edge. Remove pins and basting. Carefully remove the freezer paper through the gap, then use a small amount of polyester stuffing to pad the shape. Slip stitch to close the gap.

Follow the manufacturer's instructions to assemble and attach the eye or, if the hanging is for a small child, use a small circle of felt, firmly stitched in place.

4 From the lavender fabric, cut a square 2 x 2 inches and fold it in half. Press the folded corners in towards the center to form a triangle and press. Attach to the fish by stitching through the apex of the triangle, to form a tail.

5 Cut 14 squares, each 4 x 4 inches, from the calico or muslin, and on each square draw a diagonal line, then draw a line ¼ inch on each side of the diagonal line.

From each color, except lavender, cut two squares, each 4 x 4 inches. Place a calico square on a colored square and stitch them together along the two lines on either side of the diagonal line. Cut through both layers along the central, diagonal line and press the seams to one side, thus making two squares, half-calico, half-color.

6 Make 28 squares in this way, then pin a row together in the following sequence: red, orange, yellow, green, blue, and indigo. Baste then stitch the squares together with a ¼ inch seam allowance. Make another strip to match. Pin and baste one strip to the top of the square of backing fabric. Repeat at the bottom, then stitch both strips in place.

7 Make two more strips from the remaining half-calico, half-color squares, arranging the colors in the following sequence: violet, red, orange, yellow, green, blue, indigo, violet. Turn the first violet square through 180 degrees to join it to the red triangle. Pin, baste then stitch these strips to the sides of the backing square, taking care that the corner seams align. Press.

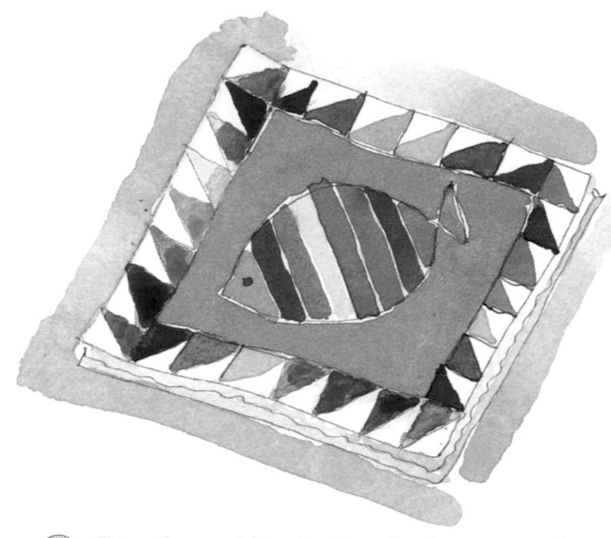

8 Trim the wadding to fit and cut a square of backing fabric to match the dimensions of the finished front section. Place the three layers together and baste, running stitches in a grid to hold the pieces securely together.

9 From the binding fabric cut four strips, each 2½ x 17 inches. Fold in half lengthwise with wrong sides together and press. With raw edges aligned and right sides facing, pin and baste a binding strip to the top and bottom edges. Stitch, then turn to wrong side, turn in the ends to neaten, and slip stitch down. Repeat on the two side edges, neatening the corners with overstitches. Slip stitch to wrong side.

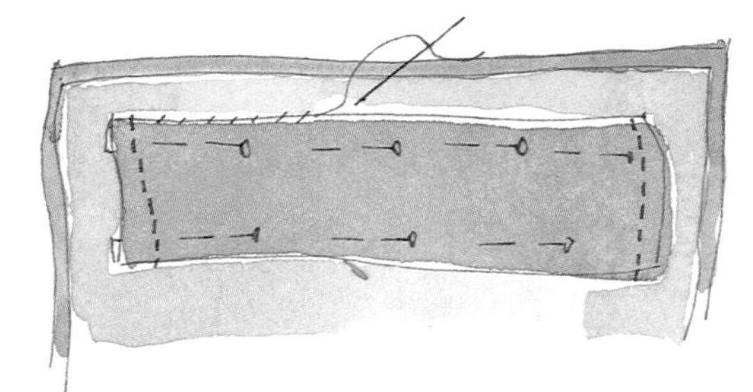

**10** Cut one strip 15 x 3 inches from the backing material. Turn in the two long edges, then turn in the short ends and press. Hem all the edges. Pin and baste the strip to the wrong side of the finished square about 1 inch from the top edge. Slip stitch the two long sides carefully in place, making sure that the stitches do not show on the right side. Remove pins and basting. Insert the dowel through the sleeve.

# PILLOWCASE WITH RIBBON APPLIQUÉ

*Finished size: 26 x 21 inches*

*The crisp broderie anglaise is hand stitched to the pillowcase or cover in a simple diamond shape. Ribbon is used for a trim and tiny bows have been added to complete the design. The ribbon can be chosen to suit the color of the decor, while the crisp white pillowcase and broderie anglaise would make this a perfect wedding or christening gift.*

Choose an appropriate design of broderie anglaise for your purpose and complement it with contrasting ribbon.

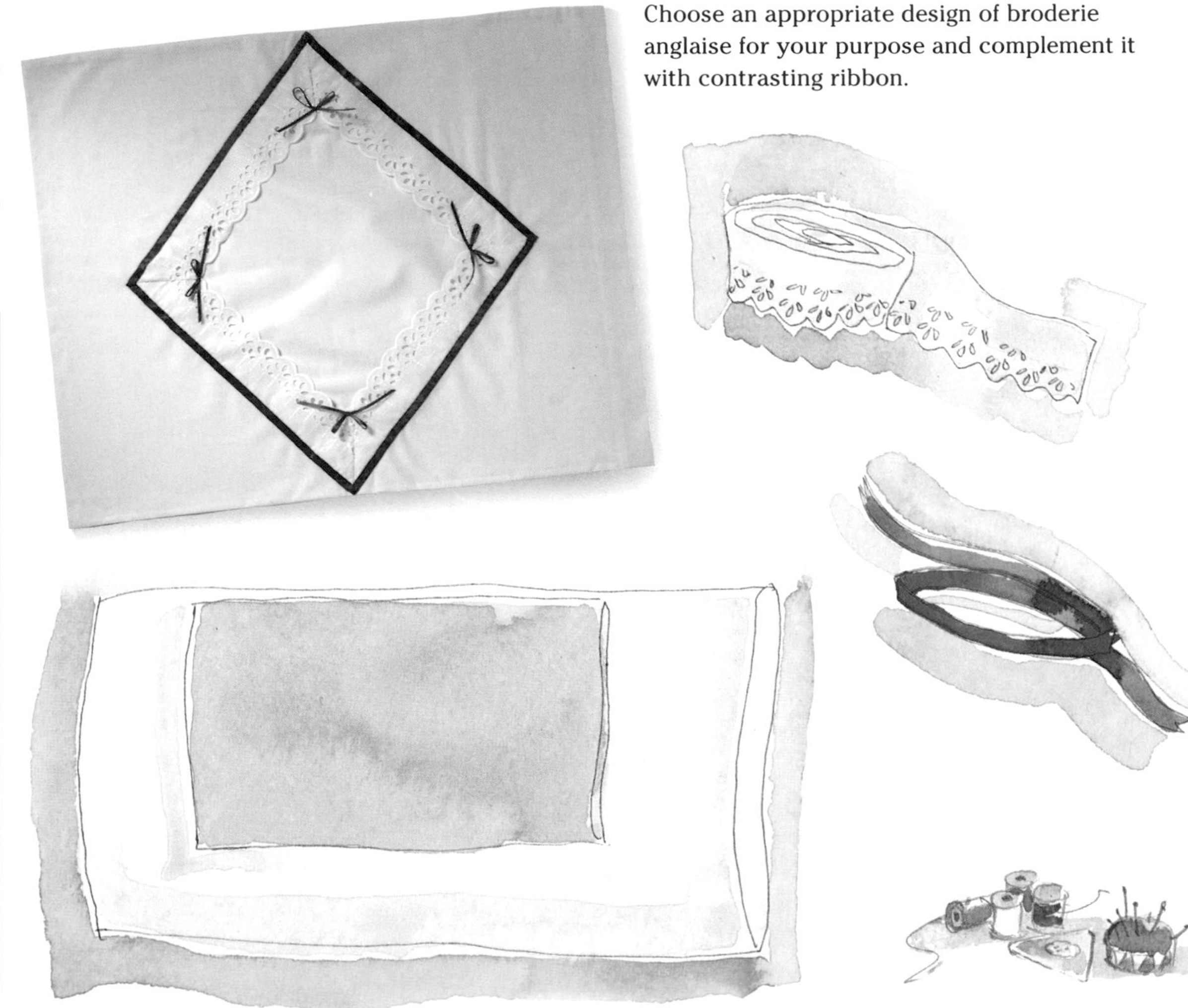

YOU WILL NEED

- 1 white pillowcase or cover
- quilter's masking tape, ¼ inch wide
- cardboard
- needles, sewing thread to match, scissors, pins
- broderie anglaise, 3 inches wide (with a raw edge): 2 yards
- ribbon, ½ inch wide: 2 yards
- ribbon, ⅛ inch wide: 1 yard

## PILLOWCASE WITH RIBBON APPLIQUÉ

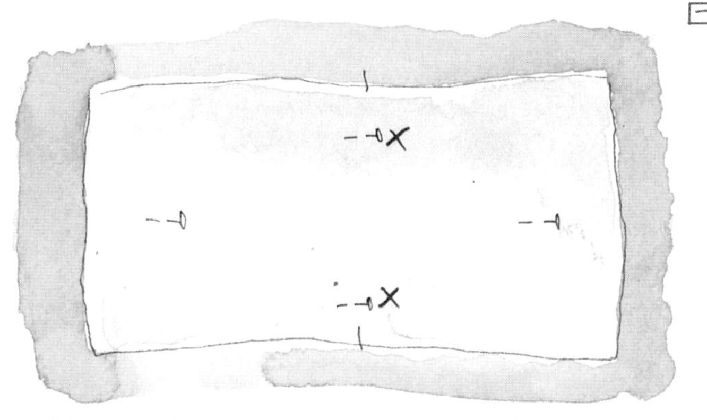

1 Place the pillowcase or cover on a flat surface. Measure and use masking tape to mark a horizontal line across the center of the pillowcase. Insert a piece of cardboard inside the pillowcase so that your stitches do not go through both layers. Place a pin about 4 inches in from each side edge and mark the central points of both long edges.

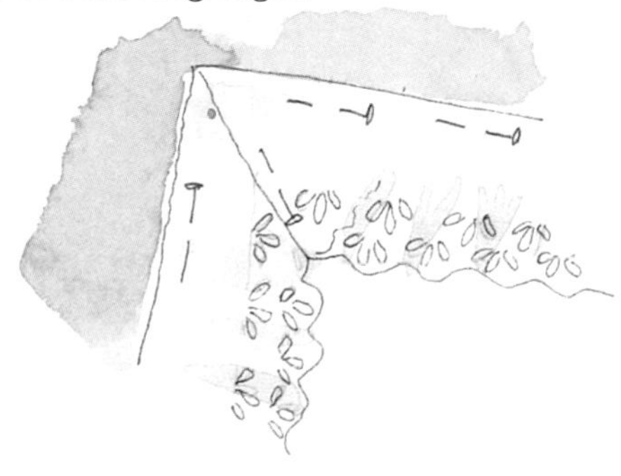

2 Placing the broderie anglaise, embroidered edge facing inward, make a diamond shape with one complete length. Begin at the center of the top edge and pin the broderie anglaise in a straight line to the point marked by the pin on the left side of the center line.

Turn the broderie anglaise with a miter fold on the wrong side and continue to pin, diagonally, in a straight line to the center point on the bottom edge. Repeat to complete the diamond.

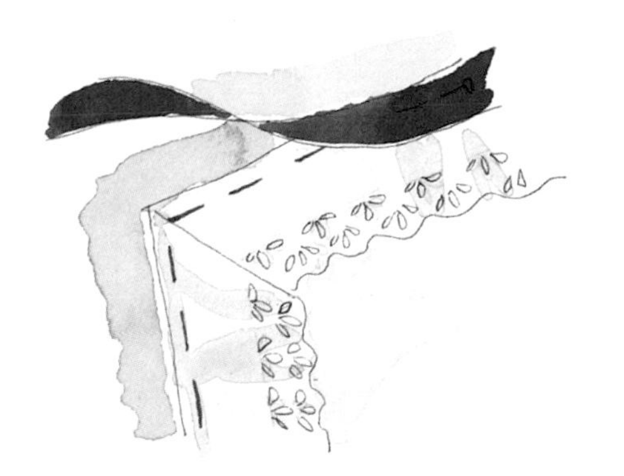

3 Baste, turning in the raw edges at the center top to neaten the fold. Remove the tape carefully, then stitch the broderie anglaise to the pillow with a small running stitch. Remove all pins and basting stitches, and press.

Place the wider ribbon over the stitched line and stitch in place, folding carefully into neat mitered angles at the corners.

4 Make four small ribbon bows and stitch them in position at the points of the diamond. Remove the cardboard.

# CHRISTMAS RING IN SHADOW APPLIQUÉ

*Finished size: 12 inches in diameter*

*You will be able to use this pretty ring as a Christmas decoration for years to come. The parcel and holly motifs are cut from brightly colored fabrics, which are placed on a white background, and these are overlaid with a layer of fine voile to give a softer, subtler effect. Hand stitching around the shapes traps them between the background fabric and the voile, and a tartan ribbon and bow add the perfect finishing touches.*

YOU WILL NEED

- voile, organza, or fine muslin: 18 x 45 inches
- white background fabric: 18 x 45 inches
- card for templates
- scraps of red, green, and patterned fabrics
- circular embroidery frame, 10 inches in diameter
- glue stick
- needles, sewing thread, scissors, pins
- pinking shears
- tartan ribbon, 1 inch wide: 2 yards
- green ribbon, ½ inch wide: 2 yards
- small brass pins

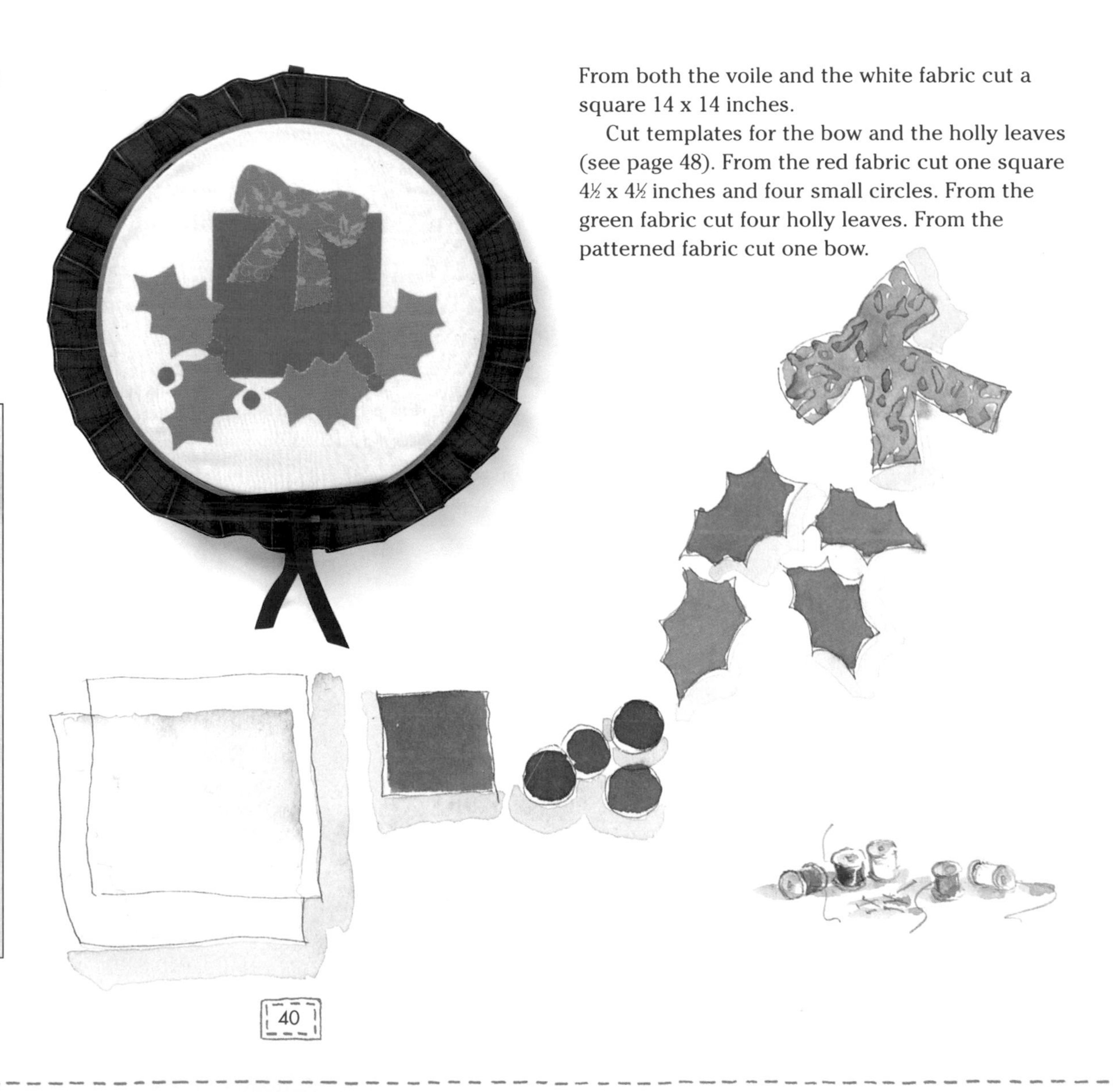

From both the voile and the white fabric cut a square 14 x 14 inches.

Cut templates for the bow and the holly leaves (see page 48). From the red fabric cut one square 4½ x 4½ inches and four small circles. From the green fabric cut four holly leaves. From the patterned fabric cut one bow.

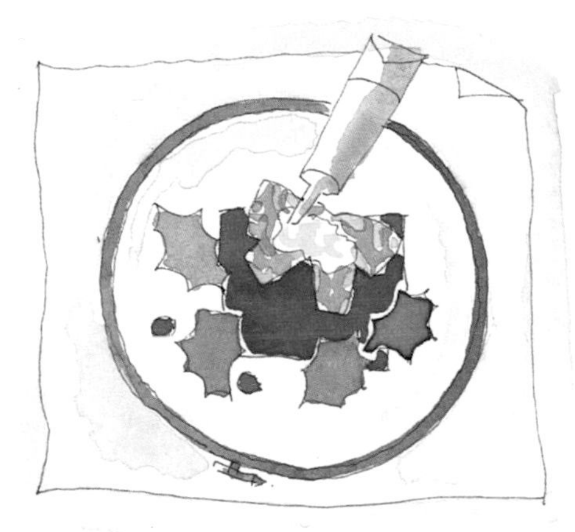

1 Place the embroidery frame on the white fabric and arrange the colored shapes within the circle. When you are satisfied with the arrangement, use a spot of adhesive to hold the shapes in place.

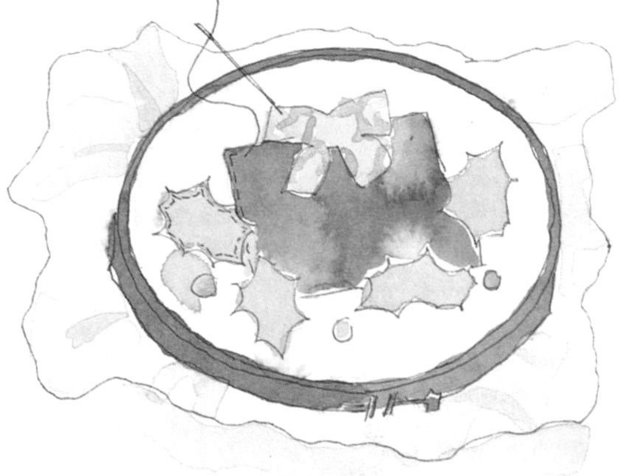

2 Lift away the embroidery frame and cover the shapes with voile. Place both layers of fabric in the embroidery frame and tighten it to hold the fabric tightly. The screw should be at the bottom of the design.

Use white sewing thread to work a small running stitch around all the shapes. The stitches should be no more than ⅛ inch from the edge of the shapes.

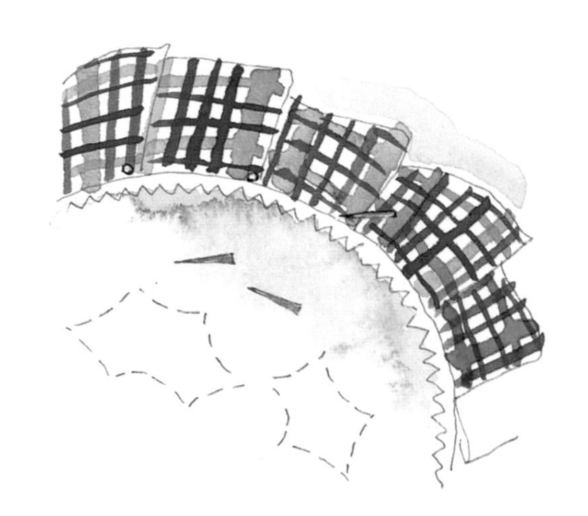

3 Trim the surplus fabric close to the edge of the ring with pinking shears.

Pleat and pin the tartan ribbon to the wrong side of the ring, overlapping it to conceal the raw edges at the bottom of the ring.

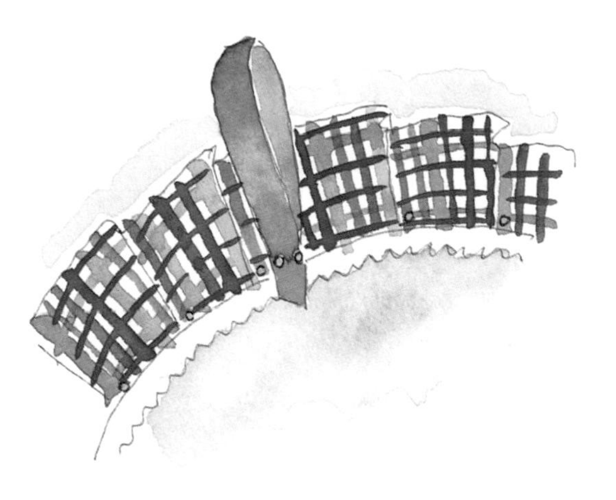

4 Glue green ribbon to the side of the ring. Trim off the surplus ribbon.

Make a small loop of green ribbon and pin it to the top of the ring.

5 Cut a length of green ribbon 10 inches long and fold the ends together at the center. Stitch in place.

Cut a length of green ribbon 12 inches long and fold it in half over the loop made in the previous step. Stitch it to the center of the loop. Place the bow at the center bottom of the frame and use very small stitches to attach it to the fabric.

# EARRING PILLOW

*Finished size: 6½ x 6½ inches*

*Keep your earrings safe and in pairs by arranging them neatly on this small pillow. The cream calico or muslin will complement any color scheme, and the reverse appliqué center is enhanced by the rich burgundy red. The edges of the open appliqué shapes have been neatened with simple overstitching.*

YOU WILL NEED

- needles, sewing thread to match, scissors, pins
- calico or muslin: 1 square 7 x 7 inches; 1 square 2½ x 2½ inches; 1 strip 1¾ inches wide and about 1 yard long
- red fabric: 2½ x 2½ inches
- cream pearl cotton (coton perlé)
- polyester wadding or batting or fine, clean sawdust

Place a ruler diagonally across the small calico square and, starting ¼ inch from one corner, draw a line 1 inch long. Repeat from the other three corners.

1 Use a small pair of sharp-pointed scissors to cut along each line to make a slit. Place this square on top of the red square. Pin and baste all four edges together.

2 Carefully fold under the cut edges of each slit to reveal the red fabric below. Use a needle or the point of a scissor blade to encourage the fabric to turn under.

Overstitch around the edges of each shape, making several stitches at the ends of each oval and making sure that the stitches go through both layers of fabric.

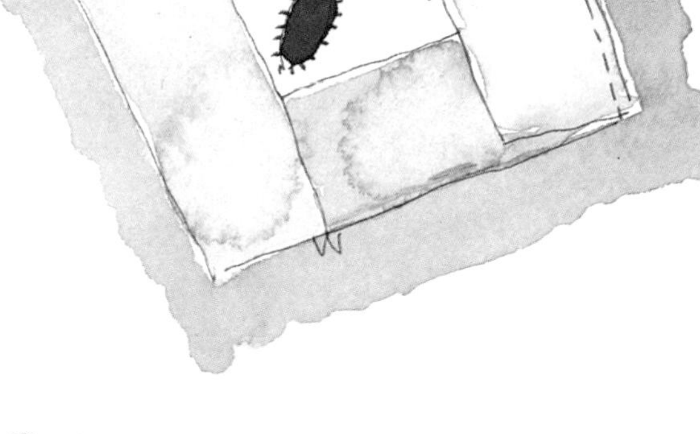

3 Cut a strip 1¾ x 2½ inches and place it, right sides facing and with raw edges aligned, along one side of the center square. Pin and baste, then stitch the two pieces together, with a seam allowance of ¼ inch.

Repeat at the opposite side, then press the seams together and outward. Take another strip, 1¾ inches wide and about 5 inches long, and place it along one of the other sides, right sides together. Pin and baste, then stitch the pieces together, stitching across the short end strips as well as along the center square. Repeat at the other side so that the center square is framed by the four strips. Press the seams together and outward.

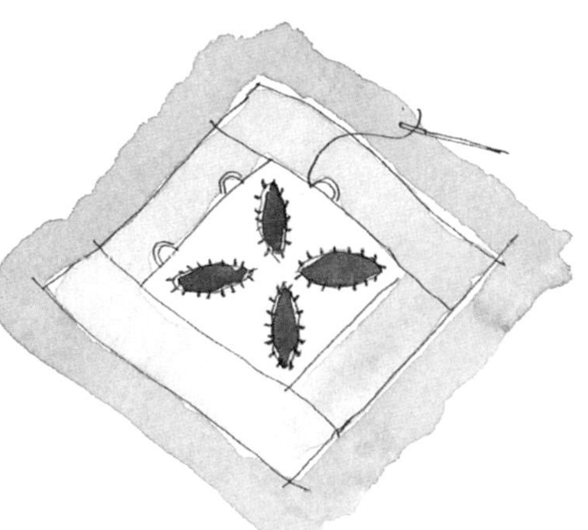

4 Use pearl cotton to make two loops along each of the four seams, positioning them evenly along the sides of the central square.

5 Add four more strips around the edge in the same way as before – that is, adding strips to two opposite sides before adding the longer strips on the two remaining sides. Press all seams outward. With right sides facing, pin and baste the finished square to the large square of calico.

6 Stitch around all the sides, with a seam allowance of ¼ inch, and leave an opening of about 2 inches in the center of one side. Trim the corners and turn the pillow to the right side, using the blunt end of a knitting needle or something similar to push the corners out. Press again.

Fill the pillow firmly with polyester wadding or sawdust before neatly overstitching the opening.

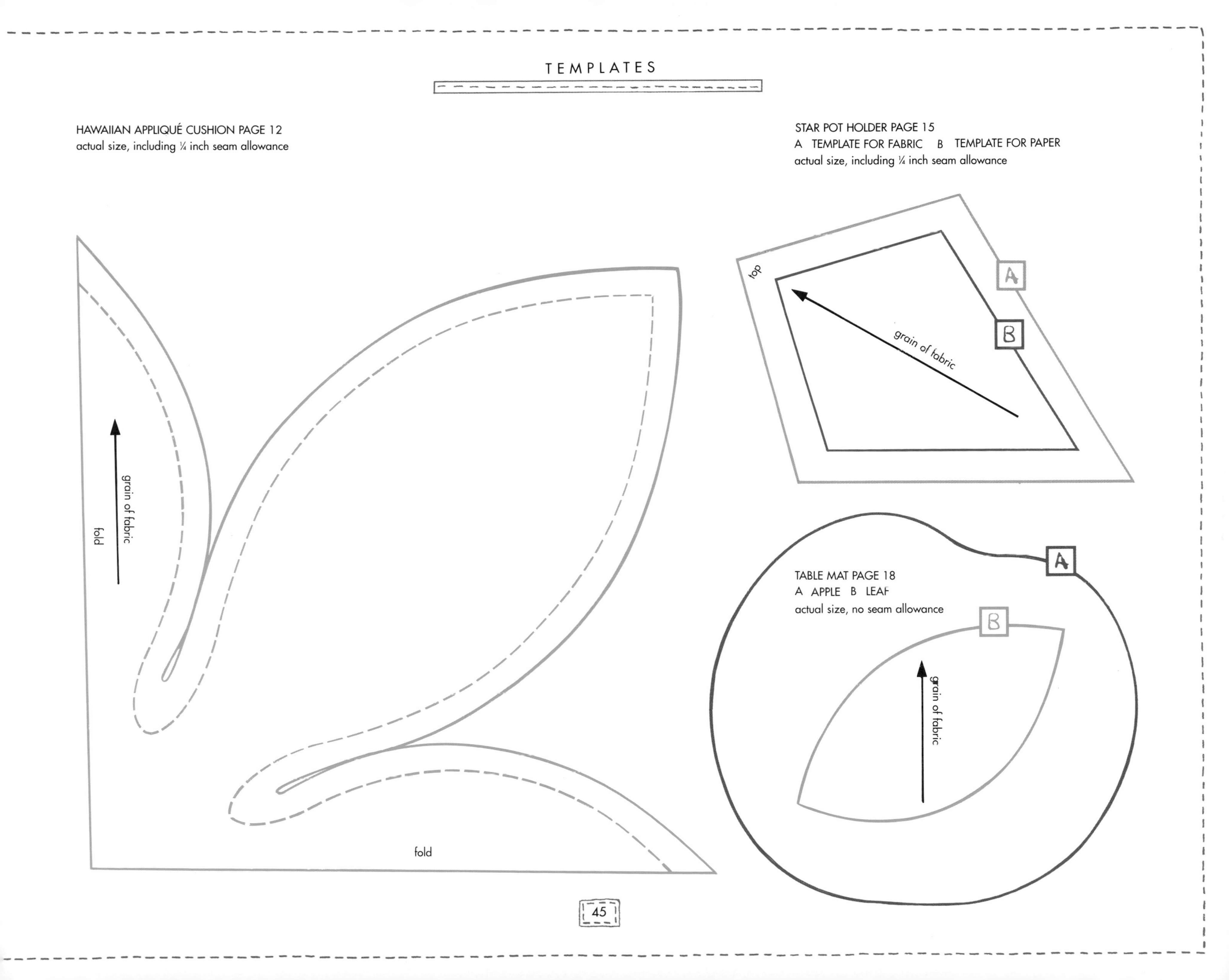
TEMPLATES
HAWAIIAN APPLIQUÉ CUSHION PAGE 12
actual size, including ¼ inch seam allowance
grain of fabric
fold
fold
STAR POT HOLDER PAGE 15
A TEMPLATE FOR FABRIC B TEMPLATE FOR PAPER
actual size, including ¼ inch seam allowance
top
A
B
grain of fabric
TABLE MAT PAGE 18
A APPLE B LEAF
actual size, no seam allowance
A
B
grain of fabric

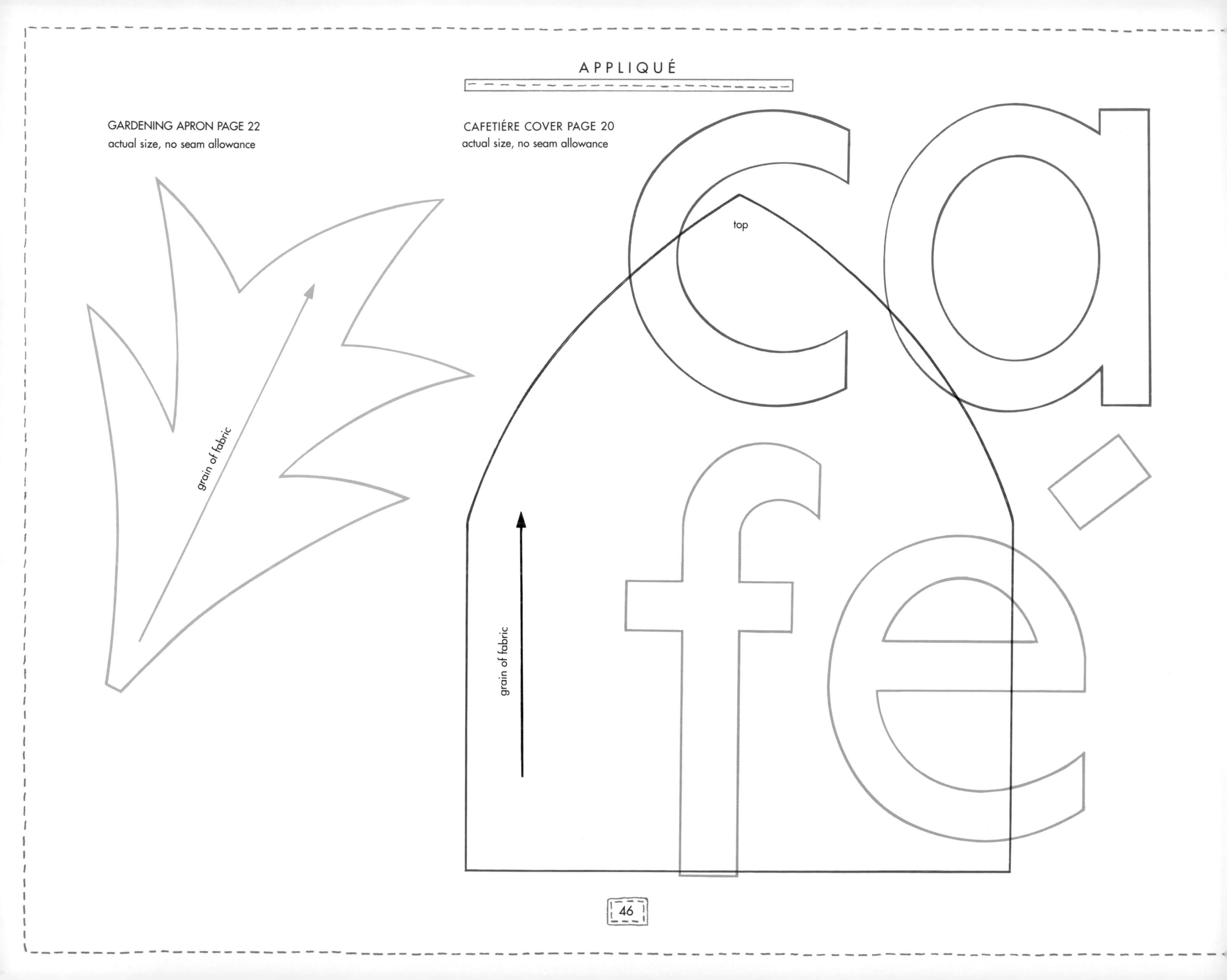
GARDENING APRON PAGE 22
actual size, no seam allowance
grain of fabric
CAFETIÉRE COVER PAGE 20
actual size, no seam allowance
top
grain of fabric

# TEMPLATES

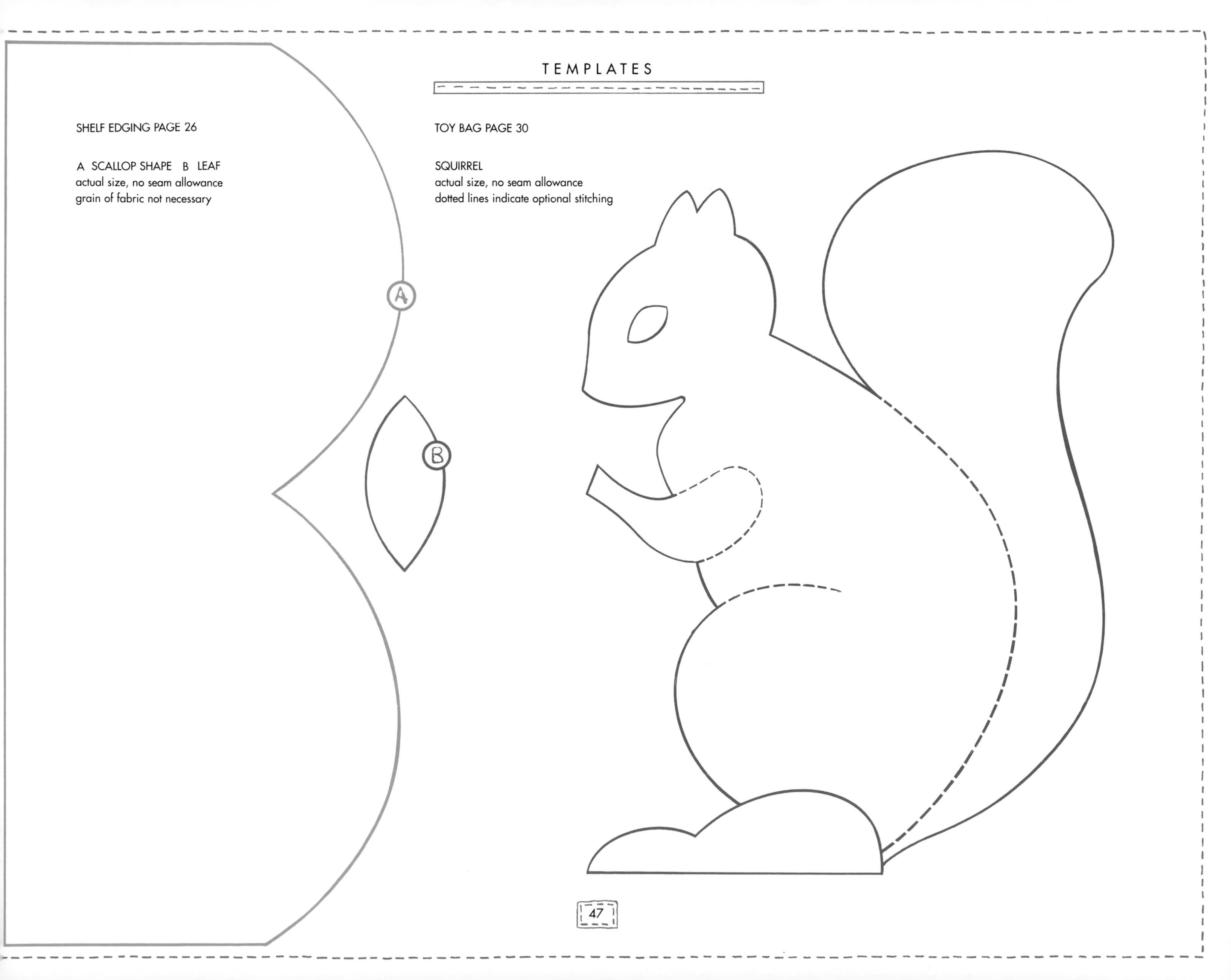

SHELF EDGING PAGE 26
A SCALLOP SHAPE B LEAF
actual size, no seam allowance
grain of fabric not necessary
A
B
TOY BAG PAGE 30
SQUIRREL
actual size, no seam allowance
dotted lines indicate optional stitching

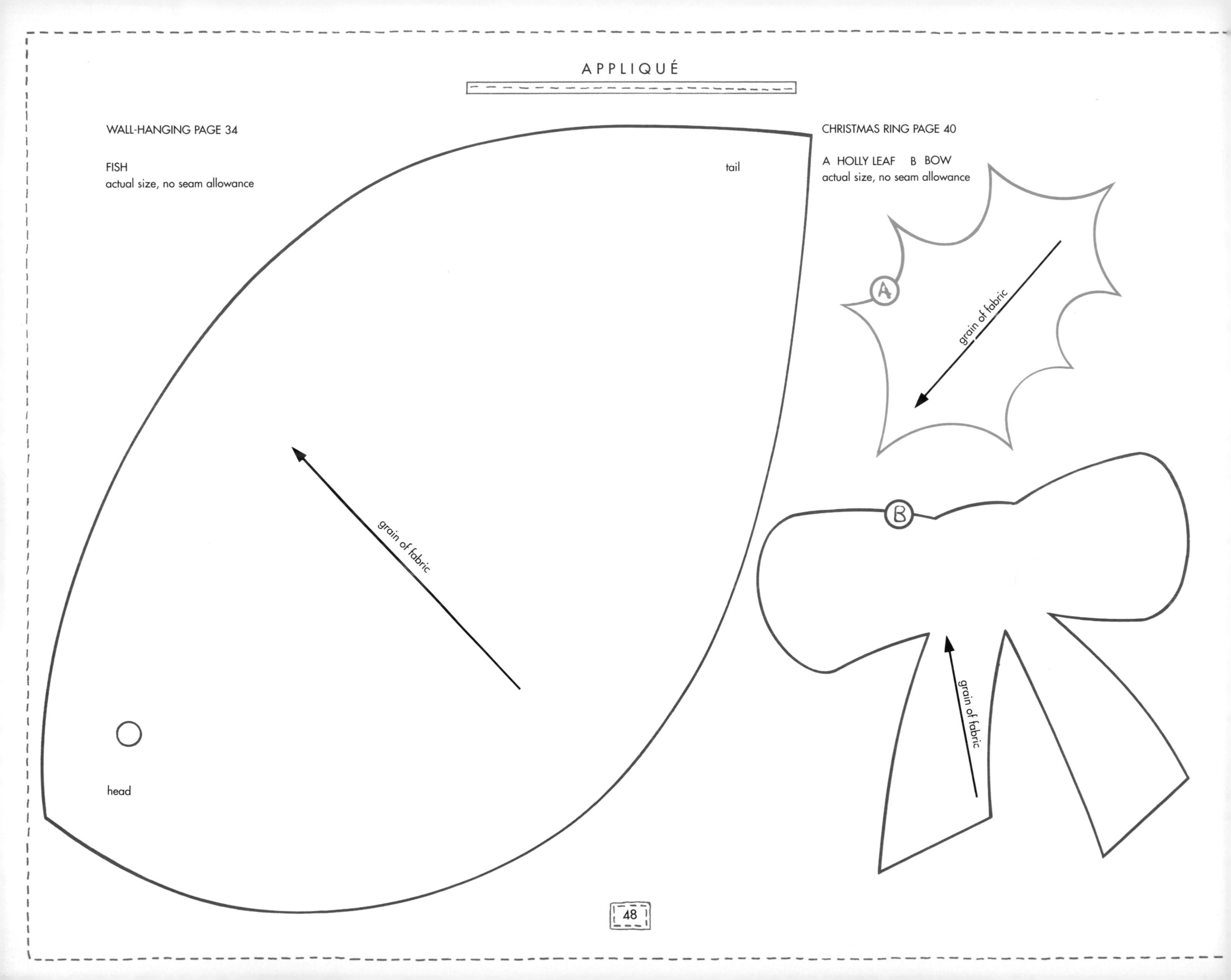
WALL-HANGING PAGE 34
FISH
actual size, no seam allowance
tail
grain of fabric
head
CHRISTMAS RING PAGE 40
A HOLLY LEAF B BOW
actual size, no seam allowance
A
grain of fabric
B
grain of fabric

# PATCHWORK & QUILTING

*Beautiful, long-lasting quilts and gifts to create using various popular and traditional patchwork and quilting techniques*

# INTRODUCTION

In these twelve easy projects, some of the popular traditional patchworks, such as "Flying Geese," "Checkerboard," and "Houses," are designed to introduce you to this fascinating craft and tempt you to create useful items for your home, or for your family and friends.

Both patchwork and quilting are crafts with a long-standing tradition, closely linked with social history and still enjoyed for their unique combination of functional, decorative, and creative elements. Some of the items featured are easy enough for a child or a complete beginner to attempt, such as the Play Quilt or the Fan Motif Pincushion and Needlecase set, while others present more of a challenge, like the Corded Pillow or the Curtain Tieback. A "Quillow" and a floor pillow are also featured, along with other ideas for gifts or to decorate your home.

Before you begin, read the following section, which outlines the basics of making patchwork and of quilting. Then each of the twelve projects has clear illustrations and instructions to help you achieve perfect results. The back pages provide all the templates you will need and lists cutting out details for each project.

## MATERIALS

As a general rule, pure cotton dress-weight fabrics are best to start with. These are easier to handle and will press well. A visit to a fabric store will demonstrate the wide choice of fabrics available in all sorts of designs: floral, geometric, novelty, plaids and stripes, large and small prints, as well as a large number of solid colors. Aim to include dark, medium, and light shades in your selection – many experienced quilters choose fabrics in the same way an artist selects paints, by building up a wide palette from which to choose when making quilts and other items. Patchwork suppliers are happy to cut small pieces, and many put together packs of harmonizing fabrics for the beginner.

Before starting a project, wash all fabrics to remove any residual dressing and dye, and cut off the selvages.

## EQUIPMENT

In order to begin patchwork, you will need a basic sewing kit and a few drawing and measuring tools. Although there is a vast array of specialist tools available for quilters, it is better to start simply with what you already have in the home and add to your equipment as it becomes necessary and your skills increase.

The following is all you will need to make a start:

- dressmaking scissors
- a small pair of embroidery scissors or thread snips
- needles and pins
- sewing machine if desired
- threads for basting and to match fabrics
- tape measure
- thimble
- seam ripper

For drawing and measuring:

- ruler
- pencils and eraser
- good-quality paper
- tracing paper
- cardboard or template plastic
- pencil sharpener
- craft knife or paper scissors
- colored pencils and graph paper will help with the design process

*Rotary cutting set*

Many of the simple shapes in patchwork can be easily cut without templates, using a rotary cutting set. A certain amount of practice is needed to learn how to use the cutter effectively, but once mastered it can reduce the time spent cutting out fabrics by more than half.

The basic rotary cutting equipment consists of a self-healing cutting board, the rotary ruler, and the cutter itself. Different sizes are available in all these pieces, but a good set to begin with would be a board 17 x 23 inches, a ruler 6 x 24 inches, and the large size cutter.

The sharp circular blade on the cutter is protected by a guard – get into the habit of putting the guard on each time you put the cutter down and always cut away from your body. A new blade can cut through up to eight layers of fabric and should last well if care is taken to protect it.

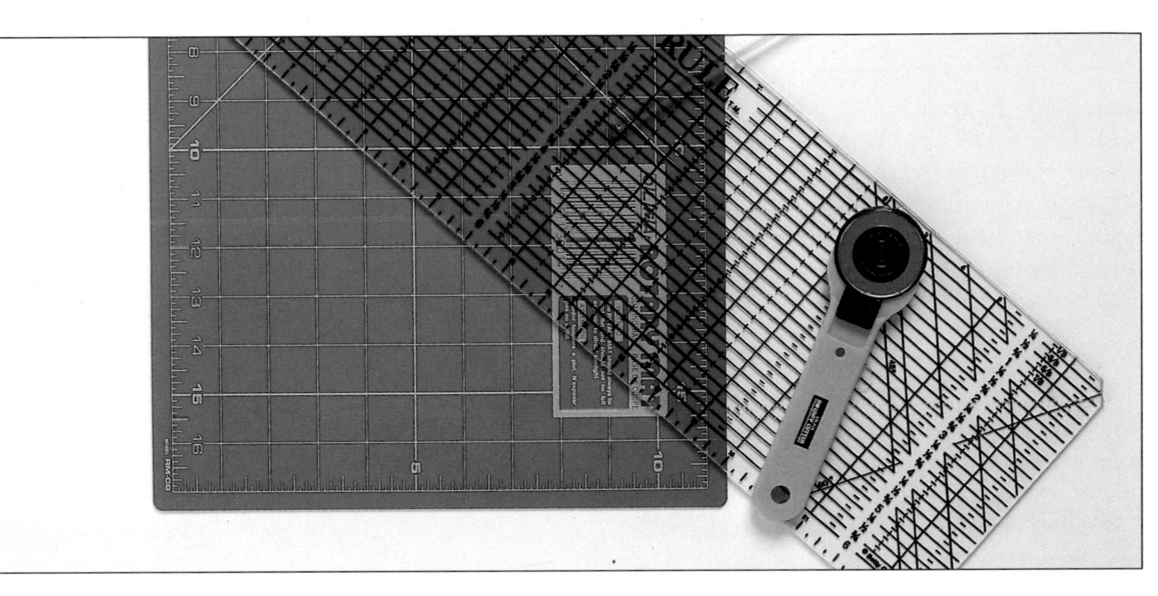

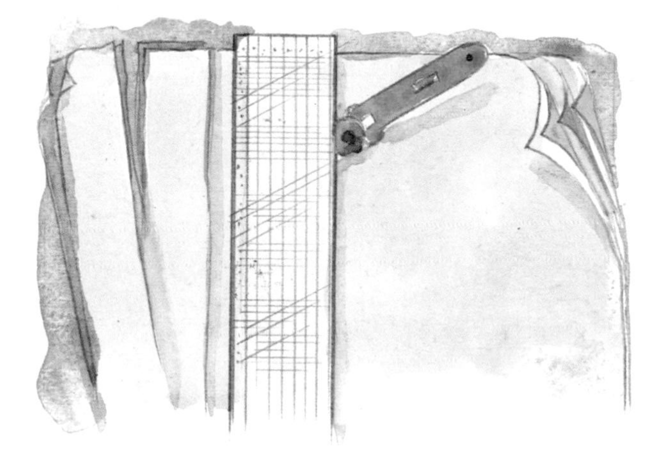

Using the grid on the rotary ruler – align the appropriate line on the ruler with the edge of the fabric and cut.

The board and the ruler are both marked with a grid, and the ruler has a non-beveled edge to stop the blade from slipping across when in use. Never use a rotary cutter with a flat or beveled ruler as this could be dangerous.

Prepare the fabric for cutting out patches by first straightening and squaring the crosswise grain (selvage to selvage across the width) as follows: fold the fabric in half with selvages together, then fold again, placing the second fold in line with the selvage edges. Smooth the layers together and steam press, then place the fabric on the board. Position the ruler on the fabric with one of the horizontal grid lines level with the double fold, which should be at the front of the board. Slide the ruler to the edge of the fabric, then hold it firmly down while you push the cutter along the edge of the ruler to trim and straighten the edges of the fabric. By creating a 90-degree angle in the fabric as you cut, aligning a horizontal line on the ruler with the folded edges and the vertical edge of the ruler on the edges to be cut, you will ensure that the strips of fabric will not be distorted or form a "V" shape. When the edge has been straightened, fabric can be cut into strips, squares, rectangles, and triangles by using either the grid on the board or on the ruler.

To use the grid on the board, place the fabric in line with both horizontal and vertical grid lines and cut the required sizes by lining up the ruler with the measurements on the board. To use the grid on the ruler, line up the appropriate line on the ruler with the cut edge of the fabric, thus holding the fabric under the ruler, and cut. The bulk of the fabric should be on the right if you are right-handed, and on the left if you are left-handed.

Once strips are cut, they can be subcut into squares and rectangles. To cut half-square triangles, first cut squares, then divide them across from corner to corner.

## Basic techniques

Most of the projects in this book are self-explanatory, but a few basic techniques are a useful foundation to build on. It is important to realize that accuracy is necessary in all stages of patchwork, from making the templates through to cutting out the fabrics and stitching the patches together.

### *Making templates*

Trace or draw the template using the measurements given and transfer to a firm material such as cardboard or template plastic. The seam allowance used in patchwork is ¼ inch, and this can be added to the template or to the fabric as you cut out the patches. Templates given in this book have a sewing line (dotted) and a cutting line (solid).

Usually, templates for *hand* piecing are the finished size of the patch, i.e. no seam allowance, and templates for *machine* piecing have seam allowance added.

### *Marking and cutting the fabrics*

Place the template on the wrong side of the fabric, aligning the straight grain correctly and mark around the outer edges. For hand piecing, this line is your sewing guideline. Add a seam allowance as you cut the fabric. Remember to leave a large enough gap between the patches to accommodate the seam allowances.

For machine piecing, cut on the line as the template already has the seam allowance added. Patches can therefore be marked edge to edge on the fabric.

### *Sewing the patches together*

Patches are placed right sides together and stitched with a running stitch by hand or machine. When hand piecing, use small stitches with an occasional backstitch to strengthen the seam. Begin and end the seam with two or three backstitches and sew on the marked lines. When machine stitching seams, position the presser foot to give the correct seam allowance and guide the fabrics through the machine right across from edge to edge. Press seams to one side; the darker side if possible. Where several seams come together, press the final seam open to avoid bulk.

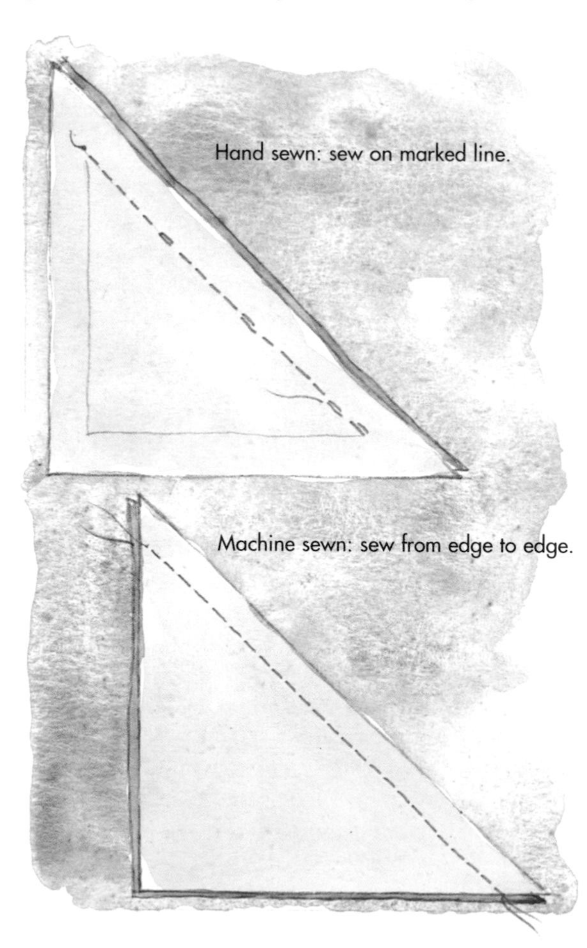


### *Building up the patchwork*

Start with the smaller patches and stitch in straight lines wherever possible. All projects have piecing order diagrams and follow logical sequences. When experimenting with new blocks, study the diagrams to work out the best way to build up the design.

## Finishing techniques

Finishing techniques for most of the projects are included with the instructions, so this section will deal only with one or two which are common to several items.

### *Quilting*

Quilting serves the dual purpose of fastening the layers of the quilt together and forming a decorative texture on the surface. It is done with a running stitch, traditionally by hand, but machine quilting is gaining in popularity as it is so much quicker. The layers of the quilted item – the top, the batting, and the backing fabric must be fastened together so that the layers will not shift, either with a grid of basting stitches or safety pins placed at regular intervals. Quilt from the center out if possible and try to keep your stitches as even as possible. To begin and end each length of thread, tie a knot and pop it through into the middle layer of the quilt "sandwich" to keep the work looking neat on the front and back.

### *Making a fabric loop*

Cut a strip of fabric the required length and width. Fold in half lengthwise, right sides together, and stitch along the long edge. Press the seam open and into the center of the back, then stitch across one short end. Turn the loop through to the right side with a blunt ended knitting needle and press again. Trim loop to required length.

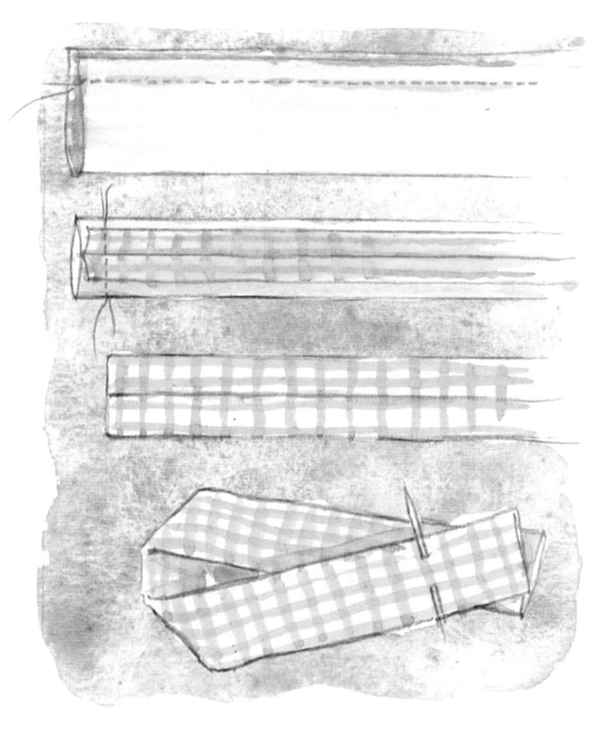

### *Binding*

For items which need to be bound, cut binding strips from coordinating fabric to match the patchwork, between 2–2½ inches wide according to the project, and use double for more durability. Fold the strips right side out and place the side with raw edges along the top side of the quilt. Stitch through all layers. The folded edge can then be hemmed down onto the back of the quilt, enclosing all raw edges. For a quick machine binding, stitch the binding along the edges of the quilt on the *wrong* side, then fold over to the right side of the quilt and machine stitch along the folded edge.

Finish the short ends at the corners neatly or with a folded miter.

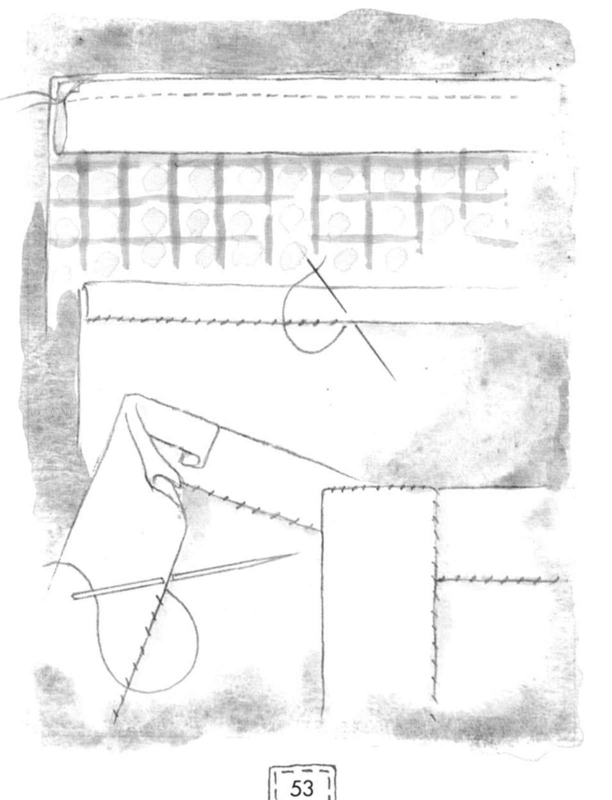

# PICNIC OR PLAY QUILT

*Finished size: 41 x 41 inches*

*Suitable for a picnic or for a baby's play pen, this practical quilt is an ideal project for someone who is just beginning to work with patchwork. It can be quickly made from squares and rectangles, and the quilting, which is in straight lines, can be done by hand or by machine.*

YOU WILL NEED

- needle, threads to match, pins, scissors
- patterned fabrics: a total of 1½ yards scrap fabrics, pieces larger than 5½ inches square
- solid fabrics: ½ yard in pieces larger than 5½ x 3½ inches
- backing fabric: 1½ yards
- lightweight polyester batting: 45 x 45 inches
- coordinated fabric for binding: ½ yard

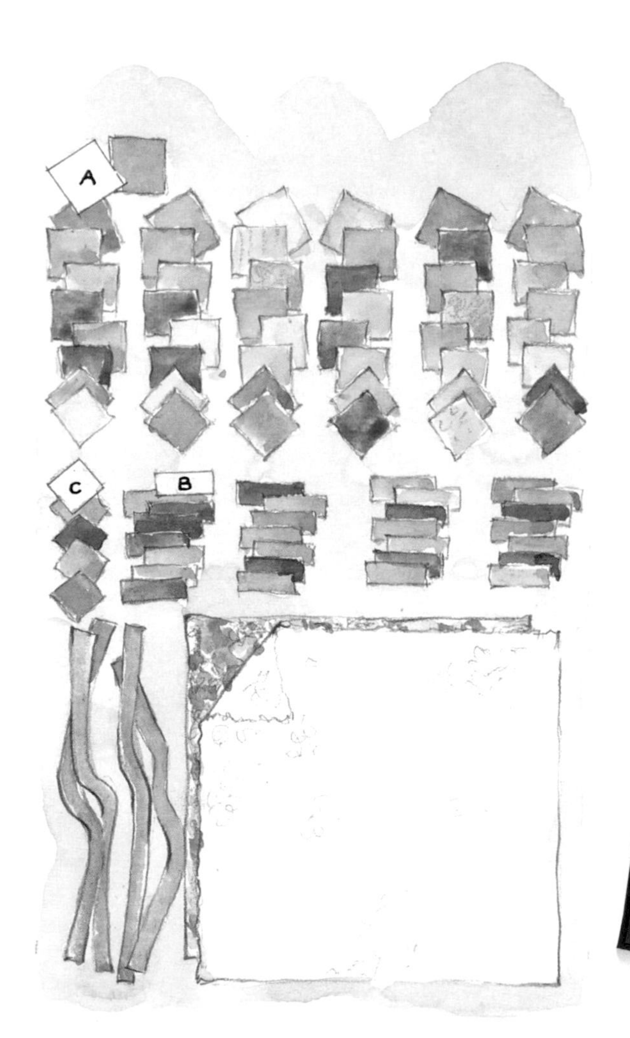


1 Trace and make templates shown on page 89 from cardboard or plastic. Follow cutting instructions on page 89.

2 Taking ¼-inch seam allowances, piece the squares together in rows of seven, alternating the fabrics to achieve a checkerboard effect. Press seams toward the darker fabric. Stitch the rows together, making sure the seams align. Press long seams to one side. Then join the rectangles in four sets of seven to make borders. Add a corner square to each end of two of these.

3 **Adding the borders.** Stitch the borders to the sides of the quilt, with the long strips on two opposite sides of the patchwork.

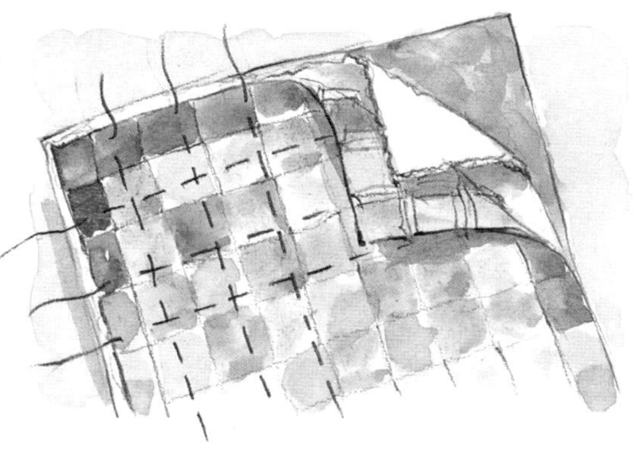

4 **Quilting.** Place the backing fabric, wrong side up, on a flat surface and place the batting on top. Place the finished patchwork right side up in the center. Pin, then baste the three layers together, making rows of stitches both horizontally and vertically about 4 inches apart. Quilt by hand or machine, using the seams as a guide. Trim the backing and batting even with the patchwork.

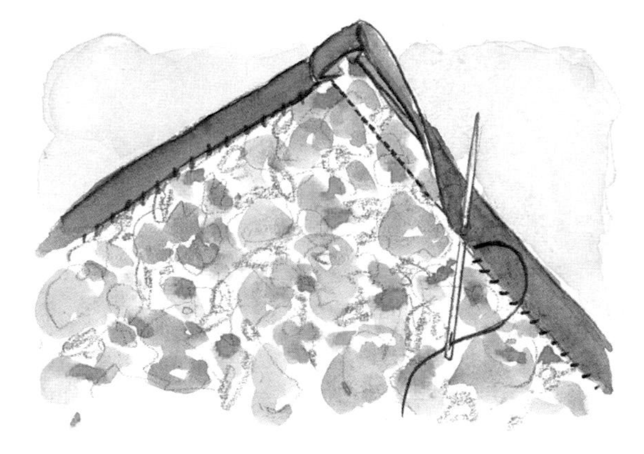

5 Complete the quilt by binding the raw edges. For a quick machine binding, or hand stitched binding, see the technique explained on page 53.

# Housewarming Floor Pillow

*Finished size: 36 x 36 inches*

*A simple pictorial block is repeated four times in the center of the pillow, which has multiple borders, some with corner squares. We have made it in plaids and striped fabrics, which give it a homey appearance. The front of the pillow cover is machine pieced for strength and machine quilted, but if preferred, it could be hand quilted.*

YOU WILL NEED

- needle, threads to match, pins, scissors
- cardboard for templates
- colored fabrics (six shades for each block): 9 x 36 inches (in total for each block); 1 yard for the borders; 1¾ yards for the outer border and back
- lightweight polyester batting: 40 x 40 inches
- lining for back of cover: 1½ yards
- zipper: 35 inches long
- pillow form: 36 x 36 inches

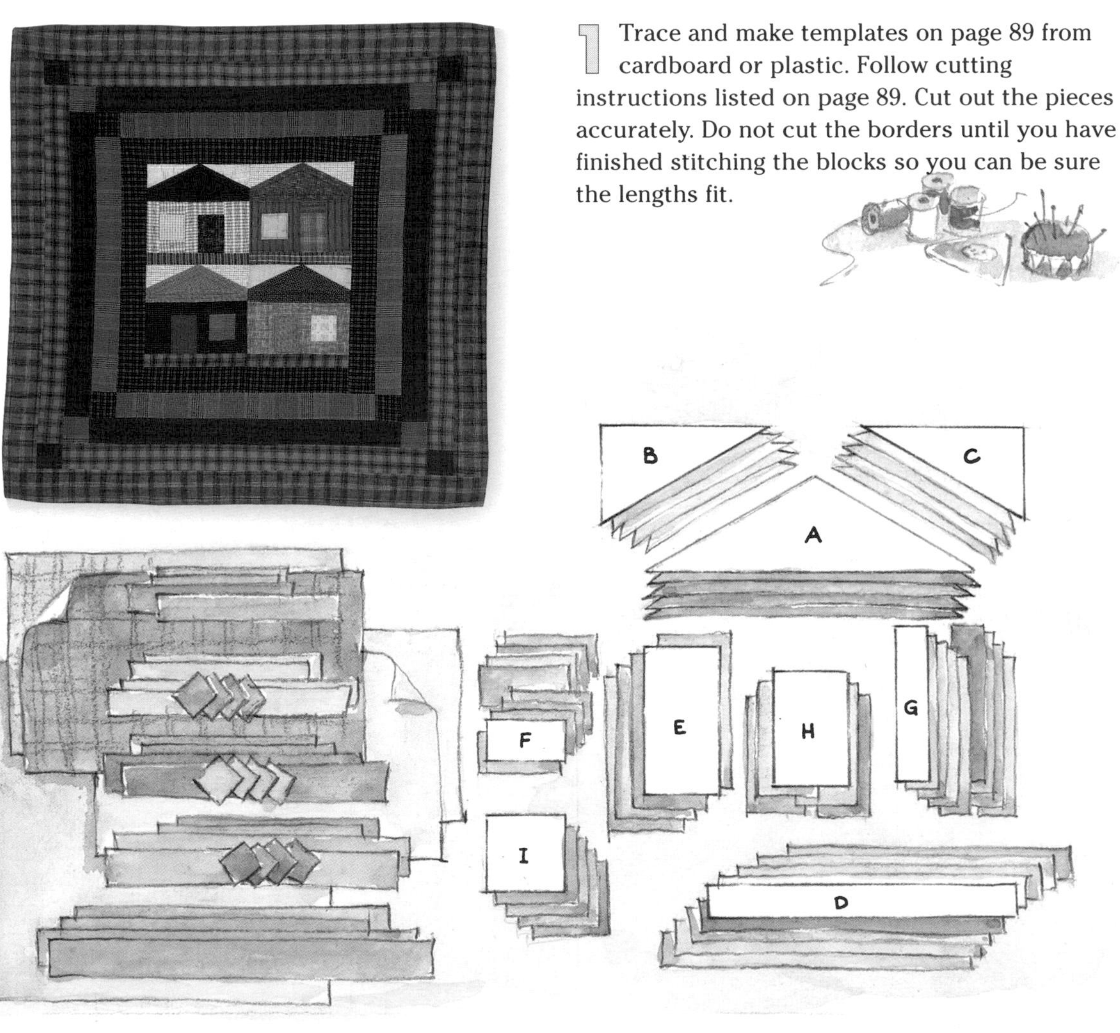


1 Trace and make templates on page 89 from cardboard or plastic. Follow cutting instructions listed on page 89. Cut out the pieces accurately. Do not cut the borders until you have finished stitching the blocks so you can be sure the lengths fit.

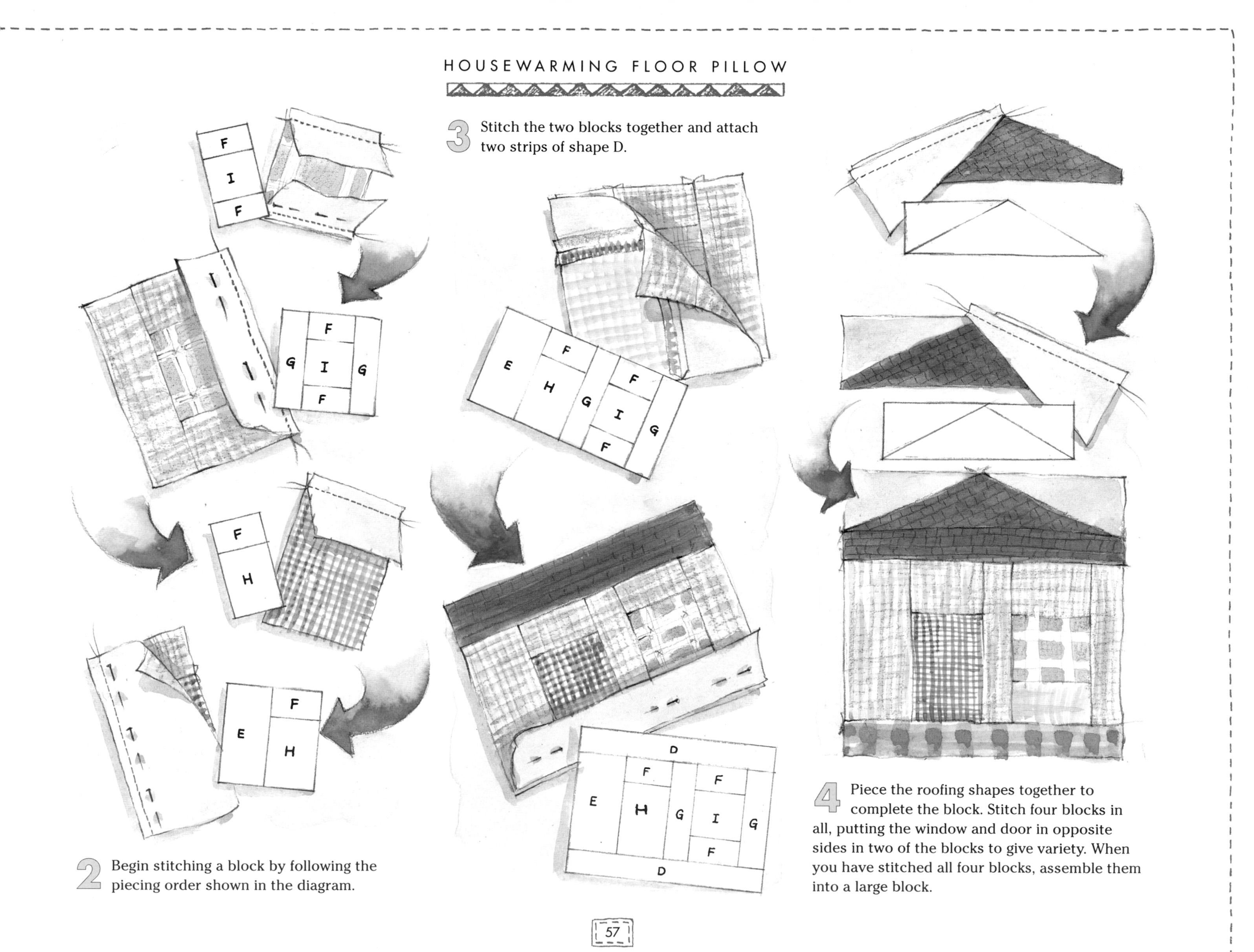


2 Begin stitching a block by following the piecing order shown in the diagram.

3 Stitch the two blocks together and attach two strips of shape D.

4 Piece the roofing shapes together to complete the block. Stitch four blocks in all, putting the window and door in opposite sides in two of the blocks to give variety. When you have stitched all four blocks, assemble them into a large block.

**5 Adding the borders.** Cut two strips 2½ x 16½ inches (check the length before cutting) and stitch them in place at the top and bottom of the center panel. Cut two more strips, 2½ x 20½ inches, for the sides, again checking length before cutting.

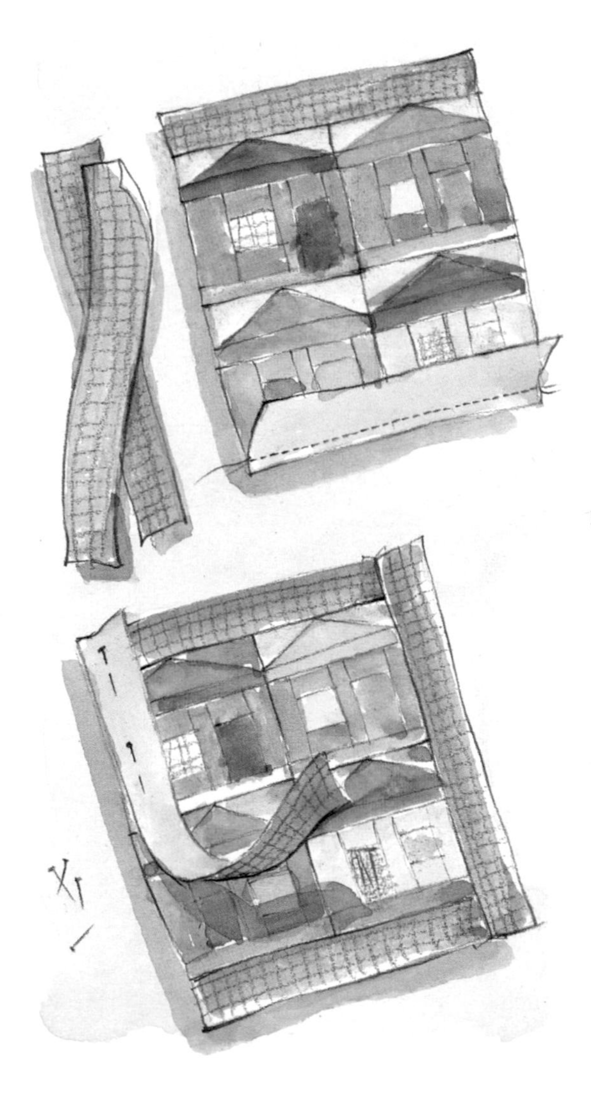

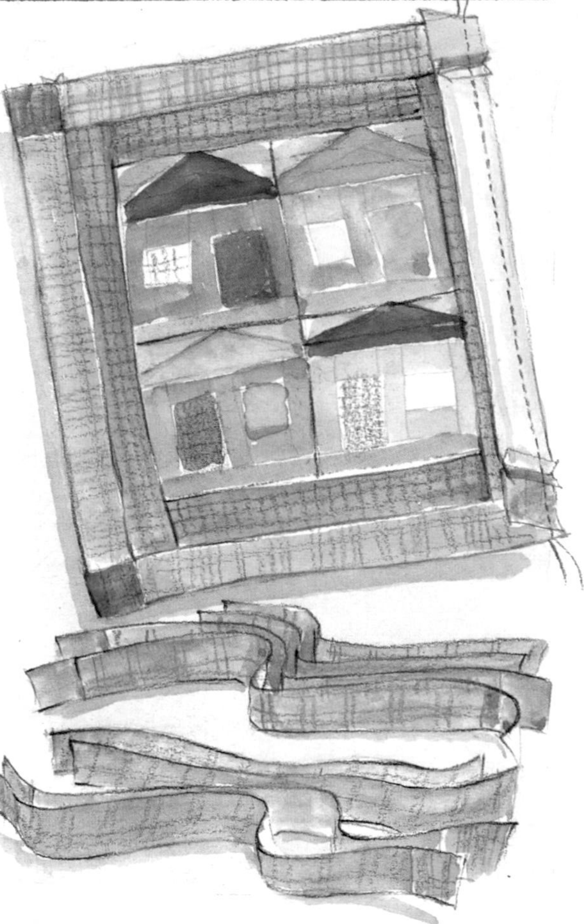

**6** Cut four strips the length of the sides and 2½ inches wide. Cut four 2½-inch squares in contrasting fabric for the corners. Make the third and fourth borders in the same way, joining strips if necessary to make the strips long enough.

**7** The fifth border is cut from the material used for the back of the pillow. Cut strips 3¼ inches wide and stitch them as for the first border (i.e. top and bottom first, then running right up the sides).

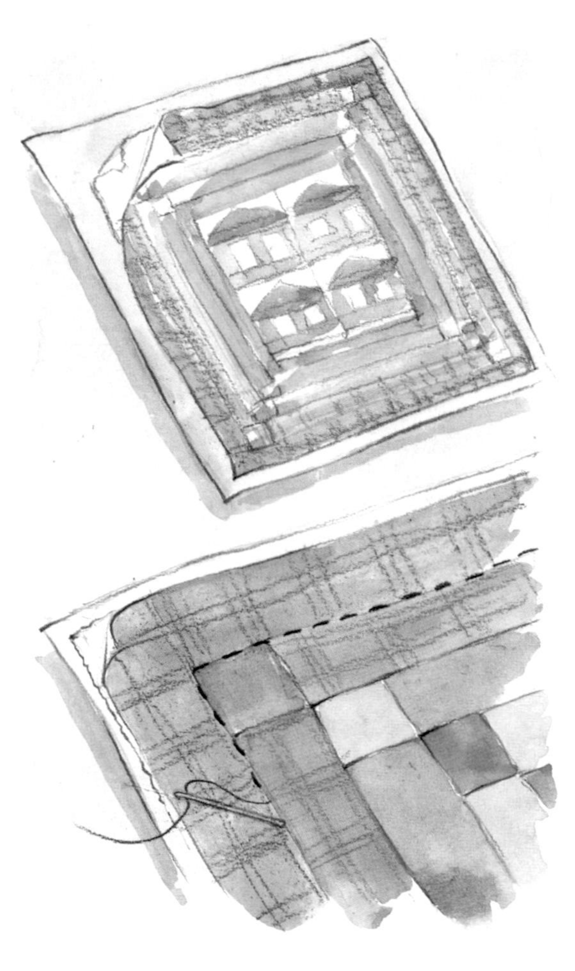

**8 Quilting.** Cut a square of backing fabric 1 inch larger all around than the finished patchwork and lay it, right side down, on a flat surface. Place the batting on top and the patchwork, right side up, on top. Smooth carefully, then pin and baste the layers together, stitching vertically and horizontally in rows about 4 inches apart to form a grid. Quilt by machine or hand, following the contours of the patchwork.

**9** From the remaining fabric for the back, cut two pieces, each 22 x 39 inches. Cut two pieces the same size from the lining fabric. Place together right sides facing, and stitch along one long edge, with ¼-inch seam allowances. Turn right side out and press a new fold in the fabric so that the seam lies 1½ inches from the new edge. Repeat with the other two pieces. Insert the zipper between the two sections of the back, concealing it by overlapping one back section by 1 inch.

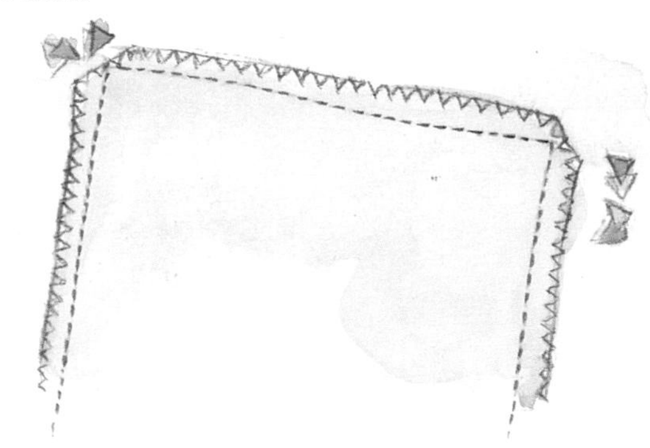

**10** Place the pillow front and back pieces together, right sides facing, and smooth carefully. Pin and baste together, then, with the patchwork on top, stitch around the edge, taking a seam allowance of ¼ inch. Trim the seams and corners, then overcast all seams before turning right side out. Insert the pillow form.

# Corded and Quilted Pillow

*Finished size: 14 x 14 inches*

*The leaf motif on this pillow cover was achieved by a technique known as Italian quilting or corded quilting, which is ideal for linear patterns. The raised effect is achieved by threading quilting wool through stitched channels, and we have enhanced the simple corded design by additional quilting.*

YOU WILL NEED

- needle, threads to match, pins, scissors
- cream fabric: 27 x 36 inches
- cardboard or plastic for templates
- gauze or loosely woven fabric: 27 x 36 inches
- dressmaker's chalk
- quilting wool and large tapestry needle
- lightweight polyester batting: 16 x 16 inches
- lining fabric or gauze: 16 x 16 inches
- quilting thread
- masking tape: ½-inch wide
- zipper: 12 inches long
- pillow form: 12 x 12 inches

1 Trace and make the templates shown on page 89. Follow the cutting instructions listed on page 89. Note the cut on the bias.

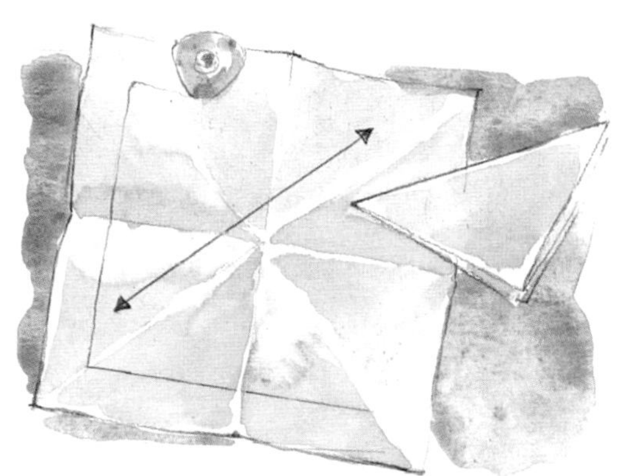

2 Cut the 16 x 16-inch square on the bias of the cream fabric for the front of the pillow. Press to mark the vertical and horizontal midlines. Fold in half and half again across the diagonals and press lightly to mark the corner to corner lines. Draw a 12 x 12-inch square as an outer guideline.

3 Position the larger template so that a horizontal line passes through the points of the leaf. The end marked with X should be toward the center. Transfer the outline to the fabric. Repeat on the opposite side and on the two vertical lines and on the two diagonal lines.

4 Use the smaller template to draw lines inside the large leaf shapes.

5 Baste the gauze to the back of the pillow front, taking lines of stitches horizontally and vertically across the pillow to make a grid.

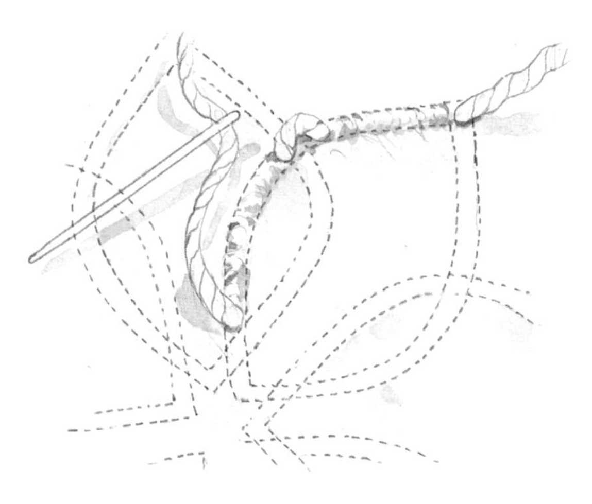

6 Stitch along the marked outlines of the leaf with a small, even running stitch. Where the lines intersect, pass the needle under the back of the diagonal leaves.

7 Beginning with the diagonal leaves, thread a tapestry needle with quilting wool. Push the needle through the gauze into the back of a stitched channel, at one of the points of a leaf. Slide the needle along the channel as far as you can, then bring it out through the gauze.
Pull the wool through the channel so that an end of ¼ inch is left, then reinsert the needle through the same opening and continue, leaving a small loop so that the fabric does not pucker.
Bring the wool out of the starting point and cut it off. Stitch the two ends together to prevent them from slipping through the channel. Work the other three diagonal shapes in the same way.

8 Then work the horizontal and vertical leaves. Where the lines intersect, bring the wool out of the channel and reinsert on the other side of the line.

9 Place a square of lining or gauze, 16 x 16 inches, the batting and pillow front in layers and pin and baste together.

10 Stipple quilt (small random stitches as illustrated) in the outer vertical and horizontal leaf shapes and in the central area.

11 Use masking tape to mark a diagonal grid of quilting lines and quilt as illustrated. Trim the pillow front to 15 x 15 inches.

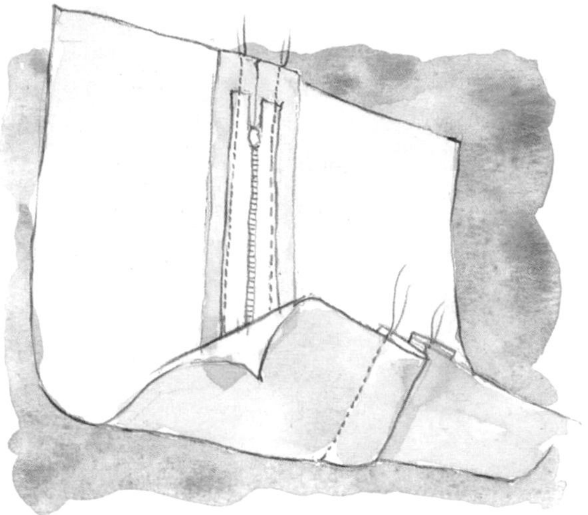

12 Cut two pieces of cream fabric, each 16 x 19 inches, for the back of the pillow. Insert the zipper.

13 Place the front and back right sides together and stitch around all outer edges. Trim the seams and corners and turn right side out.

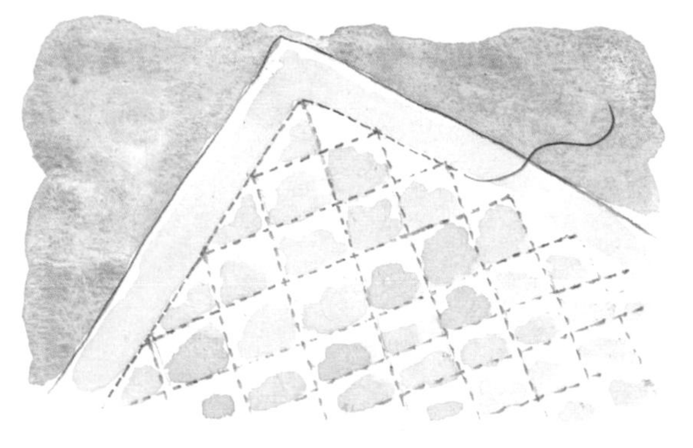

14 Stitch around the outer edge, through all thicknesses, on the 12-inch square line marked in step 2, to form a border. Insert the pillow form.

# STAR AND PINWHEEL SHOULDER BAG

*Finished size: 16 x 16 inches*

*We have used four Friendship Star blocks arranged around a central pinwheel for this decorative shoulder bag, which is large enough to hold all the bits and pieces you need.*

YOU WILL NEED

- needle, threads to match, pins, scissors
- template plastic or cardboard
- white fabric: 18 x 36 inches
- blue fabric: 27 x 36 inches
- red fabric: 8 x 8 inches
- lightweight polyester batting: 18 x 38 inches
- lining fabric: 18 x 38 inches
- 1 button

1 Trace and make templates shown on page 90 from cardboard or plastic. Follow the cutting instructions listed on page 90.

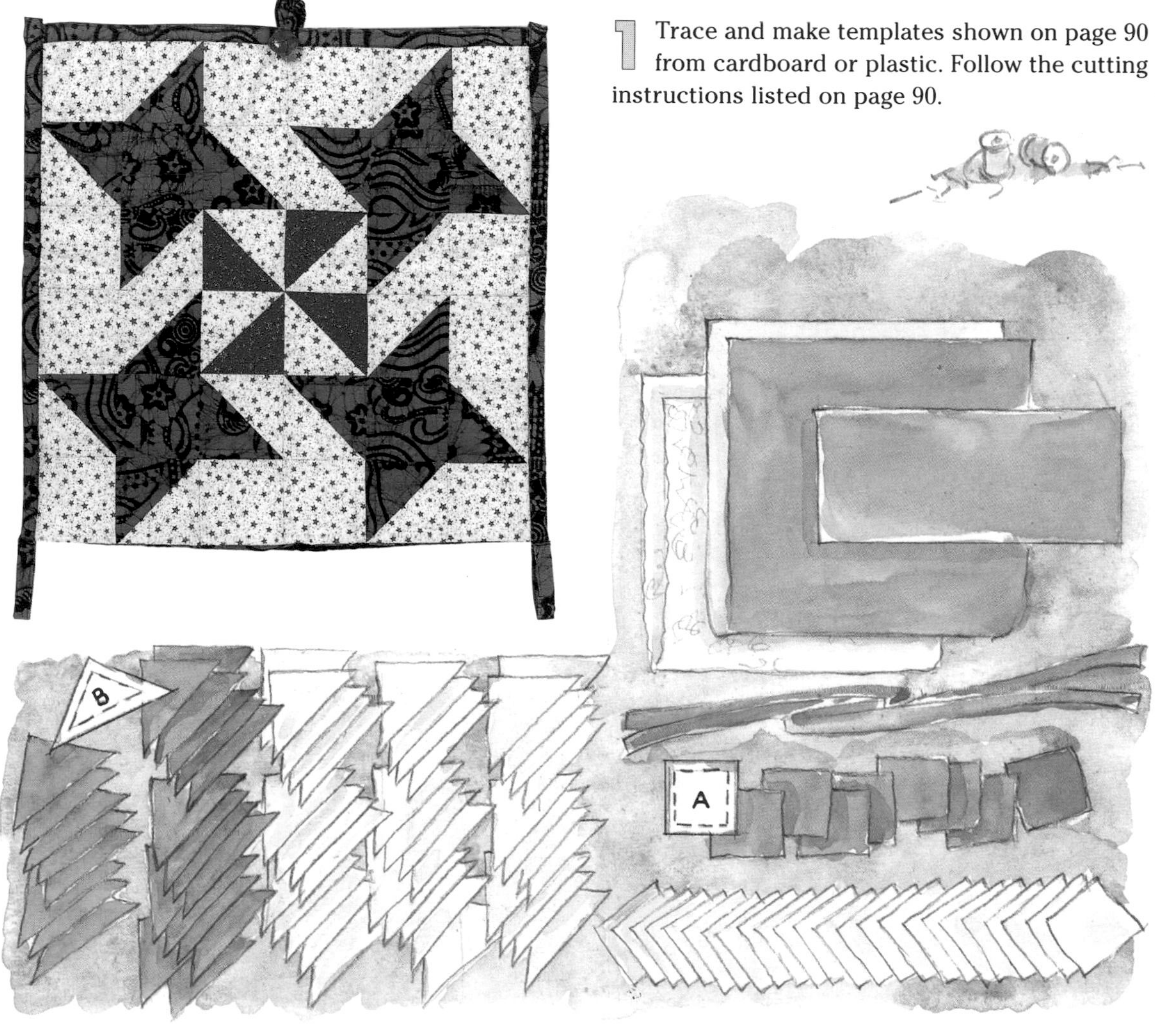

2 Follow the piecing diagram above to assemble eight blocks and join these into two blocks of four as shown. Use a seam allowance of ¼ inch on all patchwork pieces.

3 Stitch the blue fabric strip between the two blocks to form the gusset at the base.

4 Place the lining fabric wrong side up. Lay the batting on it and place the patchwork, right side up on the batting to form a sandwich. Pin and baste the three layers together, making sure you have lines of stitches at intervals of 4 inches, both horizontally and vertically.

5 Quilt by hand or machine, using the seams between the patchwork pieces as a guide. Trim the lining and batting so they are level with the patchwork edges.

6 Cut two strips of blue fabric, 2½ x 15½ inches, and fold them in half lengthwise with wrong sides facing. Press. Make a straight binding to cover both short edges of the bag (see page 53).

7 Make a fabric loop through which the button will pass. Insert the loop halfway along one side, under the edge binding.

8 With the patchwork outward and the top edges together, pin and baste the sides of the bag together, folding the gusset in half so that it lies inside the bag. Stitch the sides of the bag together through all thicknesses of fabric.

9 Make two more lengths of folded binding for the straps, 2½ x 44 inches, and stitch them to the sides of the bag, extending the line of stitches along the whole length of each strip.

10 Leave 5 inches extending at the bottom on each side and fold these pieces up to form decorative loops at the base of the bag. Knot the straps together so that the bag hangs at a comfortable length and attach the button to the center of the front edge.

# Curtain Tieback

*Finished size: 3 x 30 inches*

*This is a neat way of tying back curtains, and you can select colors that contrast with or are the same shade as the curtains themselves. The checked effect looks complicated, but although it requires some patience, the technique is surprisingly simple.*

YOU WILL NEED

- needle, threads to match, pins, scissors
- light fabric: ⅞ yard
- dark fabric: ⅝ yard

1 Cutting from selvage to selvage, cut 2 dark strips 1½ inches wide and 2 light and 1 dark strip 1¼ inches wide.

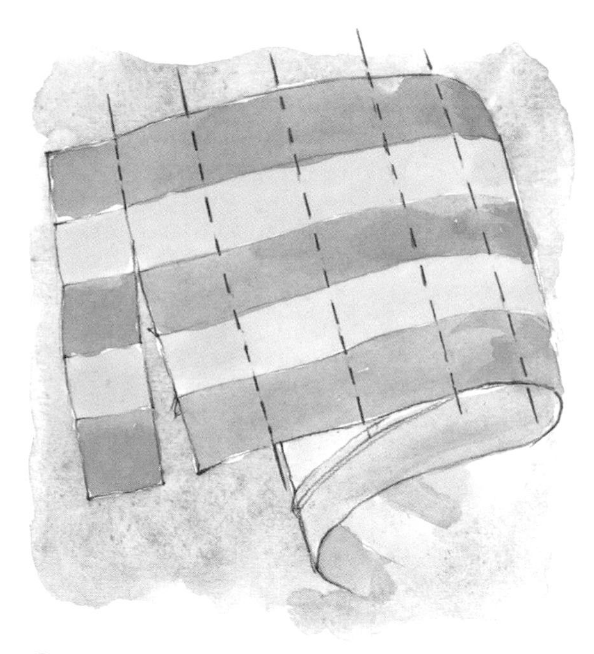

2 Taking a ¼-inch seam allowance, attach the strips in the sequence shown. Press seams toward darker fabric.

Cut the piece across into 26 strips, each 1¼ inches wide. Reposition so that dark and light shades are offset by one strip. Sew strips together, taking care to match the seams. Press the seams on the back.

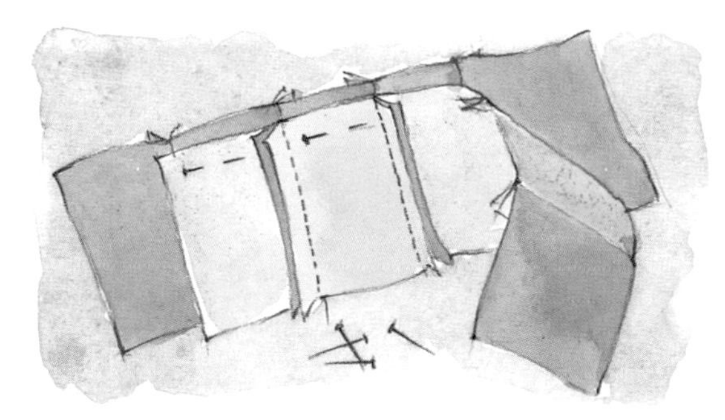

3 Lay the strip flat and mark a vertical line halfway. Cut along the vertical line and reverse the two pieces so that the vertical cuts are at each end and the original end pieces are now adjacent in the center. Stitch these two strips together.

4 Trim the triangles from the edges, leaving ¼ inch beyond the corners of the outer rows of squares.

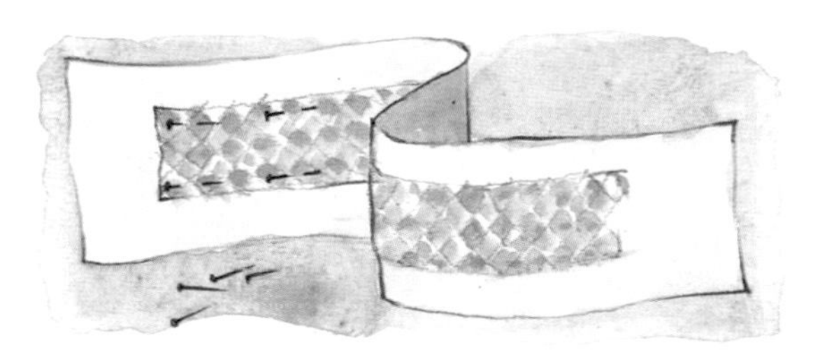

5 Cut a rectangle of light fabric 6 inches wide and 7 inches longer than the patchwork. Place the patchwork exactly in the center, wrong sides together. Pin and baste.

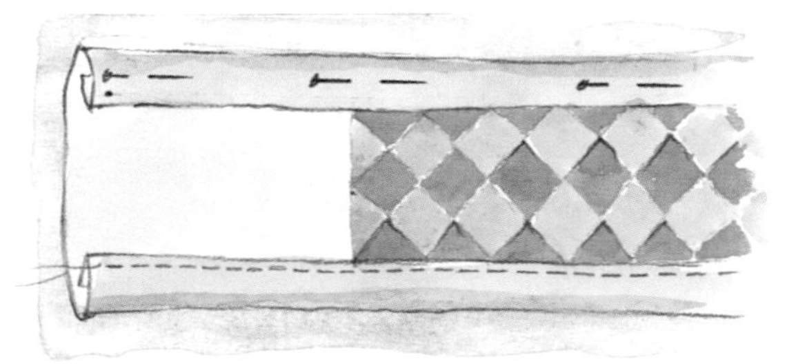

6 On the two long sides, take a double fold to bring the backing over to the right side of the patchwork, so that the edge of the fold is exactly on the corners of the squares in the outer rows. Stitch through the folded edges and the patchwork to hold the turned edge down.

7 At the short end, fold the excess back at an angle of 45 degrees to the bottom edge. Trim and tuck all raw edges neatly inside. Insert a narrow loop, about 4 inches, in each corner at each end and overcast. Reinforce the loops by stitching twice over the corners.

# Christmas Table Mats

*Finished size of each mat: 15 x 12 inches*

*Give your Christmas table setting a festive look with these practical mats. You can either stitch the patchwork by hand, with a running stitch, or machine stitch the pieces together. Similarly, the quilting stitches holding the patchwork, batting, and back together, can be worked by hand or by machine.*

YOU WILL NEED FOR FOUR MATS

- needle, threads to match, pins, scissors
- cardboard or plastic for templates
- three patterned fabrics: ⅜ yard of each
- backing fabric: ½ yard
- lightweight batting: 4 pieces, each 14 x 17 inches

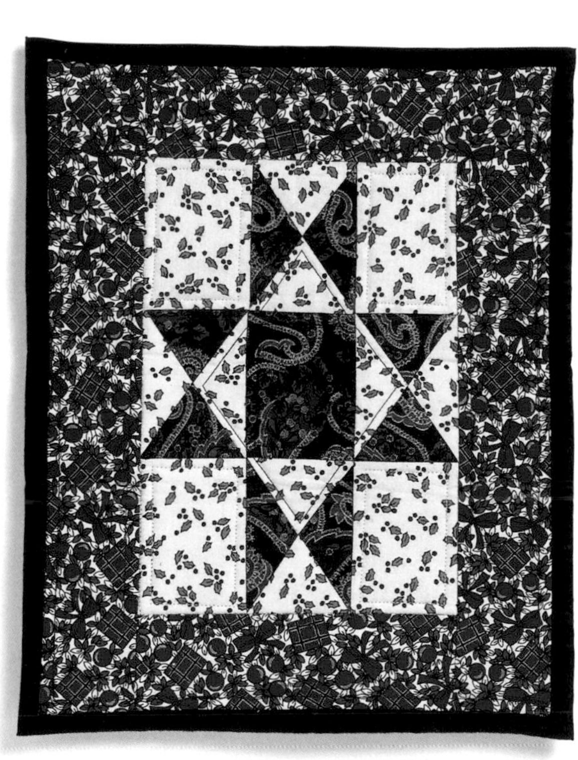

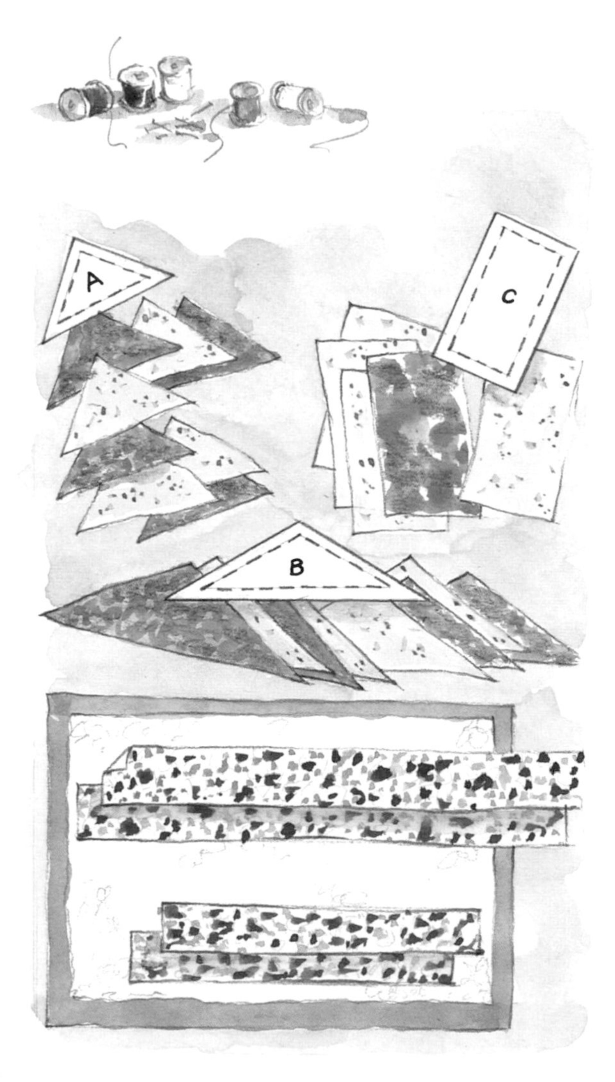


1 Trace and make templates on page 90 from cardboard or plastic. Follow cutting instructions listed on page 90. Cut out the pieces accurately. Do not cut the borders until you have finished stitching the blocks.

2 Make star points by piecing A and B as shown. Match the center lines. Arrange the rectangles with C pieces and stitch together in three columns. Complete the block by stitching the two long seams. Press well front and back.

3 **Adding the borders.** Stitch the two short borders on first. Add the longer borders to the top and bottom edges and press.

4 **Quilting.** Trim the batting to the exact size of the patchwork and place it on the backing piece. Cut it 1 inch larger all around. Place the patchwork on top. Smooth carefully, then pin and baste before quilting by hand or machine, following the contours of the patchwork.

5 Bring the backing fabric over to the right side of the mat by folding it double and enclosing the raw edges. At the corners, fold the backing so that the point just touches the corner. Trim off the small triangle along the crease, then double-fold around the corner, making a neat miter. Hand or machine hem the edge of the backing to form a neat self-binding.

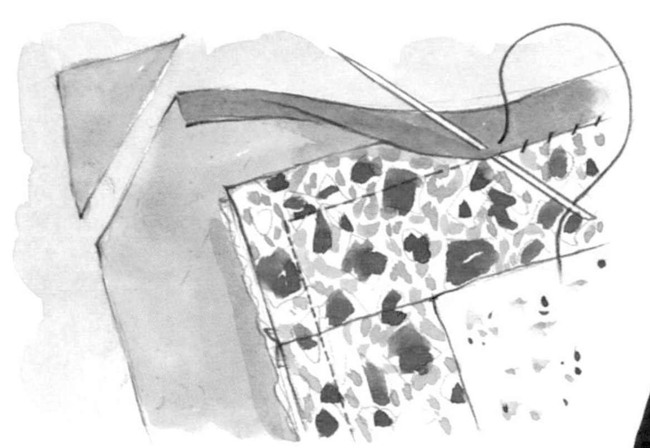

# FAN MOTIF PINCUSHION AND NEEDLECASE

*Finished size: 4 inches*

*The motif for the pincushion and needlecase is made by the paper-piecing method. Each fabric patch is basted to a piece of paper before the patches are stitched together, and when you are working with geometric shapes such as hexagons and diamonds, or with the sections of a motif such as this fan, this method is a good way of making sure that the pieces fit accurately together.*

YOU WILL NEED

- needle, threads to match, pins, scissors
- cardboard or plastic for templates
- heavy paper
- scraps of patterned fabric (3 colors)
- solid fabric: 5 x 20 inches
- small quantity polyester stuffing (for pincushion)
- lining fabric: 4½ x 10 inches (for needlecase)
- felt: 2 pieces, each 3¾ inches (for needlecase)
- embroidery thread

1 Trace and make the templates on page 91. from cardboard or plastic. Draw around the templates onto heavy paper. *For each item* cut four fan sections and one corner piece.

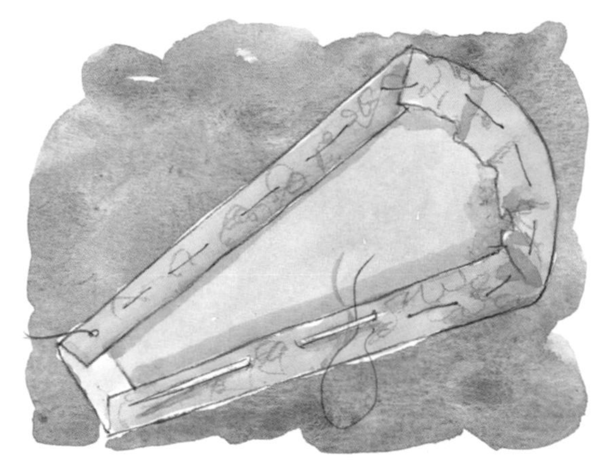

**2** **To make the motif:** Pin the five paper sections to the wrong side of the pattern fabric and cut each one out, adding ¼ inch all around for turning. Baste the paper to the fabric, except at the narrow ends of the fan pieces and the two straight edges of the corner piece.

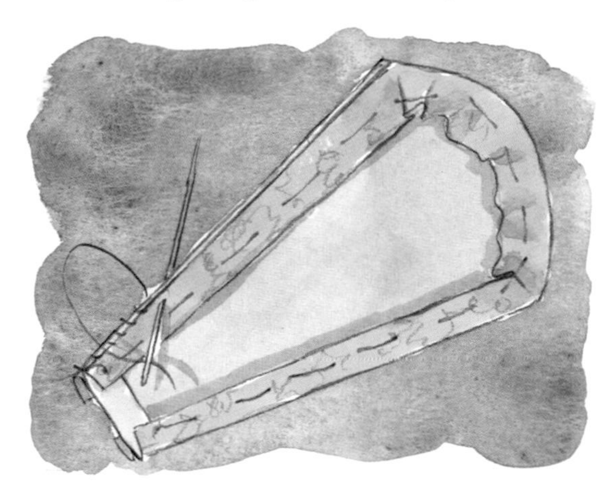

**3** Press all the pieces to finish the edges, then whipstitch the fan segments together. Carefully remove basting stitches and the paper from each section.

**4** Apply interfacing to the 4½-inch squares of solid fabric. Using small slipstitches, appliqué the four pieces of the fan section to the corner of the square.

**5** Remove the basting and paper from the corner piece and position it over the fan section. Appliqué in place.

**6** **To make the pincushion:** Place the two squares right sides together, and machine stitch around the outer edges, taking a seam allowance of ¼ inch and leaving a gap of 2½ inches on one side. Trim the corners and turn right side out. Stuff firmly and overstitch the gap by hand.

**7** **To make the needlecase:** Place the two squares, right sides facing, and stitch down one side so that the base of the fan motif is in the lower right-hand corner of the front. Press the seam open.

8 With right sides facing, pin and baste the lining fabric and outside of the case together. Stitch the two pieces together, with a ¼-inch seam allowance and leaving a gap of 3½ inches on one side. Clip corners and seams and turn right side out. Press and topstitch all four sides, closing the gap as you do so.

9 Use pinking shears to trim the two pieces of felt to fit inside the case and stitch them in place down the center.

10 Make a tassel by wrapping embroidery thread around a piece of cardboard 3 inches deep. Slide the threads off, wrap another piece of thread around the top, trim the bottom and stitch to the corner of the fan motif.

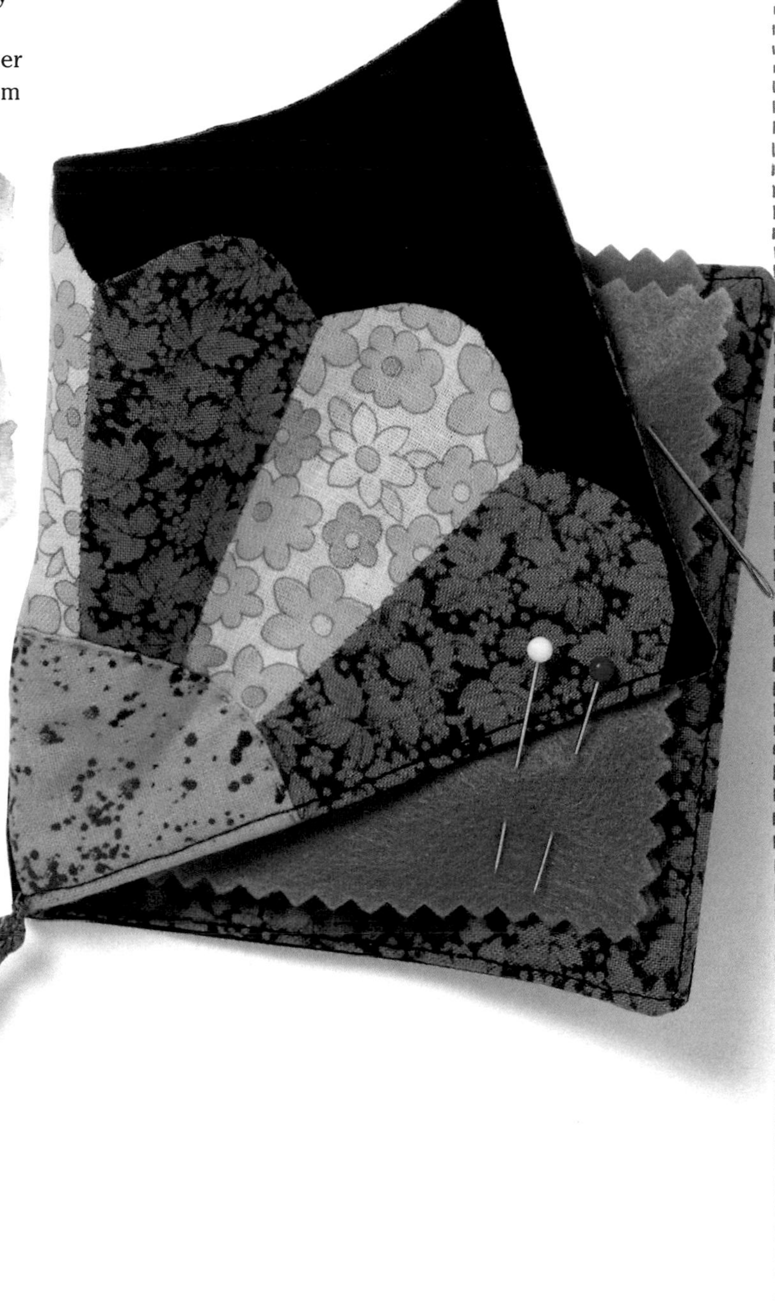

# "QUILLOW" OR LAP QUILT

*Finished size: 43 x 55 inches*

*When it is not being used, this lap quilt can be folded away and tucked into a matching pocket stitched to the back, so that it can do double-duty as a cushion or pillow. The patchwork top is made from two easy designs – Churn Dash and Ohio Star – which work well together. A thick batting has been used for extra warmth, and the three layers are tie-quilted.*

YOU WILL NEED

- needle, threads to match, pins, scissors
- purple print: 1⅜ yards
- green print: ¾ yard
- yellow print: 1¼ yards
- beige print: ¾ yard
- medium-weight polyester batting: 46 x 58 inches
- lightweight polyester batting: 19 x 19 inches
- backing: 1¾ yards (use material 60-inches wide or join pieces together)
- pearl cotton no. 8, in matching or contrasting color

1 Trace and make templates on page 91. Follow the cutting instructions listed on page 91. Do not cut the borders until you have finished stitching the blocks so you can be sure the length fits.

2 The patchwork top is made of 12 blocks; the pillow panel on the back requires one block. You will need six Churn Dash blocks and seven Ohio Star blocks.

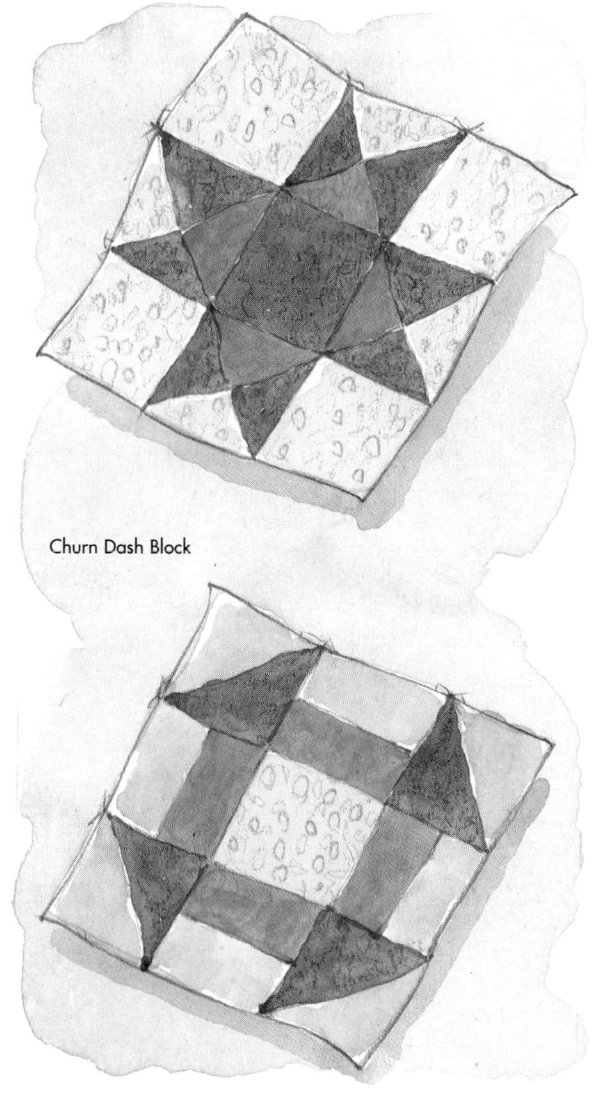

Churn Dash Block

Ohio Star Block

3 Follow the diagram to piece the patchwork into six Churn Dash blocks.

4 Follow the diagram to piece the patchwork into seven Ohio Star blocks.

**5** Stitch the blocks alternately together into a 3 x 4 panel. Retain one Ohio Star block for the pillow.

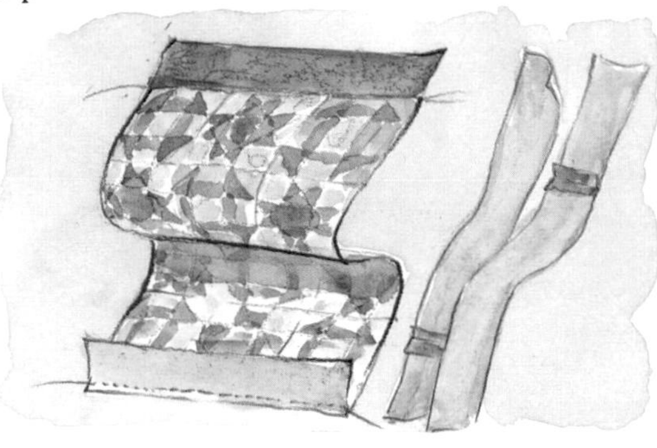

**6** **Adding the borders.** Cut strips of purple fabric, 4½ inches wide, to edge the panel, stitching top and bottom first and joining strips as necessary for the sides. Press well.

**7** Place the patchwork and backing, right sides together, on top of the medium-weight batting with wrong side of patchwork on the top. Smooth and baste the three layers together around the outside edge. The backing and batting will extend beyond the patchwork. Machine stitch, taking a ¼-inch seam allowance on the patchwork and leaving a gap in one long side. Trim the excess batting and backing on all sides and corners and turn right side out.

**8** Push the corners out with a knitting needle. Baste around the edges, making sure the seams lie neatly. Close the gap, then machine stitch ¼ inch from the edge.

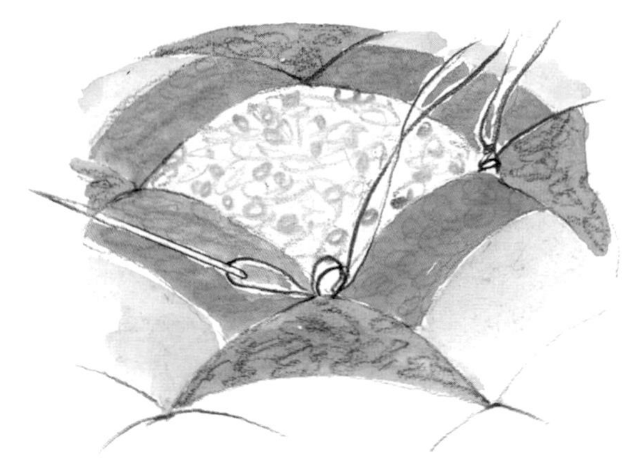

**9** Thread a needle with a long strand of pearl cotton and pull it double. Make a stitch through all layers of the quilt, leaving a tail, then make a backstitch over the first and bring the needle out on the same side of the fabric. Tie the ends in a square knot, then trim to about 1inch long. Alternatively, use French knots, buttons, or beads instead of, or in addition to, the knots.

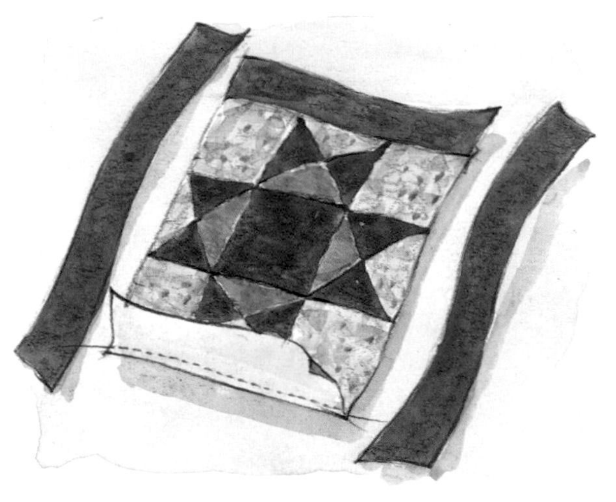

**10** Make the pocket by cutting from the border fabric two strips 3 x 12½ inches, and two strips, each 3 x 17½ inches. Stitch the two shorter strips to opposite sides of the remaining Ohio Star block, then add the two longer strips to make a square 17½ x 17½ inches.

**11** Cut a piece of backing fabric, 18½ x 18½ inches, and place the block and the backing right sides together on top of the lightweight batting, with the wrong side of the patchwork upward. Pin and baste the layers together. Stitch around the edges, with a ¼-inch seam allowance on the patchwork and leaving a gap on one long side. Trim the backing and batting and clip the corners, then turn right side out.

**12** Push out the corners, baste around the edge, making sure the seams are straight, and close the gap. Machine stitch ¼ inch around the edge.

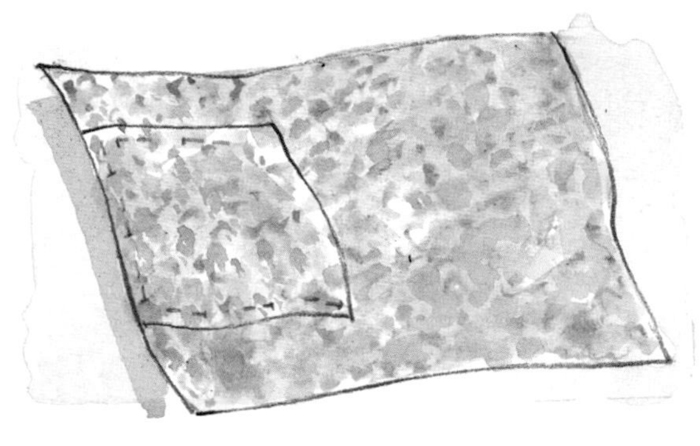

**13** Position the pocket on the back of the quilt, pinning it with the patchwork side inward. Slipstitch around three sides, reinforcing the corners of the open side with extra stitches.

Make the quilt into a pillow by making two lengthwise folds in line with the sides of the pocket. Turn the pocket to the outside, pulling the bottom part of the quilt as you do so, pushing out the corners. Fold down the top end of the quilt to the edge of the pocket and tuck it inside.

# FLYING GEESE STORAGE TUBE

*Finished size: 10 x 24 inches*

*Keep your plastic bags neat and handy with this ingenious tube. You simply push the bags in the top, then pull them out through the elasticized base when you need them.*

YOU WILL NEED

- needle, threads to match, pins, scissors
- cardboard or plastic for templates
- main fabric: ⅞ yard
- contrasting fabric: ⅜ yard
- shirring elastic: 6 inches

1 Trace and make the templates on page 91 from cardboard or plastic. Follow cutting instructions listed on page 91. Note the direction of the grain.

2 Piece together the patchwork panel from the triangles, taking ¼-inch seam allowance throughout. Press seams open.

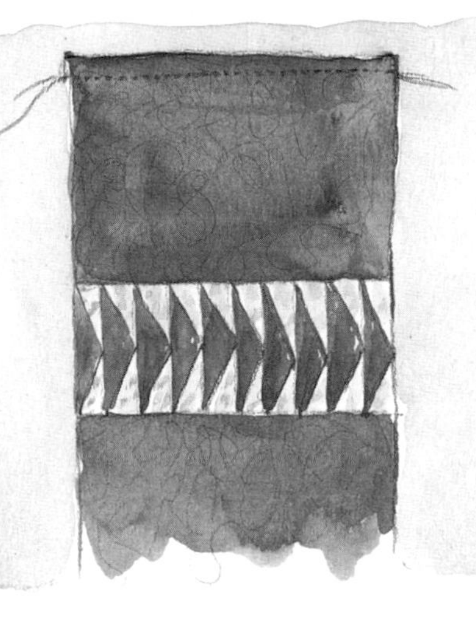

3 From the main fabric cut 1 piece 8 x 20½ inches and 1 piece 20½ x 26 inches. Stitch the patchwork panel between these two pieces. Turn, press, and stitch a narrow hem along both remaining short ends.

4 Fold the piece in half lengthwise, right sides together, and matching the patchwork panel. Pin and baste, then stitch the long sides together to make a tube.

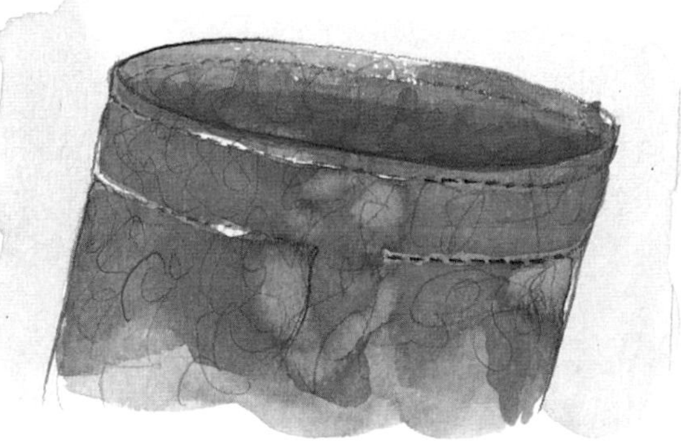

5 Turn the tube in half, with the short ends aligned and with wrong sides facing. The larger piece of fabric (the cuff and lining) should be on the inside. Pin the two open ends together matching the seams.

Make a casing for the elastic by stitching around the bottom 1 inch from the edge, then again ¼ inch in, leaving a gap in the second row through which you can thread the elastic. Pull the elastic tight, knot it, trim the ends and close the gap with a few stitches.

**6** Smooth the tube so that the lining and outer fabric lie neatly together. Topstitch around the fold and attach a 10-inch long hanging loop (see page 53), made in the outer fabric, near the seam.

# WALL POCKETS

*Finished size: 21 x 27 inches*

*These useful wall pockets, decorated with bright colored triangles, will provide extra storage space for a host of everyday items – string, scissors, note-pad, pens, and pencils.*

YOU WILL NEED

- needle, threads to match, pins, scissors
- base fabric: 2¼ yards
- lining: 2¼ yards
- lightweight batting: 22 x 28 inches
- colored fabrics: a total of ⅝ yard in different solid colors for the strips and triangles
- firm muslin: ⅝ yard
- hanging rod

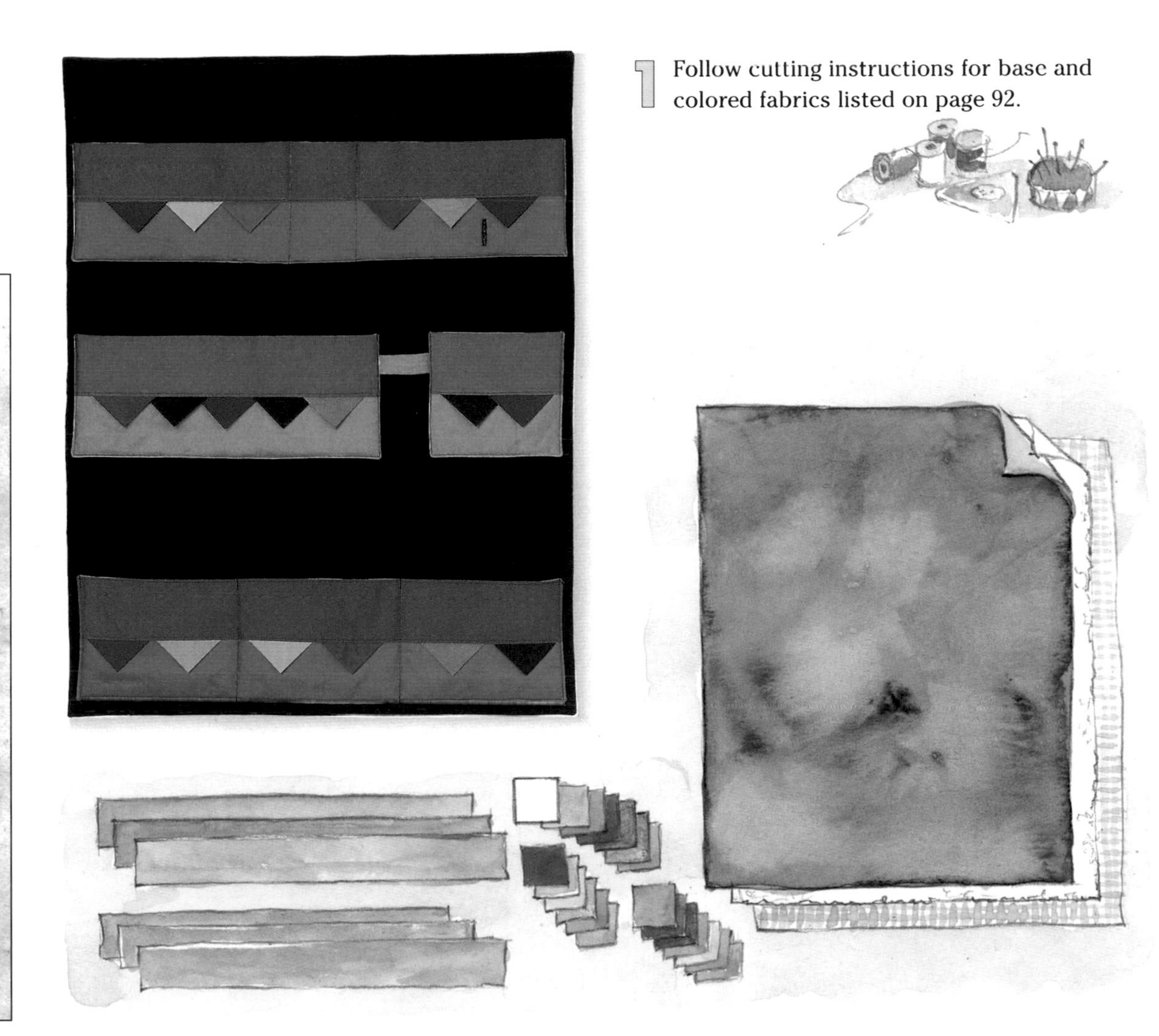

1 Follow cutting instructions for base and colored fabrics listed on page 92.

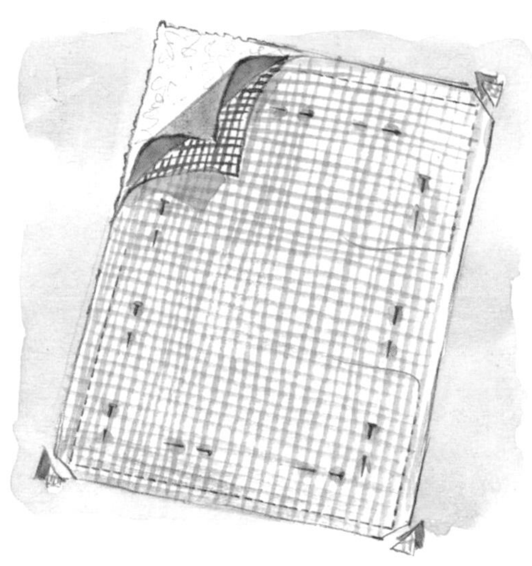

2 Baste the base fabric and lining right sides facing, with wadding underneath. Stitch ½in/1.25cm from the edge, leaving a 6in/15cm gap on one side. Trim seams and turn to the right side. Top stitch ¼in/5mm from the edge, closing the gap as you do.

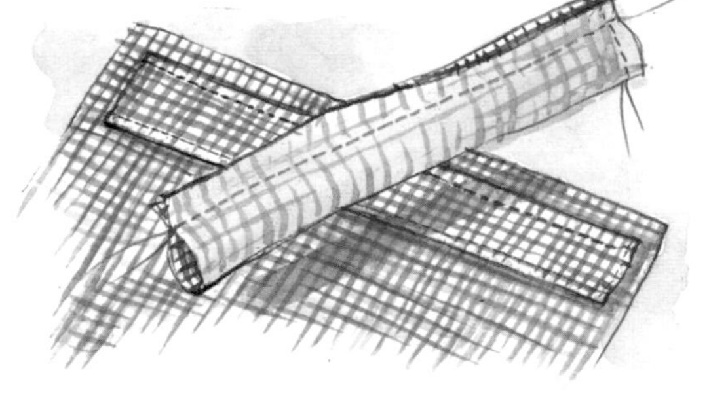

3 Fold the base fabric strip in half, right sides together, and stitch along the long edge. Press the seam open in the centre of the tube. Stitch across one short end. Turn to right side and neaten the other short end. With the seam underneath, stitch to the top of the base along the long edges, leaving the short ends open to accommodate a hanging rod.

4 Fold and press 12 colored squares in half and in half again diagonally. Make the lower pocket by marking one contrasting color strip into thirds, then arranging six triangles, in three groups of two along one edge. Make the top pocket by arranging the remaining triangles in two sets of three. Place the second contrasting strip, right side down, over the first strip. Stitch together, trapping the triangles in the seam. Topstitch on front.

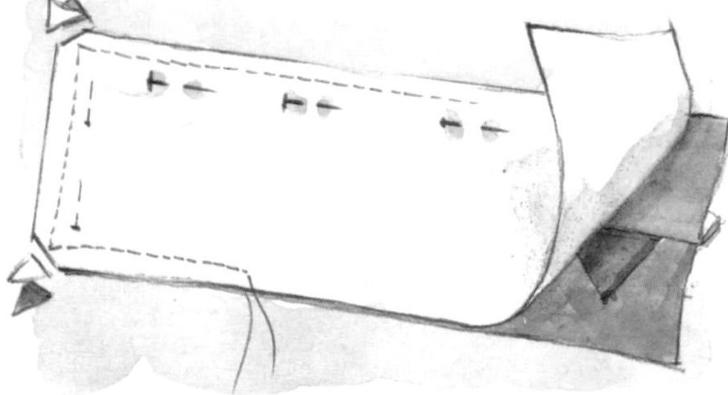

5 Place the pockets, right sides down, on the muslin and cut lining to match. Stitch the pockets to the lining, leaving a gap on the lower edge. Trim and turn right side out. Press.

6 Make the center pockets in the same way as the lower and top, but cut strips 3 x 13 inches for the left-hand pocket and 3 x 6 inches for the right-hand pocket. Position seven more triangles.

7 Make a loop, for scissors, from a strip of fabric 2 x 6 inches (see page 53).

8 Position the lower pockets along the bottom of the base and stitch around the sides and bottom edge. Divide the pocket in three and stitch the vertical lines.

9 Draw a line on the base, 5 inches above the lower pockets. Position the center pockets on this line, with the scissor loop between them and under the sides of the pockets. Stitch sides and bottom edges.

10 Work a buttonhole to hold string on one side of the top pockets. Position the top pockets 3 inches from the top edge. Stitch sides and bottom edges, divide into three and stitch vertical lines, making a narrow section for pens and pencils.

Trim all ends and insert the hanging rod.

# Belt or Shoulder Purse

*Finished size: 7 x 8 inches*

*When you are traveling, this is the ideal way to keep your passport and other valuables safe. The purse will fit onto a belt or you can thread a length of cord through the side loops for a shoulder strap.*

YOU WILL NEED

- needle, threads to match, pins, scissors
- scraps of pattern fabric for patchwork panel: 19 pieces, each 1½ x 3½ inches
- paper for templates
- fabric for side panels: ¼ yard
- lining fabric: ¼ yard
- iron-on interfacing: 8 x 19 inches
- snap fastener

1 Trace and make templates on page 92 from cardboard or plastic. Follow the cutting instructions listed on page 92.

**2** Stitch 19 patchwork pieces in a long strip, taking a ¼-inch seam allowance. Press seams to one side. Stitch two side panels, right sides facing, aligning the straight ends with the bottom of the strip. Press seams to the side. Topstitch on side panels ¼ inch from seam.

**3** Iron the interfacing to the wrong side of the patchwork piece.

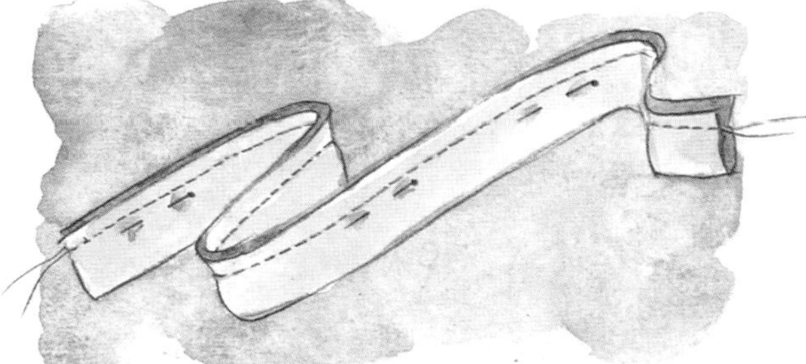

**4** Make the side loop by folding the strip of fabric in half lengthwise, right sides together, and stitch the long edge. Trim seam and turn right side out. Press the seam at center back.

**5** Cut the loops into two equal pieces and fold each piece in half. Pin them, one at each side, to the edge of the patchwork piece.

**6** Place the patchwork and lining together, right sides facing. Stitch around the outer edge, trapping the loops in the stitching, but leaving a gap on one of the long sides. Trim the seam and turn right side out. Press.

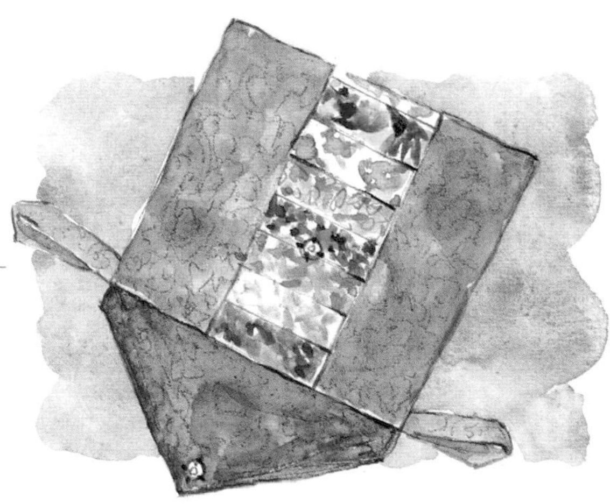

**7** Fold up the bottom 7 inches and baste the sides together to form a square. Stitch the two sides, closing the gap and creating a pocket. Sew on the snap to close the purse.

# Crazy Patchwork Wall Hanging

*Finished size: 31 x 38 inches*

*Crazy patchwork is an excellent method of using up scraps of fabric. It was especially popular in the 19th century, when all kinds of exotic materials, left over from elaborate dresses, were used, together with scraps of ribbon, lace, embroidered details, and even sentimental mementoes. This wall hanging is made from 12 individual blocks, with linking strips in the single color. Although the scraps are irregular shapes, they should all have straight sides.*

YOU WILL NEED

- needle, threads to match, pins, scissors
- scraps of silk, taffeta, satin, etc.
- medium-weight muslin: 1¼ yards
- embroidery thread
- sashing: ⅝ yard
- solid cotton for border: ⅝ yard
- backing fabric: 1¼ yards
- lightweight polyester batting: 1¼ yards
- black binding fabric: ⅝ yard

1 Follow the cutting instructions on page 92. Do not cut the border strips until you have completed the block to be sure they fit.

**2** Place a 4- or 5-sided scrap of fabric in the corner of a muslin square, right side up. Press and pin. Following the diagram, place a second scrap over the first, right sides together, aligning one straight edge. Stitch through both layers of silk and muslin. Press and unfold the second piece. Trim the sides so the straight edge of the first patch extends along the second. Continue in this way, varying the shapes and sizes of the patches, until you have completed 12 large and 4 small squares. Trim the blocks to square them up and baste around the edges to fasten the scraps to the muslin. Embroider the seams with a linear stitch, such as herringbone, feather stitch or fly stitch.

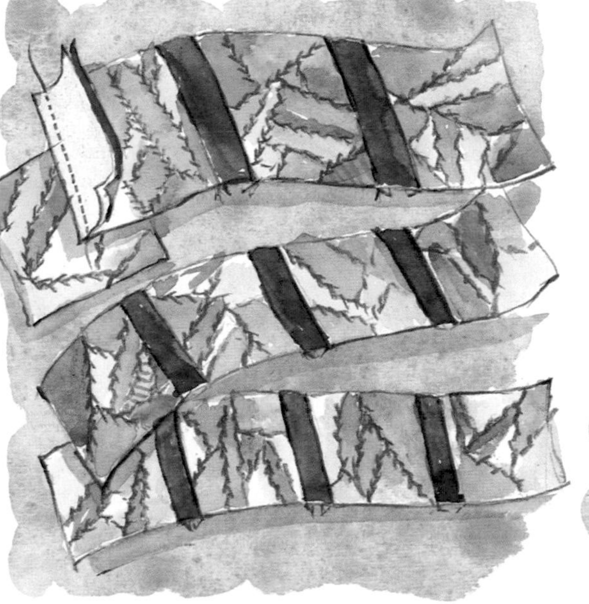

**3** Back the sashing with muslin so it is a similar weight to the blocks. Use the short sashing strips to join the large squares in three rows of four squares each.

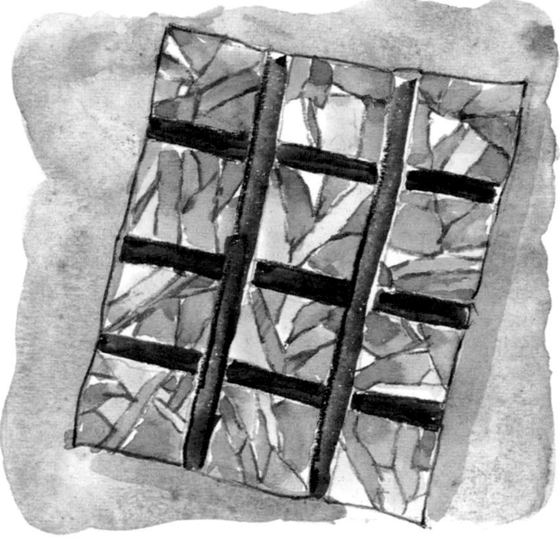

**4** Use the two longer strips of sashing to join the three strips. Trim all edges.

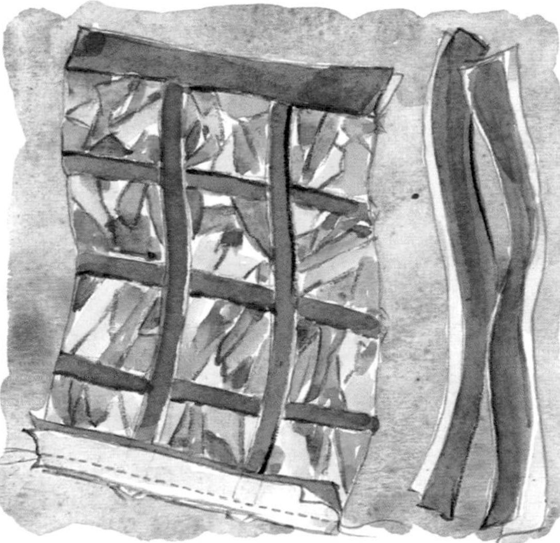

**5** Adding the inner border: Measure the length of the finished work and cut four border strips in sashing 2 inches wide. Back with muslin. Stitch pieces in position.

6 Adding the outer border: Again check the correct lengths of the finished work, and cut four strips 4 inches wide. Stitch the longer sides first. Stitch the small patchwork squares to each end of the shorter border strips, then add the shorter border strips, top and bottom. Topstitch the outer edge of the border

7 Make a sandwich of the backing fabric, batting, and the finished patchwork and pin and baste in horizontal and vertical rows at intervals of 6 inches. Quilt around each block and each border piece by machine or by hand. Remove basting stitches.

8 Cut strips of binding 2½ inches wide, joining as necessary to make a strip long enough to go right around the finished work. Fold in half lengthwise and press. Stitch to the right side of the patchwork, miter the corners (see page 53). Turn the binding to the back and hem by hand. To accommodate a hanging rod, follow Step 3 on page 82 (Wall Pockets).

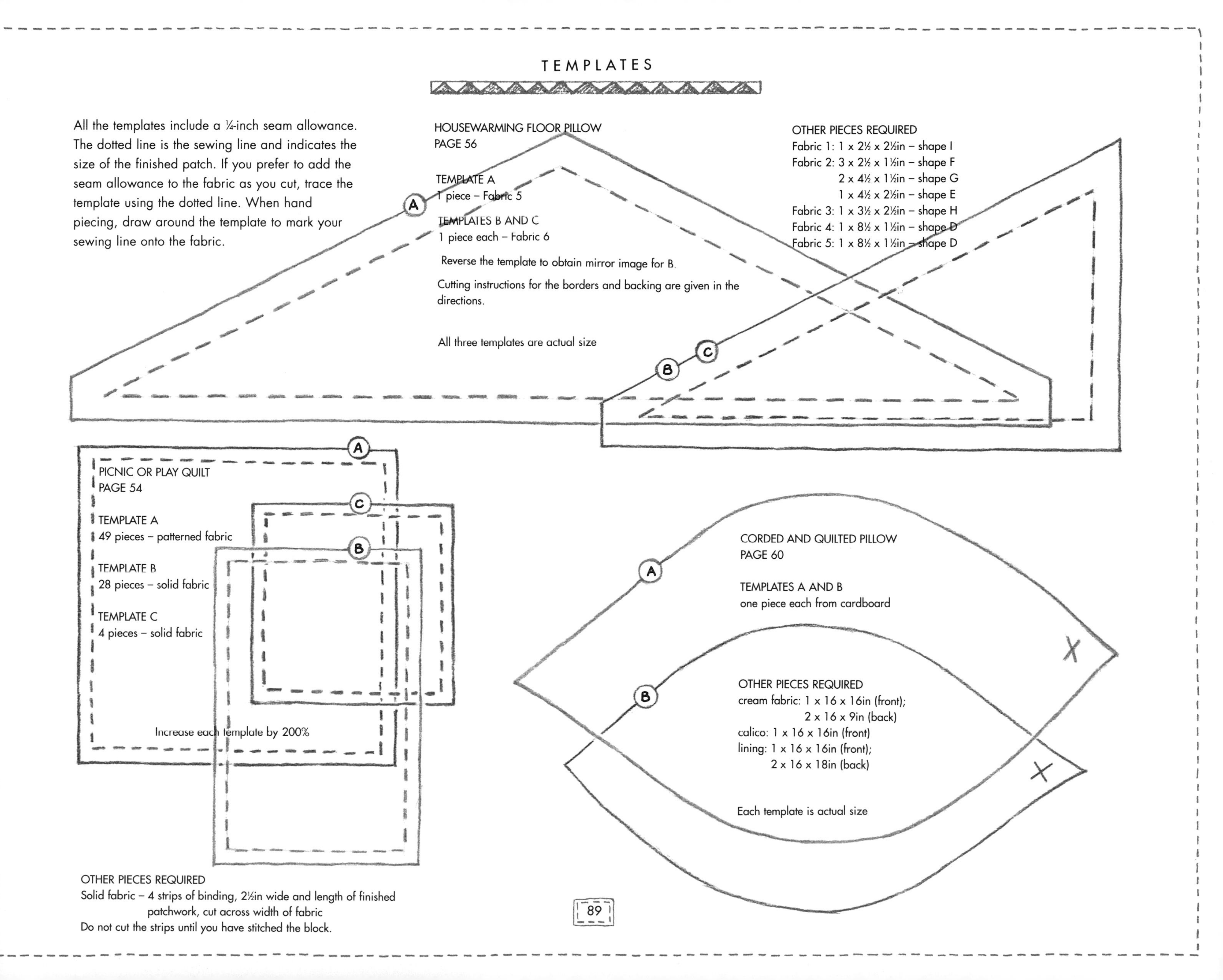




All the templates include a ¼-inch seam allowance. The dotted line is the sewing line and indicates the size of the finished patch. If you prefer to add the seam allowance to the fabric as you cut, trace the template using the dotted line. When hand piecing, draw around the template to mark your sewing line onto the fabric.

HOUSEWARMING FLOOR PILLOW
PAGE 56

TEMPLATE A
1 piece – Fabric 5

TEMPLATES B AND C
1 piece each – Fabric 6

Reverse the template to obtain mirror image for B.

Cutting instructions for the borders and backing are given in the directions.

All three templates are actual size

OTHER PIECES REQUIRED
Fabric 1: 1 x 2½ x 2½in – shape I
Fabric 2: 3 x 2½ x 1½in – shape F
2 x 4½ x 1½in – shape G
1 x 4½ x 2½in – shape E
Fabric 3: 1 x 3½ x 2½in – shape H
Fabric 4: 1 x 8½ x 1½in – shape D
Fabric 5: 1 x 8½ x 1½in – shape D

PICNIC OR PLAY QUILT
PAGE 54

TEMPLATE A
49 pieces – patterned fabric

TEMPLATE B
28 pieces – solid fabric

TEMPLATE C
4 pieces – solid fabric

Increase each template by 200%

OTHER PIECES REQUIRED
Solid fabric – 4 strips of binding, 2½in wide and length of finished patchwork, cut across width of fabric
Do not cut the strips until you have stitched the block.

CORDED AND QUILTED PILLOW
PAGE 60

TEMPLATES A AND B
one piece each from cardboard

OTHER PIECES REQUIRED
cream fabric: 1 x 16 x 16in (front);
2 x 16 x 9in (back)
calico: 1 x 16 x 16in (front)
lining: 1 x 16 x 16in (front);
2 x 16 x 18in (back)

Each template is actual size

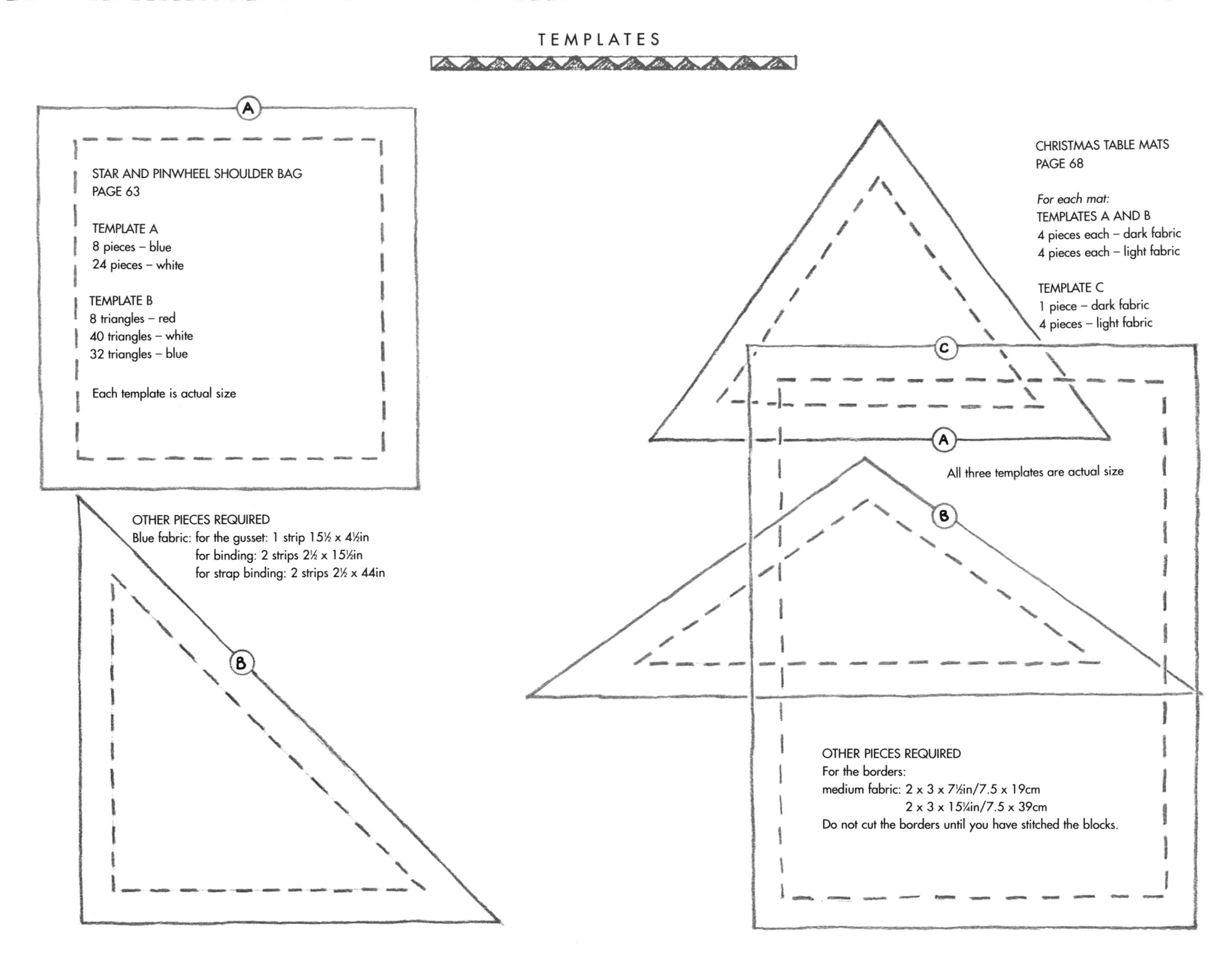
TEMPLATES
A
STAR AND PINWHEEL SHOULDER BAG
PAGE 63
TEMPLATE A
8 pieces – blue
24 pieces – white
TEMPLATE B
8 triangles – red
40 triangles – white
32 triangles – blue
Each template is actual size
B
OTHER PIECES REQUIRED
Blue fabric: for the gusset: 1 strip 15½ x 4½in
for binding: 2 strips 2½ x 15½in
for strap binding: 2 strips 2½ x 44in
CHRISTMAS TABLE MATS
PAGE 68
For each mat:
TEMPLATES A AND B
4 pieces each – dark fabric
4 pieces each – light fabric
TEMPLATE C
1 piece – dark fabric
4 pieces – light fabric
C
A
All three templates are actual size
B
OTHER PIECES REQUIRED
For the borders:
medium fabric: 2 x 3 x 7½in/7.5 x 19cm
2 x 3 x 15¼in/7.5 x 39cm
Do not cut the borders until you have stitched the blocks.

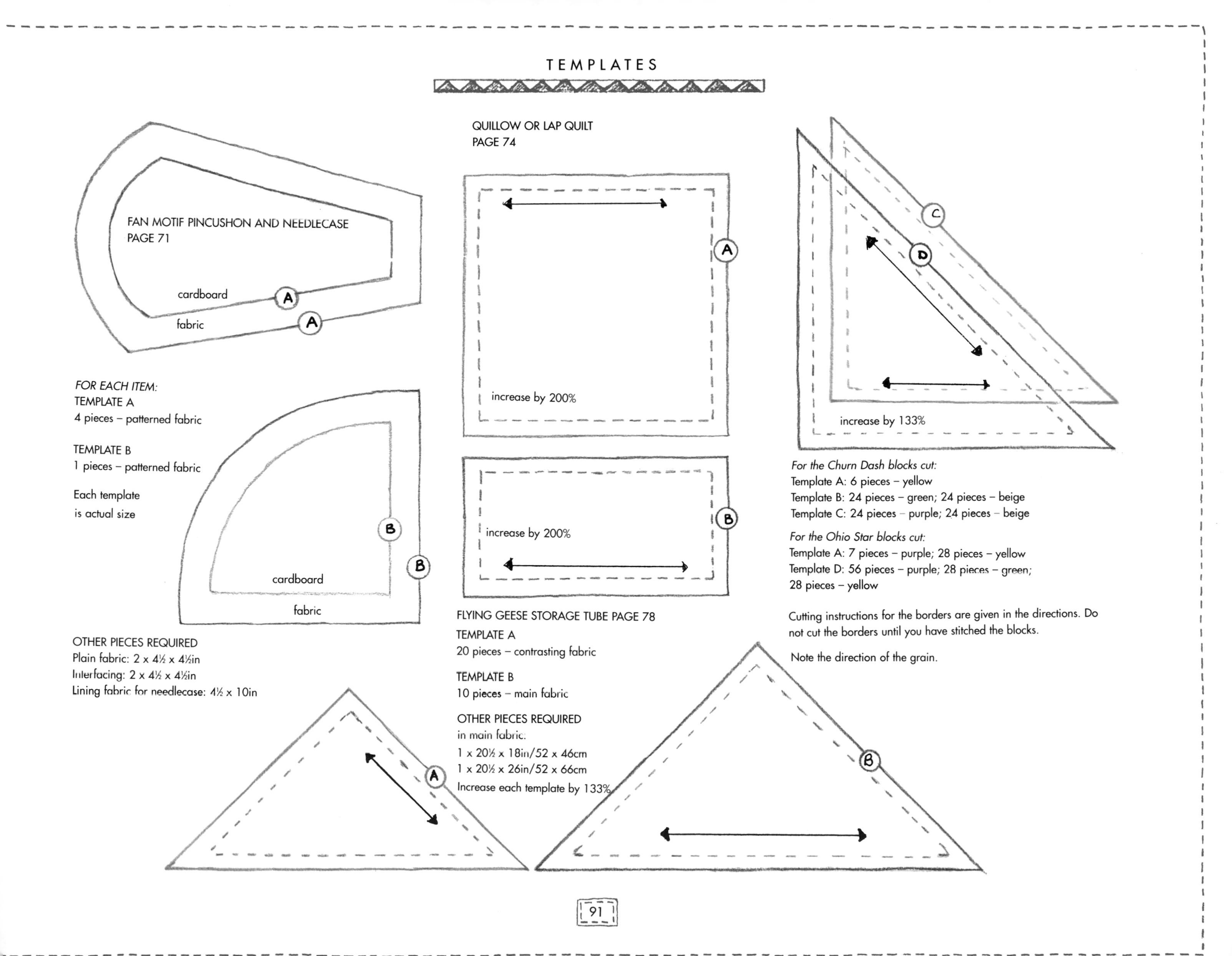
TEMPLATES
FAN MOTIF PINCUSHON AND NEEDLECASE
PAGE 71
cardboard
A
fabric
A
FOR EACH ITEM:
TEMPLATE A
4 pieces – patterned fabric
TEMPLATE B
1 pieces – patterned fabric
Each template
is actual size
B
B
cardboard
fabric
OTHER PIECES REQUIRED
Plain fabric: 2 x 4½ x 4½in
Interfacing: 2 x 4½ x 4½in
Lining fabric for needlecase: 4½ x 10in
QUILLOW OR LAP QUILT
PAGE 74
A
increase by 200%
B
increase by 200%
FLYING GEESE STORAGE TUBE PAGE 78
TEMPLATE A
20 pieces – contrasting fabric
TEMPLATE B
10 pieces – main fabric
OTHER PIECES REQUIRED
in main fabric:
1 x 20½ x 18in/52 x 46cm
1 x 20½ x 26in/52 x 66cm
Increase each template by 133%
A
B
C
D
increase by 133%
For the Churn Dash blocks cut:
Template A: 6 pieces – yellow
Template B: 24 pieces – green; 24 pieces – beige
Template C: 24 pieces – purple; 24 pieces – beige
For the Ohio Star blocks cut:
Template A: 7 pieces – purple; 28 pieces – yellow
Template D: 56 pieces – purple; 28 pieces – green;
28 pieces – yellow
Cutting instructions for the borders are given in the directions. Do not cut the borders until you have stitched the blocks.
Note the direction of the grain.
91

CRAZY PATCHWORK WALL-HANGING
PAGE 86

PIECES REQUIRED
muslin: 12 squares 7 x 7in
4 squares 4 x 4in
1 x 18 x 36in (optional)
sashing: 9 x 7 x 2in
2 x 32 x 2in
inner border: 2 x 21½ x 2in
2 x 31½ x 2in
outer border: 2 x 27 x 4in
2 x 34 x 4in
binding fabric: 1 x 18 x 36in
Do not cut the borders until you have stitched the block.

WALL POCKETS
PAGE 81

PIECES REQUIRED
Base fabric: 1 rectangle: 21½ x 27½in
1 strip: 22 x 6in
1 strip: 2 x 6in (for scissor loop)
Lining: 1 rectangle: 21½ x 27½in
Colored fabrics: 19 squares: 3 x 3in
4 strips: 21 x 3in
2 strips: 13 x 3in
2 strips: 6 x 3in

B

A

BELT OR SHOULDER PURSE
PAGE 84

TEMPLATE A
2 pieces – side panel fabric

TEMPLATE B
1 piece – lining
1 piece – interfacing

OTHER PIECES REQUIRED
Scraps of fabric: 19 x 3½ x 1½in
Side panel fabric: 1 strip 1½ x 14in (for side loops)

Increase each template by 220%

# CROSS-STITCH

*Special, yet simple, personal gifts, to create while learning traditional cross-stitch embroidery techniques*

# INTRODUCTION

Cross-stitch embroidery is an immensely satisfying and rewarding craft, offering tremendous scope for making beautiful gifts and adding to your own personal skills. The book contains a broad selection of practical projects to suit all tastes and occasions – each one carefully chosen for the simple skills involved in making it. Indeed, some projects, such as the jampot covers, paperweights and greetings cards, are "made up" without any additional sewing. The bookmark, for example, is so easy to complete that even a beginner to cross-stitch and general sewing could make it in an evening!

Once you have a little practice in cross-stitch, you may like to "mix and match" the motifs, for instance, working the wild flowers of the paperweights for greetings cards and so on.

You may also like to further personalize your embroidery with names, dates or dedications using the alphabets given on pages 45–48. The permutations are endless! Use this collection of ideas to create something special and make your cross-stitch quite unique.

## Basic Materials

### *Fabrics*

For best results, cross-stitch embroidery is worked on an evenweave fabric – this is any fabric that has the same number of threads counted in both directions, usually over 1 inch, and are generally referred to as 12, 14, 18 count or gauge, for example. The evenness of the weave ensures that all the cross-stitches are consistently square.

**Linen** is the traditional fabric for cross-stitching and is available in a good range of counts and colors. Natural colors are traditional and always popular and the slightly uneven appearance of many linens gives it a charming hand-woven look.

**Evenweave cottons** and cotton/linen mixes are also available in a great variety of colors and counts. Many of these examples can be bought as small sizes in handy packs, which is more economical than buying from the roll if you want to make only a single item. Evenweave cottons may feel very stiff due to the dressing they are given by the manufacturers. Although this can be washed out before you embroider to give a softer fabric, working on stiffened fabric may help you to stitch with an even tension.

### *Threads*

**Embroidery threads:** almost any type of embroidery thread can be used for cross-stitch embroidery, depending on the fabric count and thickness of thread. For the purposes of this book, DMC stranded embroidery cotton has been used throughout. Generally speaking, fewer strands are used on finer fabric and for suggesting fine detail, and vice versa. The exact number of strands used for the projects in the book is given with the individual instructions.

**Tacking thread** is a soft, loosely twisted cotton. The main advantages in using it are that (unlike ordinary sewing thread) it does not leave marks when pressed with an iron; should it get tangled it will break rather than damage the fabric, and it is more economical than sewing thread.

**Sewing threads** are fine, tightly twisted and strong. They are made in an excellent range of colors from cotton or cotton/polyester mixes.

### *Needles*

**Tapestry needles:** for working cross-stitch on evenweave fabrics, round-ended tapestry needles are used. Their smooth tips enable the needle to pass easily through the fabric without piercing the threads, available in sizes 18–26.

**Crewel needles:** for additional embroidery, such as the open buttonhole stitch on the shoe bag, page 11, medium-sized crewel needles are used. These have sharp points and long oval eyes and are available in sizes 1–10.

**Sharp sewing needles:** a selection will be needed for making up the projects.

### *Hoop*

Although many people prefer to work small amounts of cross-stitch in the hand, there are advantages to using a hoop. With the fabric evenly stretched, it helps to maintain an even tension to the cross-stitch. When the hoop is supported, it leaves both hands free to stitch – with one hand on top and the other below. It is possible to stitch evenly and faster this way.

### *Sewing machine*

A sewing machine is useful for making-up purposes, especially for bigger projects where longer seams are involved. In such cases, a machine-sewn seam is not only stronger than a hand-sewn one, but also quicker to complete.

### *General accessories*

You will also need the following items: stainless steel pins, a fabric tape measure, a thimble for hand sewing, especially through bulky seams, a ruler and pencil, and ideally three types of scissors: a pair of sharp dressmaker's shears for cutting out fabric, small embroidery scissors for snipping into seam allowances and trimming threads, and general purpose scissors for cutting paper, cords and so on; an iron and ironing board – preferably a thermostatically controlled iron which gives excellent results. Keep your iron and board to hand so that when you make up your projects, you can "press as you sew" to give a truly professional finish.

### *Working from a chart*

Working a cross-stitch design from a color chart is relatively easy. Each square on the chart represents one cross-stitch worked over a particular number of fabric threads; the exact number is given with each project.

Always begin your embroidery by marking the center of the fabric both ways with tacking stitches. You will see corresponding arrows on the chart which indicate the center of the design. Each chart has an accompanying color key to show matching embroidery thread colors which are identified by their numbers.

Mark the center of the chart with a small cross and begin stitching in the middle of the fabric, using the center lines on the fabric and chart as reference points for accurately counting the fabric threads and squares to center your design.

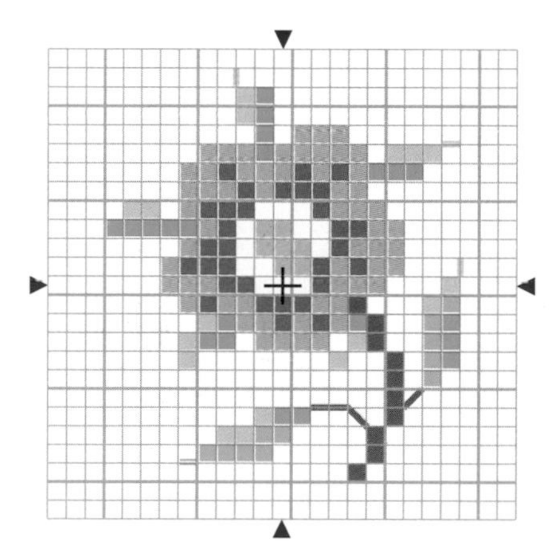

### *Alphabets*

Simple and elegant, or flamboyant and bold, alphabets have always been a popular subject for cross-stitch embroidery. The styles may vary enormously from the single line example used in the sampler on page 102 to the highly decorative type chosen for the bookmark on page 122.

Following the appropriate project instructions, use the relevant alphabets given on pages 133–136 to substitute your chosen name or initial, first drawing it on graph paper or in the space provided on the chart.

You may find it helpful to work from the alphabet charts if you have them enlarged so that the individual squares can be seen more clearly. Most photocopying services will do this for a minimum charge.

### *Preparing your fabric*

Begin by steam pressing the fabric to remove all creases. Should any remain, try to avoid those areas since it would be extremely difficult to remove them once the embroidery is worked.

Many evenweave fabrics, and linen in particular, fray easily in the hand so, once you have cut out your fabric, it is a good idea to overcast the edges using tacking thread.

### *Working in a hoop*

A hoop consists of two rings, usually of wood, which fit closely one inside the other. There is a screw attachment on the outer ring for adjusting the tension of the fabric and holding it firmly in place. Hoops are made in sizes varying from 4 inches across to large quilting hoops measuring 24 inches across.

## *Working in a hoop*

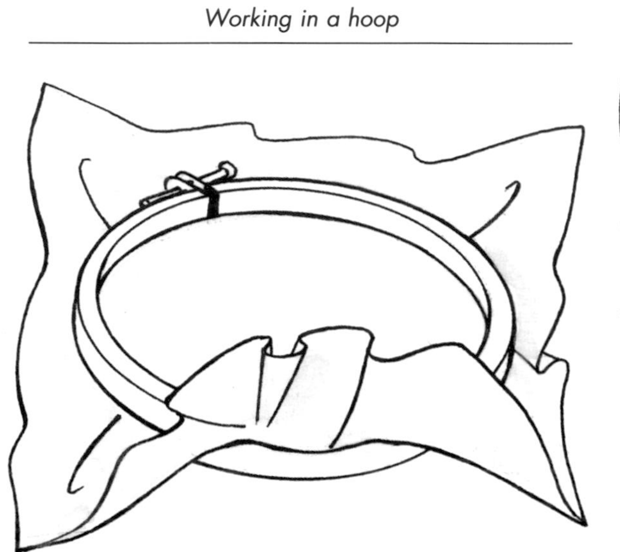

**1** To stretch your fabric in a hoop, place the area to be cross-stitched over the inner ring and press the outer ring over it with the tension screw released.

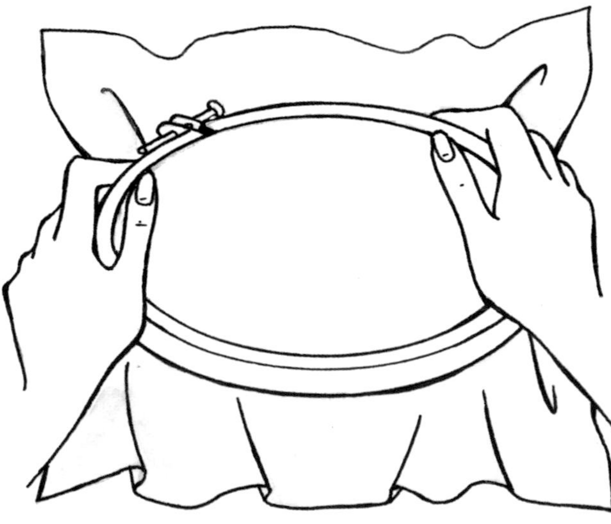

**2** Keeping the grain straight, smooth the fabric evenly and tighten the screw.

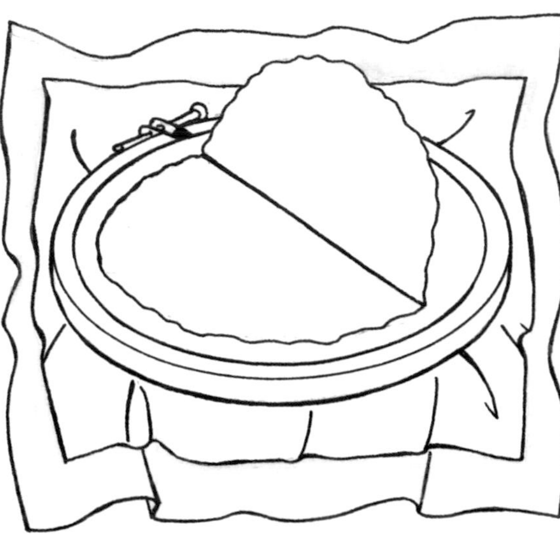

**3** To prevent the outer hoop from marking the fabric or embroidery, place tissue paper between the outer ring and the embroidery. Tear away the paper to expose the fabric as shown in the diagram.

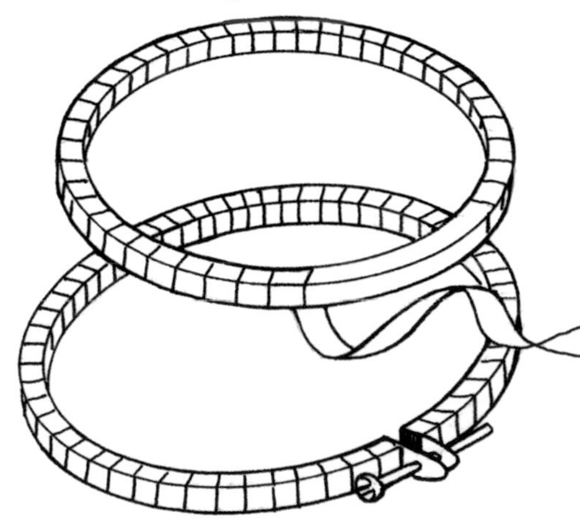

**4** Alternatively, before stretching the fabric, bind both rings with bias binding.

## *Running stitch*

Working from right to left, make small, even stitches, about ⅛ inch long, the same length as the spaces between. Pick up as many stitches as the needle will comfortably hold before pulling it through.

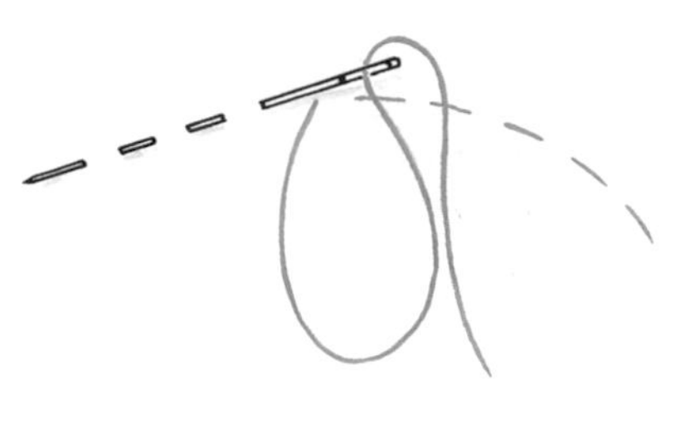

## *Slipstitch*

This small, almost invisible stitch, formed by slipping the thread under a fold of fabric, is used to join two folded edges such as the mitred corners on the table center (page 119), or one folded edge to a flat surface.

Working from right to left, bring the needle out through one folded edge. Slip the needle through the fold of the opposite edge for about ¼ inch. Bring the needle out and continue to slip the needle alternately through the two folded edges.

### *Beginning to cross-stitch*

Once you have located the center of your chart and the center of your fabric, and with the appropriately colored thread in your needle, insert it from the right side of the fabric a short distance away.

Bring the needle up through the center of the fabric leaving an 3 inches length of thread on the surface. Continue to work the cross-stitching and, when several stitches have been completed, rethread the loose end and fasten off as follows.

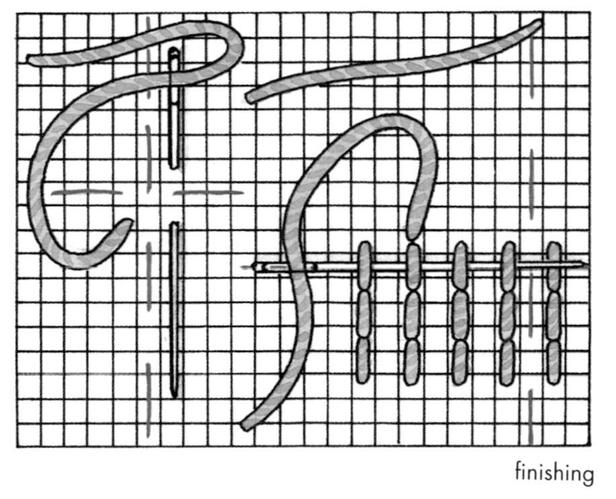


### *Fastening off*

Take the needle through to the back, reinserting it through the same hole in the fabric. Fasten off by running the needle under the previously made stitches and trim the loose end. Subsequent threads can be started in this way. Never use knots as they create a very lumpy effect.

### *Backstitch*

This simple line stitch, worked in continuous straight or diagonal lines, is used in cross-stitch essentially to outline a shape or to emphasize a shadow within a motif. It is also used for single line lettering, as in the sampler on page 104. The stitches are always worked over the same number of threads as the cross-stitching to lend uniformity to the finished embroidery.

Bring out the needle on the right side of the fabric and make the first stitch from left to right. Pass the needle behind the fabric and bring it out one stitch length ahead towards the left. Repeat and continue in this way to complete the stitchline.

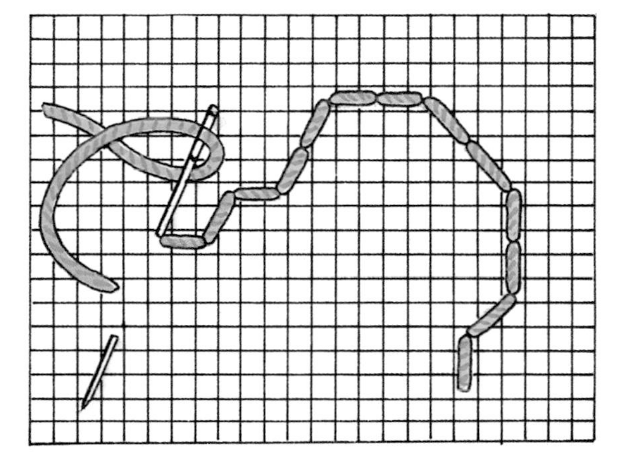

### *Cross-stitch*

The following two methods of working are used for all cross-stitch embroidery. In both cases, neat rows of straight stitches are made on the reverse side of the fabric.

**1** For stitching large solid areas, work in horizontal rows. Working from right to left, complete the first row of evenly spaced diagonal stitches over the particular number of threads given in the project instructions. Then, working from left to right, repeat the process.

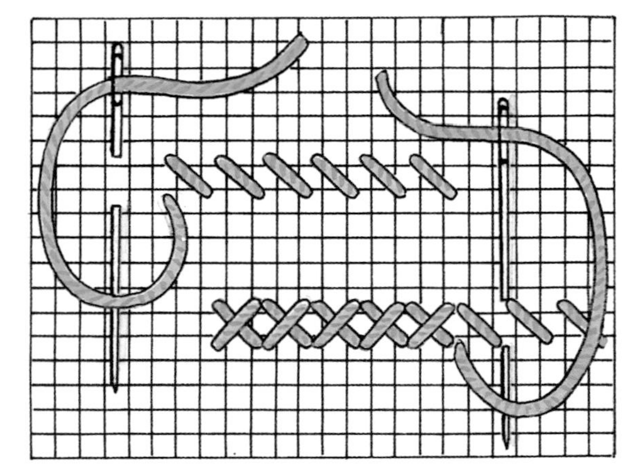

**2** For stitching diagonal lines or groups of stitches, work downwards, completing each stitch before moving to the next.

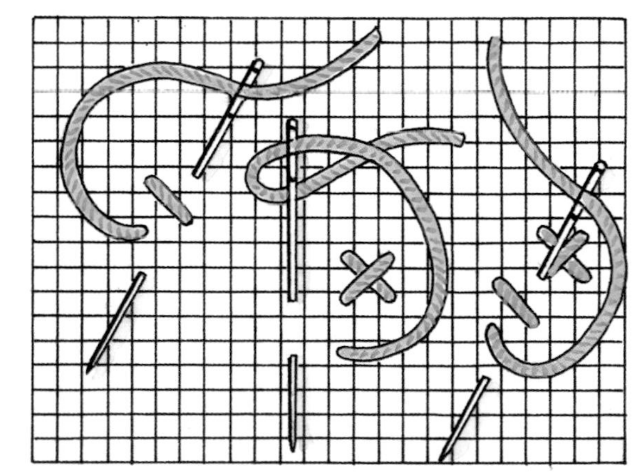

# CHILD'S SHOE BAG

*Finished size: 13½ x 12 inches*

*Make this jolly, patchwork-style drawstring show bag using a bold mixture of bright checks and plain-colored fabrics to show off the central cross-stitched name panel. Substitute your choice of name using the alphabet on page 133.*

YOU WILL NEED

- 11 x 9 inches of 27 gauge white evenweave cotton fabric
- tacking thread
- tapestry needle, size 24
- DMC stranded embroidery cotton in the following amounts and colors: one skein each of yellows 3822, 783, red 3705, greens 704, 964, 958, and blue 797
- 10 x 4 inches of both red and white small checked gingham and plain red cotton
- 18 x 15 inches of blue and white ¼ inch checked gingham
- 18 x 15 inches of bright yellow cotton
- matching sewing threads
- 2 yards of blue twisted cord, ⅛ inch thick

1 Add the name of your choice to the chart in the space provided, (page 100). Using a pencil and referring to the alphabet on page 133, center the name, evenly spacing each letter.

2 Mark the center of the fabric both lengthwise and widthwise with tacking stitches (see Techniques, page 95). Following the color key and chart, in which each square represents one stitch worked over two fabric threads, begin with embroidery in the center using two strands of thread in the needle. Working outwards from the center, complete the cross-stitching.

3 Lightly steam press the embroidery on the wrong side. Trim the edges to measure 9 x 7½ inches. With the embroidery right side up, place the two red side borders on top, with right sides facing and raw edges matching. Pin, tack and stitch, taking ½ inch seams. Press the seams open.

4 Cut a piece of blue and white checked gingham, 13 x 4 inches, for the bottom border and apply it in the same way.

5 Using the front section as a template, cut out the back section from blue and white gingham. From the yellow fabric, cut two pieces measuring 15 x 9 inches. With right sides together, stitch a yellow border to the top of both front and back sections.

6 Using three strands of green 958 in the needle, work open buttonhole stitch around the embroidered panel, neatly starting and finishing inside the seam on the wrong side. Follow the above diagram for positioning your needle, bringing it out through the seam with the thread below.

7 With right sides together, pin, tack and machine stitch around the sides and bottom of the bag, starting and finishing ¼ inch above the top seam.

8 On the yellow fabric, make narrow double turnings on the short side edges and stitch, then stitch single narrow turnings on the long edges. Fold each piece to the wrong side so that the yellow border measures 3 inches from the front. Tack across.

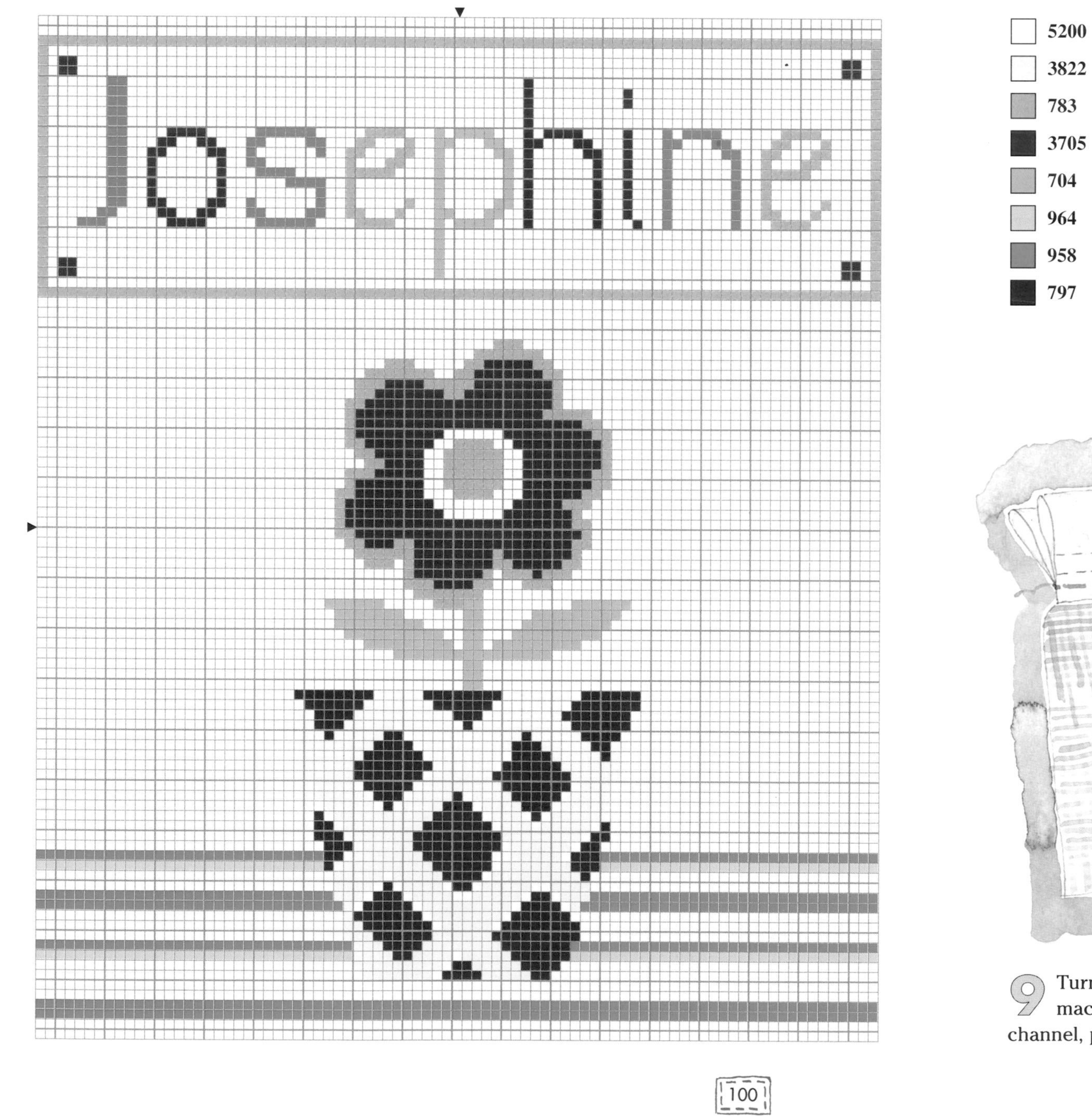

9 Turn the bag through to the right side and machine stitch a ¾ inch wide drawstring channel, positioning it 2 inches from the top.

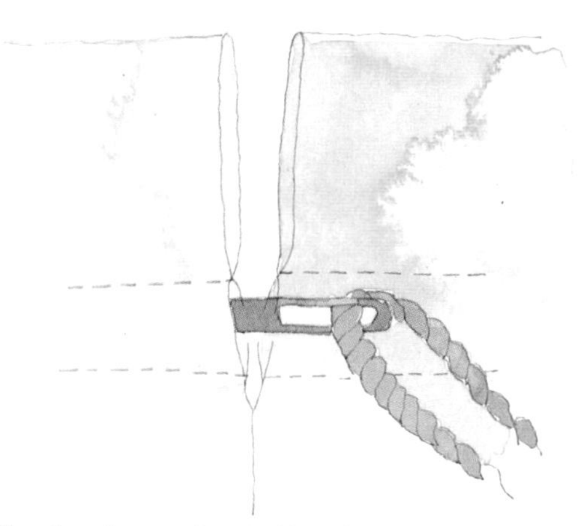

**10** Cut the cord in half and, using a ribbon threader or a large safety pin, thread each piece through the channel starting and finishing at opposite sides. Knot the ends to secure.

**11** From the remaining fabric, cut several ½ inch wide strips, about 6 inches long. Place them on top of each other, hand stitch them securely in the middle and fold in half. Bind the thread through the head of the tassel, then pass the needle upwards bringing it out at the top. Stitch neatly to each corner of the bag, oversewing on the inside seam.

# TRADITIONAL HOUSE SAMPLER

*Finished size (unframed): 10 x 8 inches*

*Inspired by the traditional samplers of the nineteenth century featuring country scenes and framed mottoes, this prettily bordered "house" sampler would make the perfect gift to celebrate moving to a new home.*

YOU WILL NEED

- 15 x 13 inches of 28 gauge off-white linen
- tacking thread
- tapestry needle, size 26
- embroidery frame (optional)
- DMC stranded embroidery cotton in the following amounts and colors: one skein each of white, greens 3364, 905, 501, 3809, blue 775, yellows 745, 3820, and reds 3712, 350
- 10 x 8 inches of medium-weight mounting board
- spray glue
- 10 x 8 inches of lightweight wadding
- masking tape for securing the mounted embroidery
- picture frame of your choice

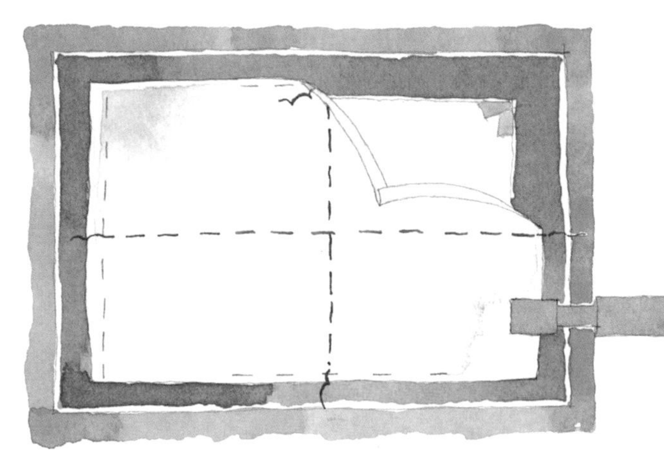

1 Mark the center of the linen both ways with tacking stitches (see Techniques, page 95) and, if preferred, stretch the fabric in either a slate frame, following the manufacturer's instructions, or staple it to a canvas stretcher or old picture frame. Make a single turning around the fabric. Staple each side to the frame, working outwards from the middle, attaching opposite sides alternately.

2 Following the color key and chart opposite, in which each square represents one stitch worked over two threads of the fabric, begin the cross-stitching in the middle using two strands of thread in the needle. Working outwards from the center, complete the cross-stitching up to the border.

Seek home for rest
For home is best...
D
H
5200
745
3820
3712
350
775
3809
3364
905
501

**3** Using three strands of thread in the needle, cross-stitch the border lines and the horizon line; backstitch (see Techniques, page 97) the curved flower stems in the outer border. Complete the remaining cross-stitching. Remove the finished embroidery from the frame but retain the tacking stitches: they will be useful in centering the embroidery on the mounting board.

**4** Coat one side of the mounting board with spray glue and press the wadding in place. Trim the edges of the wadding if necessary.

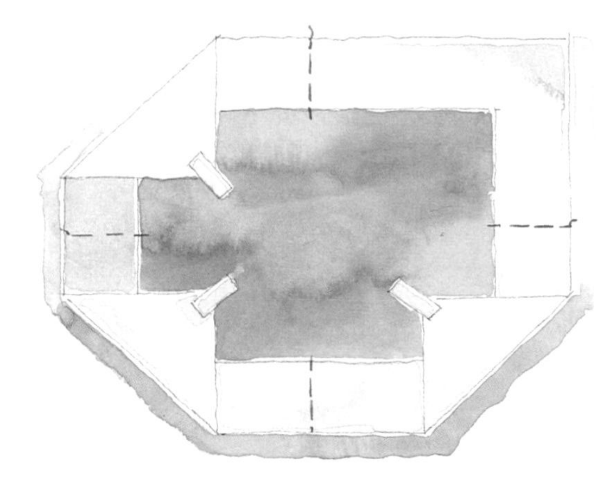

**5** To stretch the fabric over the mounting board, place the embroidery right side down on a clean surface. Mark the center both ways on the back of the mounting board and position it on top, aligning the center marks with the tacking threads. Fold over the fabric at each corner and secure well with small pieces of masking tape.

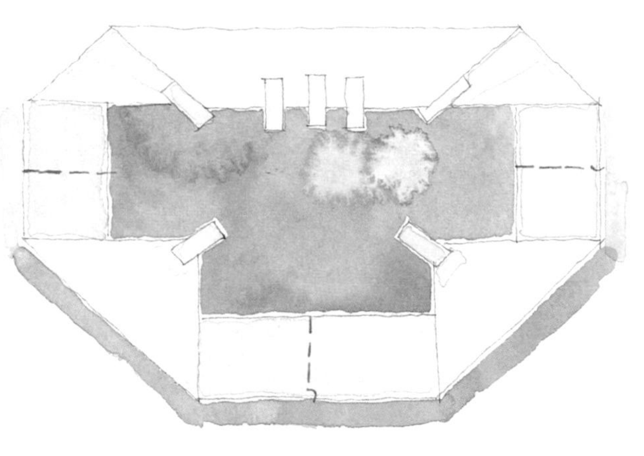

**6** Working first on one side and then on the opposite side, fold over the fabric on all four sides and secure with masking tape. Check periodically to see that the design is centered – if not, adjust the masking tape. Secure the mitred corners with tape or slipstitch them (see Techniques, page 96), if necessary. Frame the sampler following the manufacturer's instructions.

# PRETTY PINCUSHION

*Finished size: 5 x 5 inches*

*Essential for all needlecrafters – a pincushion big enough to hold plenty of pins ready for use! Stitched with a simple border design, repeated on all four sides, the pincushion is eminently suitable for beginners to cross-stitch.*

YOU WILL NEED

- 8 inch square of 28 gauge antique white linen
- tacking thread
- tapestry needle, size 26
- embroidery hoop (optional)
- DMC stranded embroidery cotton in the following amounts and colors: one skein each of pink 3805, blues 828, 792, and greens 958, 561
- 6 inch square of contrast backing fabric
- matching sewing threads
- loose synthetic wadding
- 24 inches of contrast bias binding, 1 inch wide

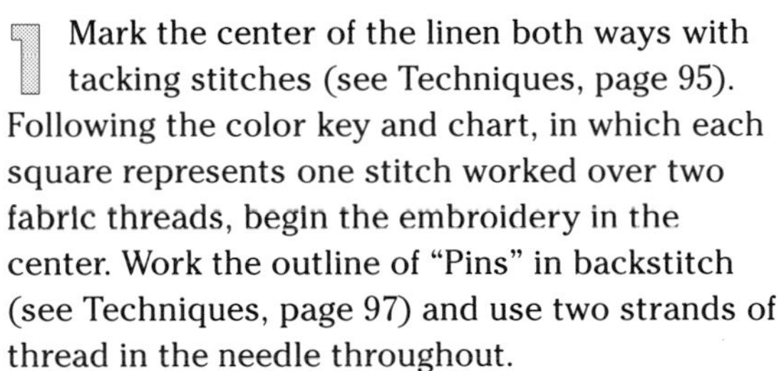

1 Mark the center of the linen both ways with tacking stitches (see Techniques, page 95). Following the color key and chart, in which each square represents one stitch worked over two fabric threads, begin the embroidery in the center. Work the outline of "Pins" in backstitch (see Techniques, page 97) and use two strands of thread in the needle throughout.

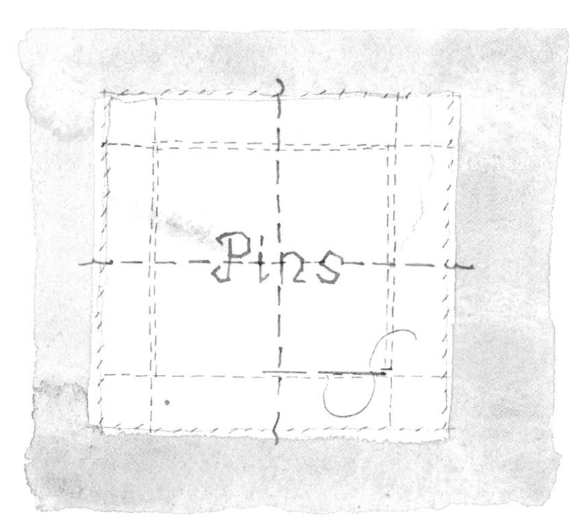


2 Working outwards from the center, embroider the border lines in backstitch too, and then complete the cross-stitching. Outline the corner diamonds with backstitch. Lightly steam press on the wrong side and remove the tacking stitches.

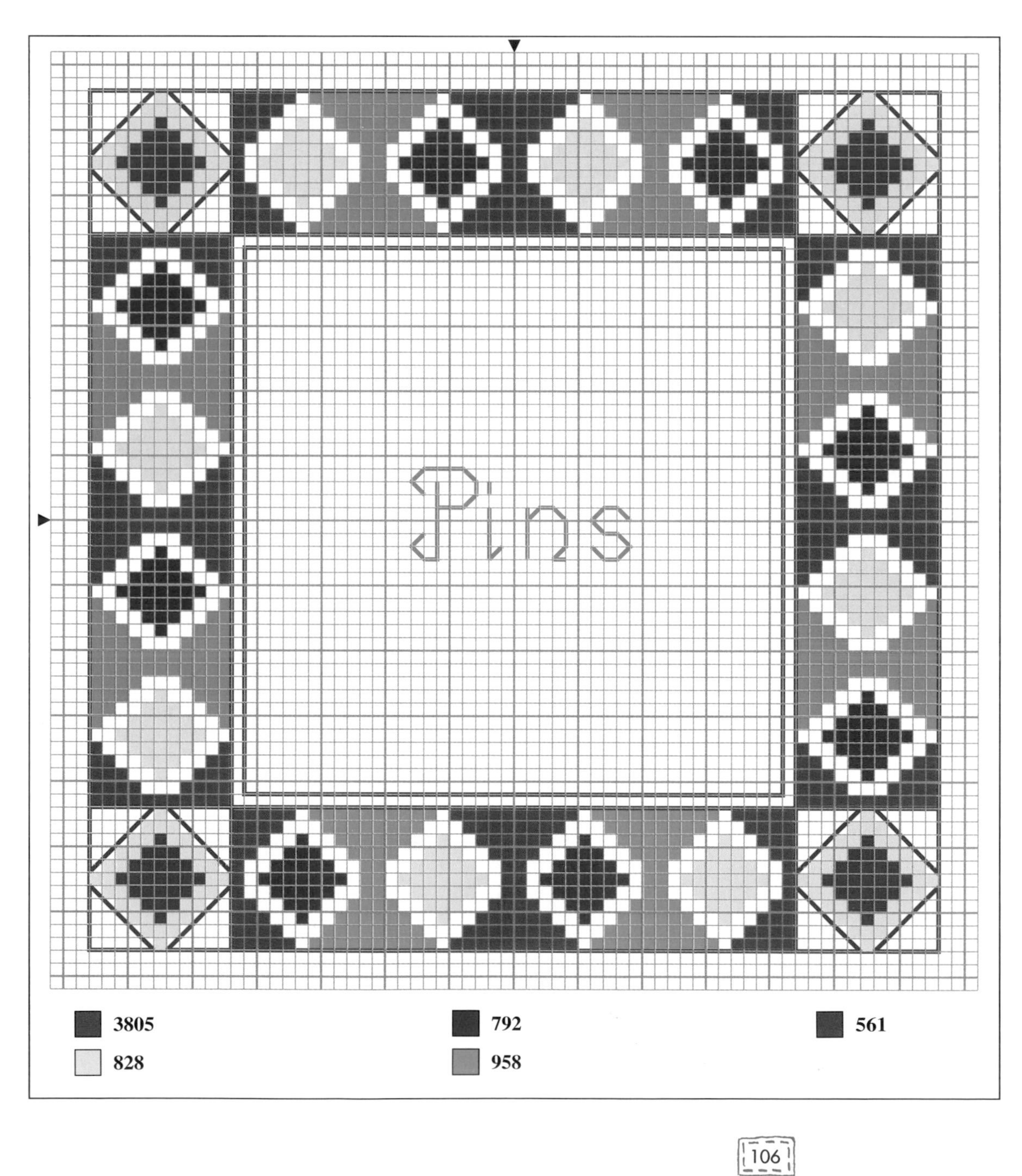

**3** Trim the edges to within ¾ inch of the embroidery. Place the backing and the embroidery together, wrong sides facing and pin to hold. Machine stitch around the edges, taking a ⅜ inch seam and leaving a 2½ inch opening in one side, as shown.

**4** Lightly stuff with well-teased wadding, using the blunt end of a knitting needle to push it into the far corners. Mold it into a smooth shape with your hands. Pin the opening together and machine stitch to close.

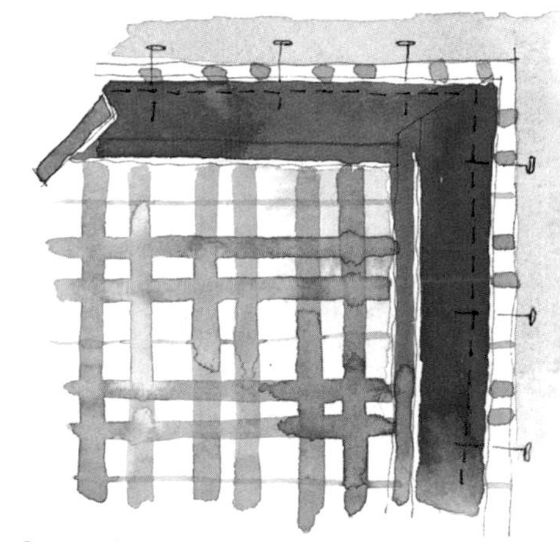

5 Cover the raw edges with bias binding. With right sides together and working from the back, fold over a diagonally cut end of the binding to the right side. Pin the binding in place with raw edges even, folding the binding diagonally at the corners. Overlap the two ends by ¾ inch and machine stitch around the edges.

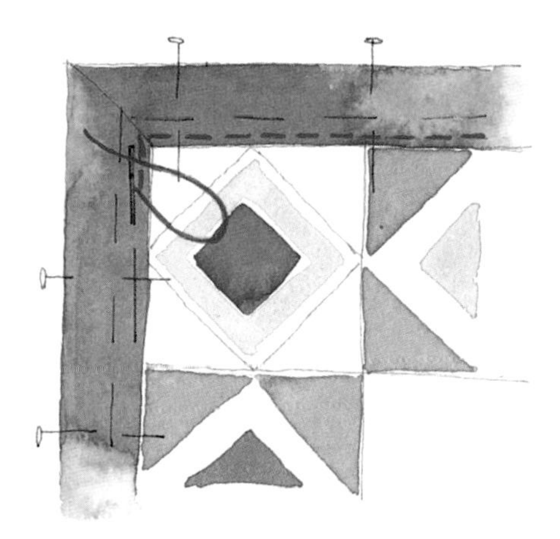

6 Turn over the binding to the right side; pin and tack. Using two strands of blue 792, stitch the binding in place with evenly spaced running stitches, ⅛ inch apart.

# SCISSORS DOLLY

*Finished size: 3½ inches high*

*How many times do we lose our embroidery scissors? Simply because they are small, they can easily get lost in a workbag or on a busy worktable. But, with a pretty, eyecatching dolly attached, you need never lose them again!*

YOU WILL NEED

- 6 x 4 inches of 26 gauge white evenweave cotton
- tacking thread
- tapestry needle, size 26
- DMC stranded embroidery cotton in the following amounts and colors: one skein each of yellow 3820, orange 971, pinks 948, 604, red 816, blues 800, 799, and green 907
- embroidery hoop (optional)
- 5 x 3½ inches of blue and white gingham
- 36 inches of blue ribbon, ⅛ inch wide
- matching sewing thread
- loose synthetic wadding

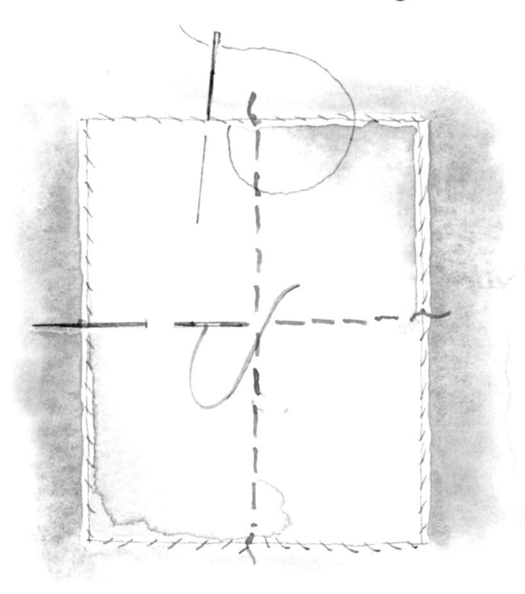

1 Overcast the raw edges of the evenweave fabric to prevent them fraying. Then tack the center both lengthwise and widthwise.

2 Following the color key and chart, in which each square represents one cross-stitch worked over two fabric threads, begin in the center using two strands of thread.

3 Complete the cross-stitching and then the backstitching (see Techniques, page 97). Lightly steam press on the wrong side. Cut out the embroidery, adding a ⅜ inch seam allowance all round. Using this as a template, cut out the gingham backing fabric.

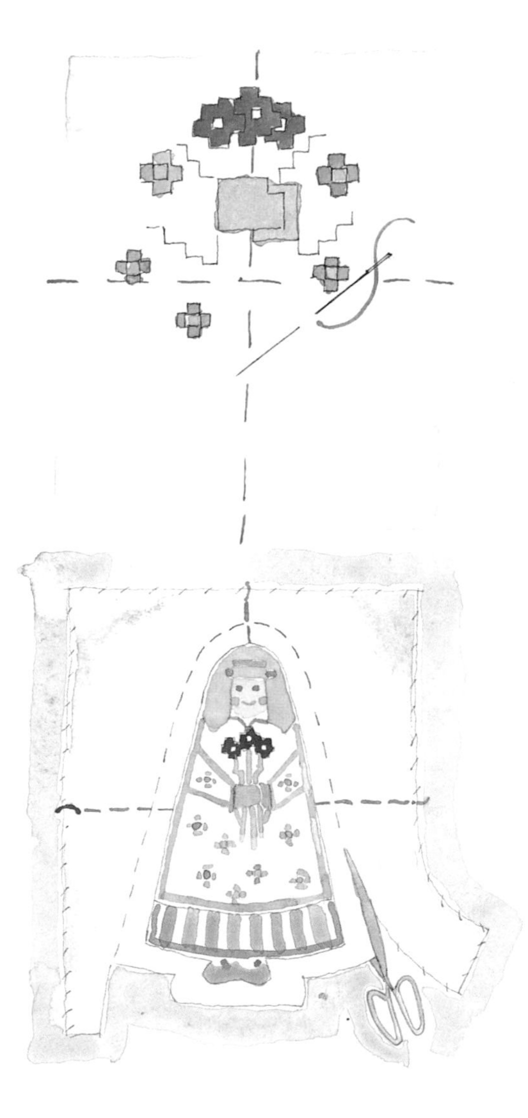

**4** From the narrow ribbon, cut off 30 inches and fold in half. Pin and tack the cut ends inside the seam allowance at the center top of the front piece. Pin and tack the front and back pieces together, right sides facing. Machine stitch around the edges close to the embroidery, leaving an opening in the side as shown.

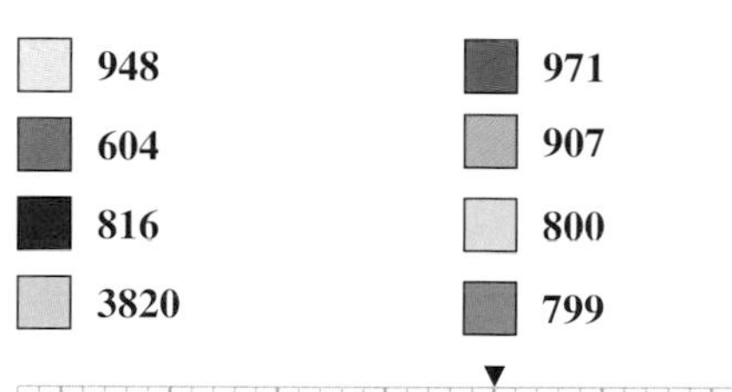


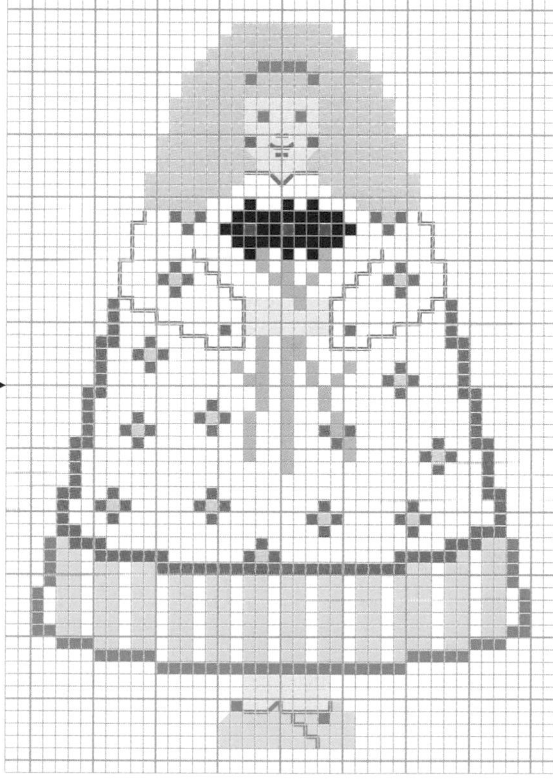

**5** Trim the seam allowance to ¼ inch. Cut across the corners, clip into the curved seam and turn through to the right side. Stuff with well-teased wadding. Turn in the opening and, using matching sewing thread, slipstitch to close (see Techniques, page 97). Stitch across the ankles through all layers.

**6** Tie the remaining length of ribbon into a bow and, working from the back of the head, attach it to the top of the head with one or two oversewing stitches.

# FRUITY PRESERVE POT COVERS

*Finished size: 6¼ inches*

*Delicious homemade preserves, made at the height of summer, can be kept and eaten during the following winter months. Cross-stitch these delightful preserve pot covers to give your gifts of preserves an extra special finishing touch.*

YOU WILL NEED

- three white, lace-edged preserve pot covers with 18 gauge evenweave centers
- tacking thread
- tapestry needle, size 26
- DMC stranded embroidery cotton in the following amounts and colors: cherries – one skein each of pink 3733, reds 3705, 347, purple 327, greens 772, 504, 3347, brown 371; blackberries – reds 3687, 816, purple 550, deep blue 823, greens 993, 3364, 943, brown 611; plums – yellow 676, pinks 776, 3706, red 3350, greens 772, 471, 3053
- embroidery hoop (optional)
- ribbon threader
- 24 inches each of green, red and yellow satin ribbon, ¼ inch wide

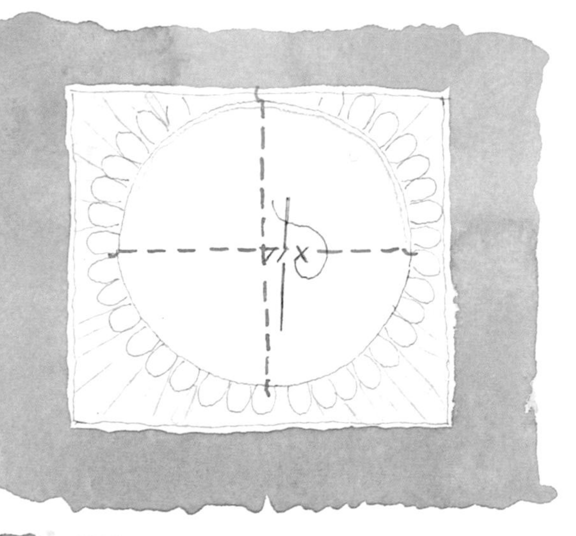

1 All three covers are embroidered in the same way. Mark the center of the evenweave fabric both lengthwise and widthwise with tacking stitches (see Techniques, page 97). Following the appropriate color key and chart, in which each square represents one stitch worked over one fabric intersection, embroider the motif starting in the middle and using two strands of embroidery thread in the needle.

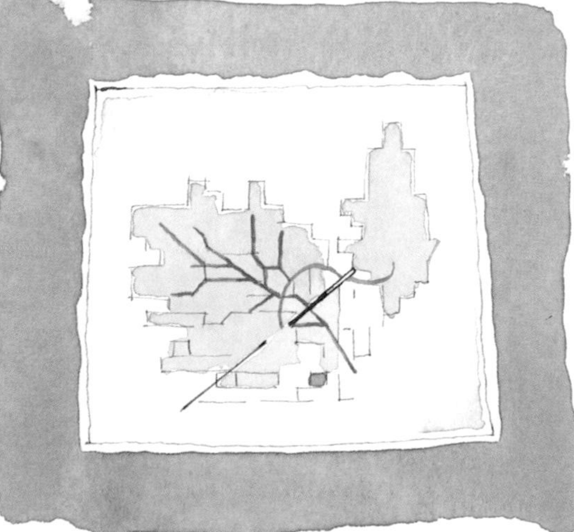

2 Working outwards from the center, complete the cross-stitching and then add the backstitching (see Techniques, page 97).

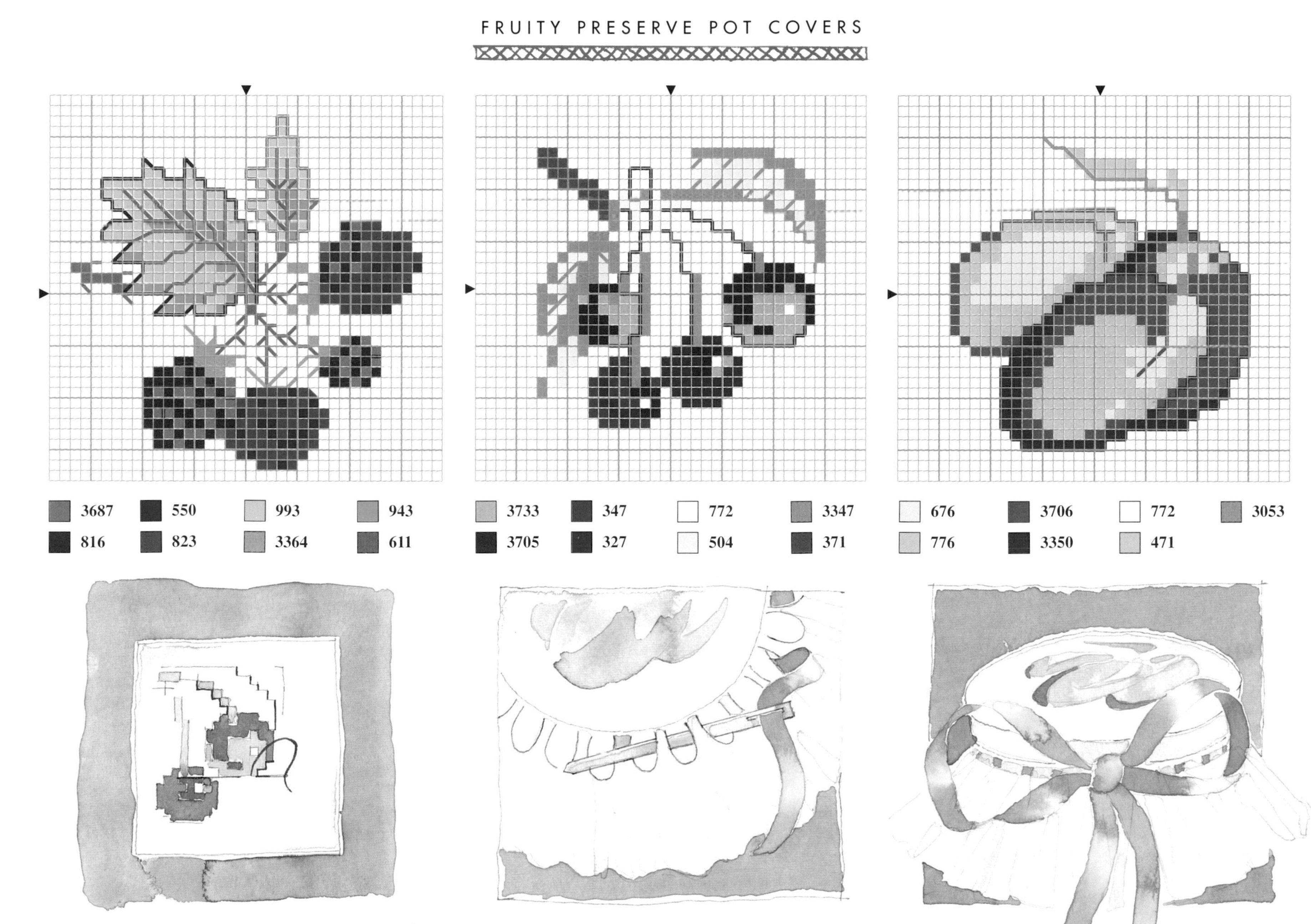


3 Backstitch the outlining where appropriate to complete the embroidery. Lightly steam press on the wrong side, if necessary.

4 Using the ribbon threader, thread the ribbon through the holes in the lace edging, close to the evenweave cover.

5 Place over the preserve pot and tie the ribbon into a pretty bow.

# COATHANGER WITH FRAGRANT SACHET

*Finished size of the coathanger, excluding the hook: 19 x 3 inches; sachet: 3½ x 3 inches*

*A padded coathanger, prettily edged with a silk frill and with a scented matching sachet, makes a welcome gift. Made from fine white linen, the hanger can be further personalized by adding the recipient's name or initials in cross-stitch.*

YOU WILL NEED

- standard wooden coathanger
- sheet of paper, 15½ x 12½ inches
- two pieces 21 x 6 inches of off-white 32 gauge linen
- 9 x 4½ inches of off-white 32 gauge linen
- tacking thread
- tapestry needle, size 26
- air-vanishing marker
- DMC stranded embroidery cotton: one skein pinks 3716, 962, lavender 341, 340, green 3817
- graph paper
- two pieces 21 x 6 inches of heavyweight synthetic wadding
- matching sewing thread
- 18 inches square of pale pink silk fabric
- lavender
- 18 inches of pink ribbon, ¼ inch wide
- 40 inches of pink ribbon, ⅜ inch wide

1 Place the coathanger on the paper and draw around the shape with a pencil. Add a second line ½ inch outside the first and cut out the paper pattern.

2 On one of the larger pieces of linen, mark the center both lengthwise and widthwise with tacking stitches. Position the paper pattern centrally on the linen and draw around it using the air-vanishing marker. Tack the outline. Fold the smaller piece of linen in half widthwise and, on the front section, mark the hem 1 inch down from the top edge. In the remaining area, mark the center both ways with tacking stitches.

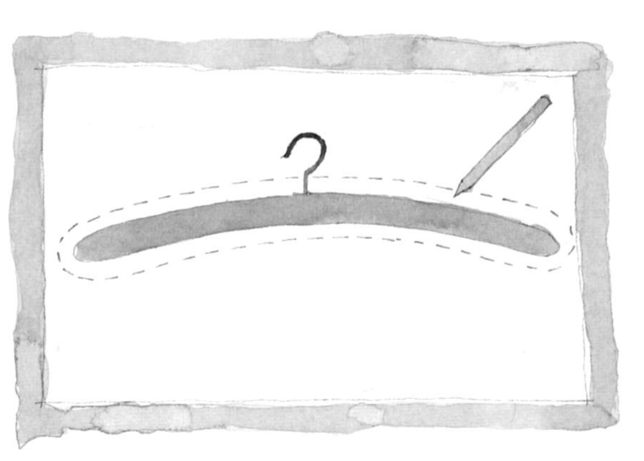

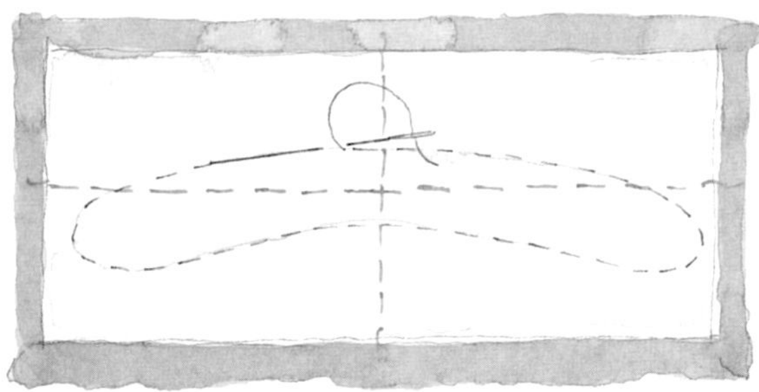

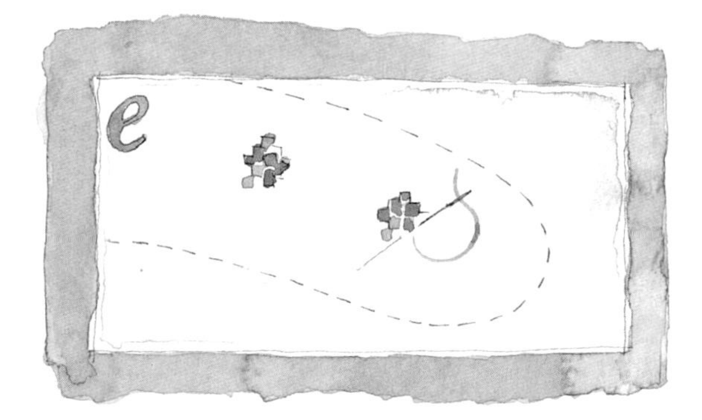

3 Following the alphabet given on page 135, draw your chosen name on graph paper, positioning it as shown in the chart, page 114. Referring to the appropriate color key and chart, in which each square represents one cross-stitch worked over two threads of fabric, begin the cross-stitching in the middle, using two strands of embroidery thread in the needle. Complete the embroidery on the hanger and the sachet and press on the wrong side.

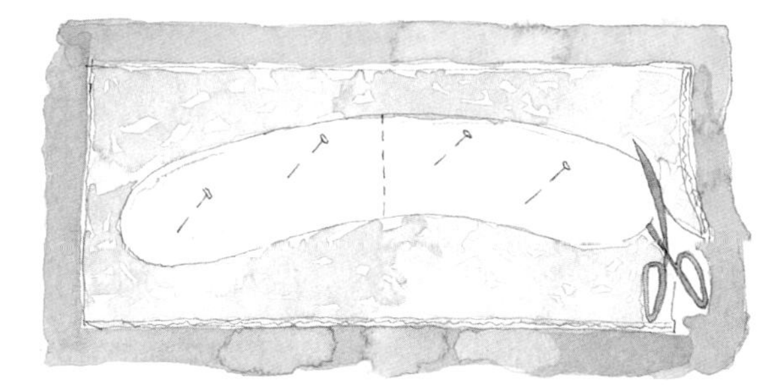

4 Following the tacked outline, cut out the embroidery, adding a ½ inch seam allowance all round. Now cut out the back section using the front as a template. Cut out two pieces of wadding using the paper pattern.

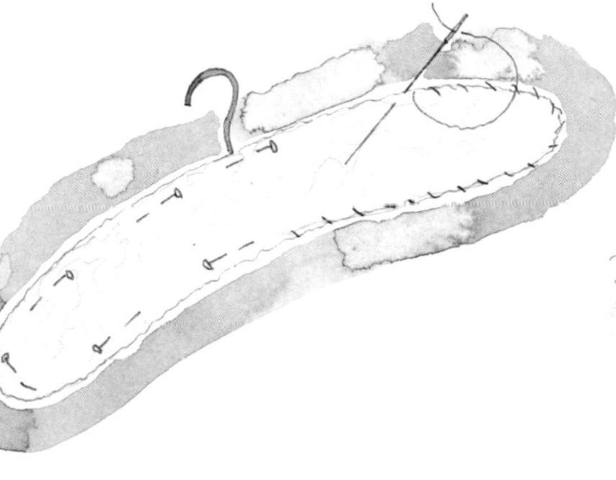

5 Place the wadding on each side of the coathanger; pin and oversew the edges together.

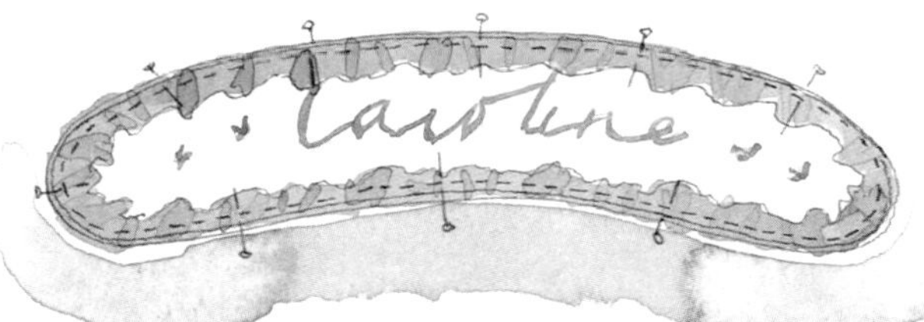

6 For the frill, cut bias strips from the silk, 2½ inches wide and join them together, as shown, to make one and a half times the length of the outside edge of the padded coathanger. Join to form a circle. Fold the silk in half lengthwise and run a gathering thread ⅜ inch from the raw edges. Place on the right side of the embroidery, pull up the gathers to fit; pin, tack and machine stitch within the seam allowance.

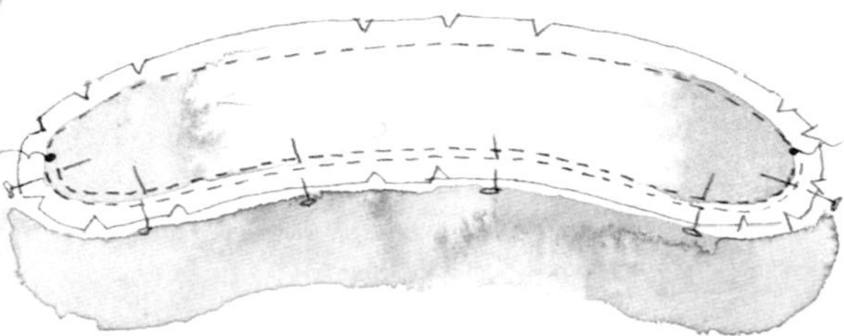

7 With right sides facing, pin, tack and stitch the front and back together, leaving the top edge open. Clip into the curved seam and turn right side out.

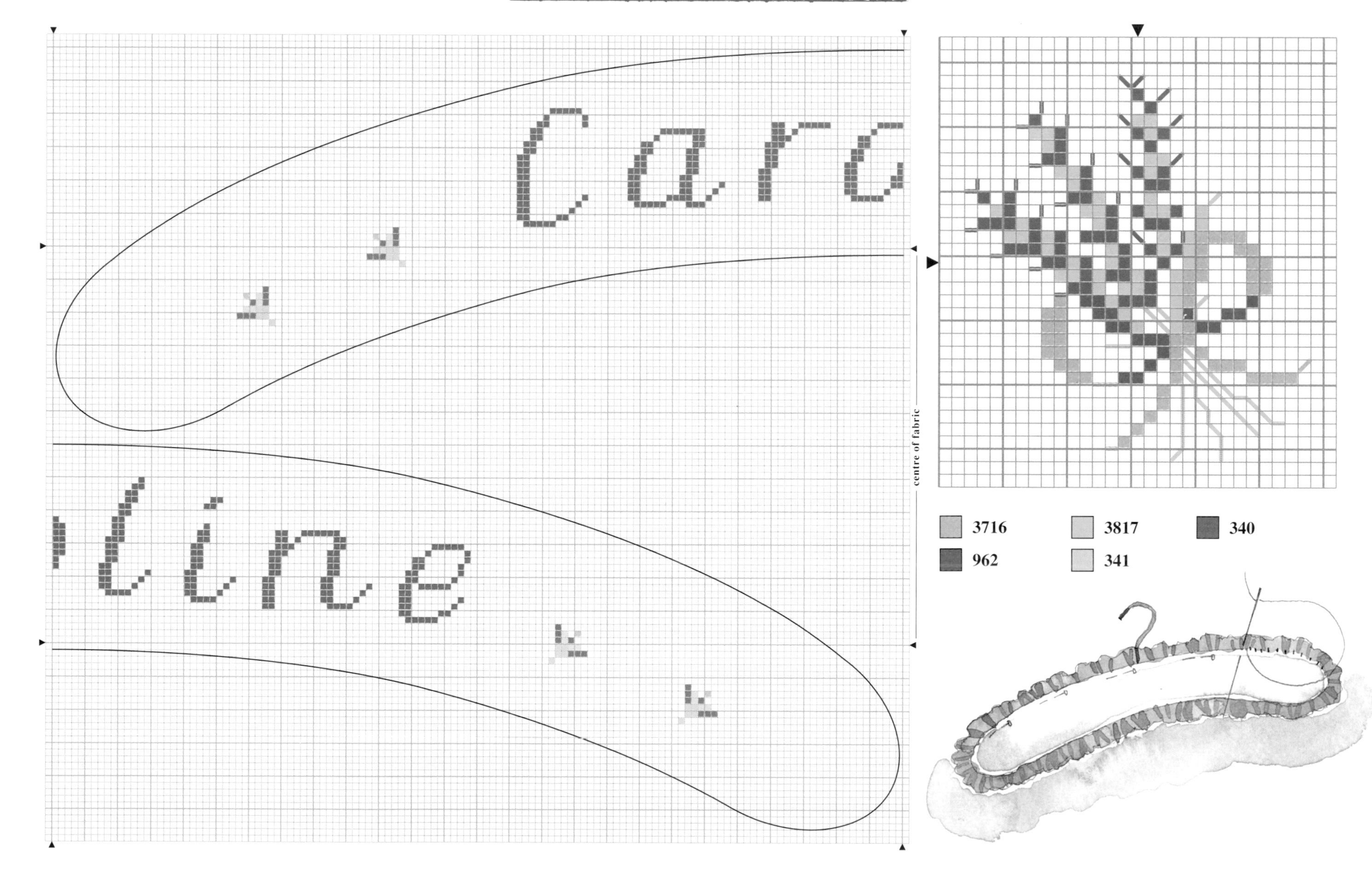


**8** Insert the padded coathanger. Working from the back, fold in the top edges; pin and slipstitch to close the opening.

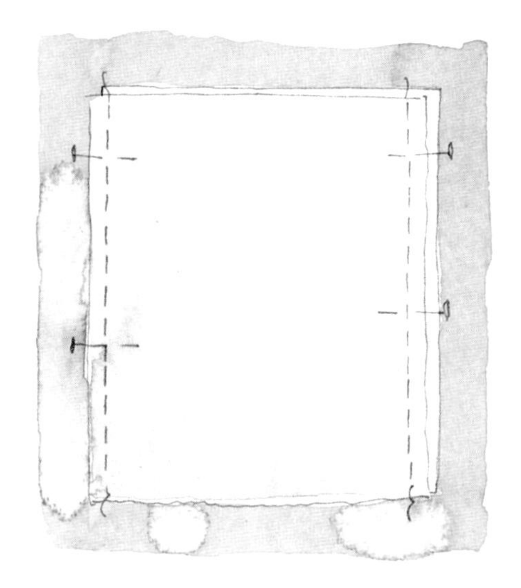

9 For the sachet, fold the fabric in half widthwise as in step two, then pin and stitch the two sides together, leaving the top open. Press the seams open.

10 Make a ½ inch double turning on the top edge; pin and stitch. Cut across the corners and turn right side out. Half fill with scented lavender.

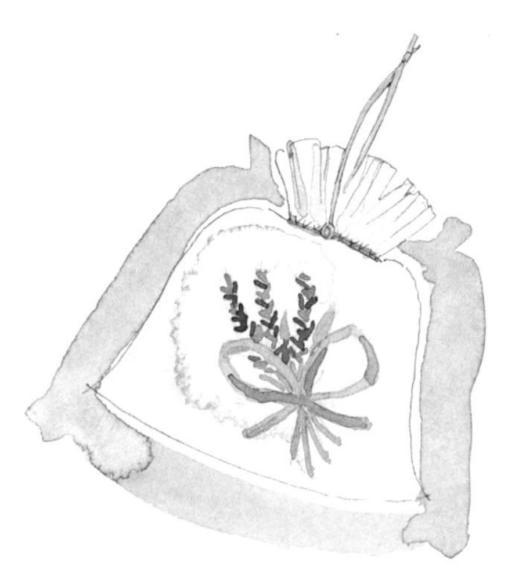

11 Gather the top, tie on the narrow ribbon and knot firmly. Knot the ends of the ribbon and slip it over the coathanger hook. Tie the remaining ribbon around the base of the hook, covering the knot of the sachet ribbon, and finish with a bow.

# WILD FLOWER PAPERWEIGHTS

*Finished size: 3¾ inches across*

*Colorful and delicate wild flowers make pretty motifs for glass paperweights. These single flower heads are quick and easy to work and, for economy, may be made from remnants of evenweave fabric.*

YOU WILL NEED

- three 6 inch squares of white 18 gauge Aida fabric
- tacking thread
- tapestry needle, size 26
- DMC stranded embroidery cotton in the following amounts and colors: ragwort – one skein each of yellows 3078, 744, 3820, greens 472, 989, 905; poppy – pinks 3326, 3712, reds 606, 326, greens 472, 966, black 310; mallow – pinks 819, 3689, 604, 3608, 3805, greens 504, 320
- three round glass-topped paperweights measuring 3¾ inches across

1 All three motifs are embroidered in the same way. Begin by marking the center of the Aida fabric both lengthwise and widthwise with tacking stitches (see Techniques, page 97). Following the appropriate color key and chart, in which each square represents one cross-stitch worked over one fabric intersection, begin the embroidery in the middle, using two strands of thread in the needle.

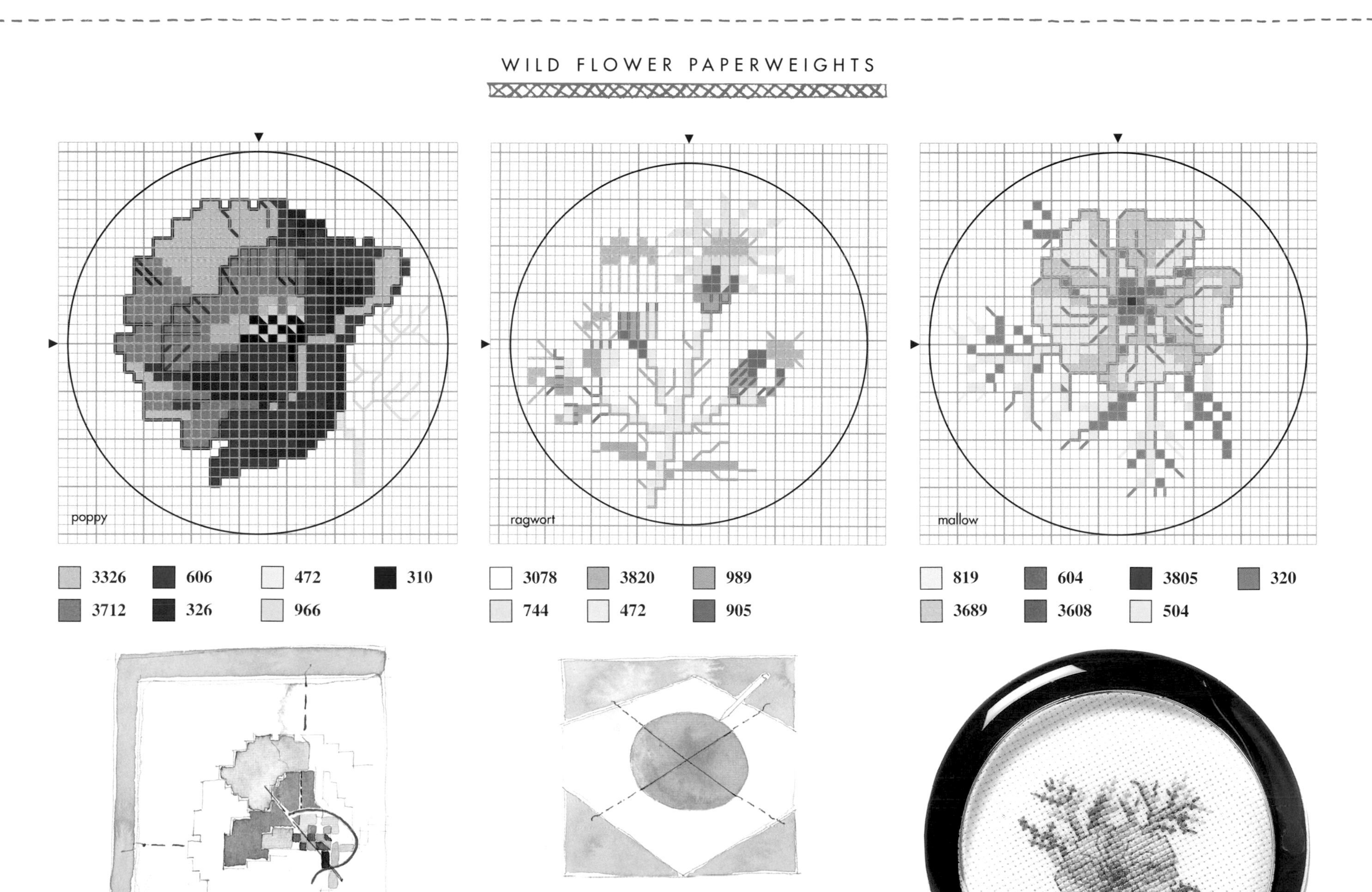


**2** Working outwards from the center, complete the cross-stitching and then work the backstitch details last (see Techniques, page 97). Lightly steam press the finished embroidery on the wrong side. Retain the tacking stitches.

**3** Place the embroidery face down. On the card template provided with the paperweight, mark the center in pencil both lengthwise and widthwise and position it on the embroidery, matching the center lines to the tacking. Draw lightly around the shape.

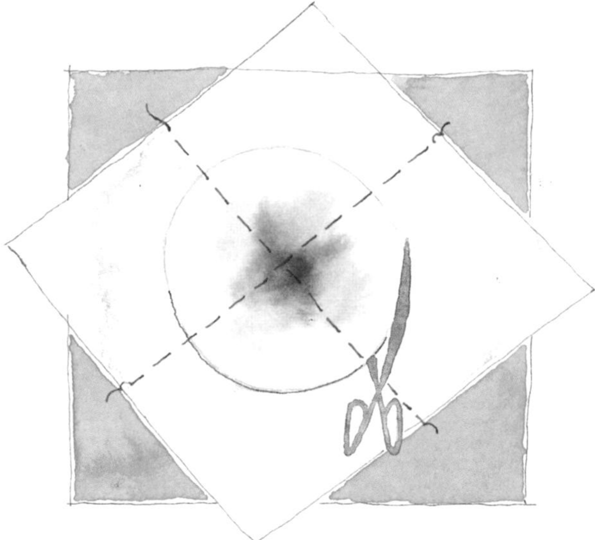

4 Make sure your embroidery is centered in the drawn circle by holding it up to the light, then cut it out. Carefully remove the remaining tacking threads.

5 Place the glass paperweight face down, and put the cut-out embroidery inside the indented circle where it will fit snugly.

6 Remove the backing paper from the self-adhesive felt backing (provided with the paperweight) and carefully cover the base of the paperweight. Press firmly to secure the embroidery.

# FLORAL TABLE CENTER

*Finished size: 22½ x 15½ inches*

*A vase of cheery summer flowers makes a pleasing design for a table center, or it could easily double as a tray cloth. Worked on off-white linen the hem is decorated with open herringbone stitch in a variety of colors; an assortment of colors is also used for the random running stitches on the inner border.*

YOU WILL NEED

- 24 x 17 inches of off-white 25 gauge linen
- tacking thread
- tapestry needle, size 26
- DMC stranded embroidery cotton in the following amounts and colors: one skein each of yellows 445, 725, 977, 741, peaches 951, 754, pinks 605, 3731, blues 775, 799, and greens 772, 3817, 913, 3012, 501
- matching sewing thread
- crewel needle, size 5

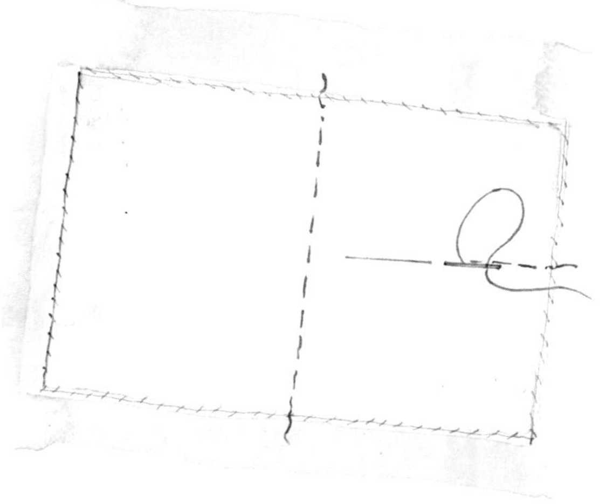

1 Overcast the raw edges of the linen to prevent it from fraying. Then mark the center both lengthwise and widthwise with tacking stitches (see Techniques, page 97).

2 Following the color key and chart, in which each square represents one cross- stitch worked over two fabric threads, start the embroidery in the middle using two strands of thread in the needle. Work outwards from the center, completing the cross-stitching before working the backstitch details (see Techniques, page 97). Lightly steam press the finished embroidery on the wrong side.

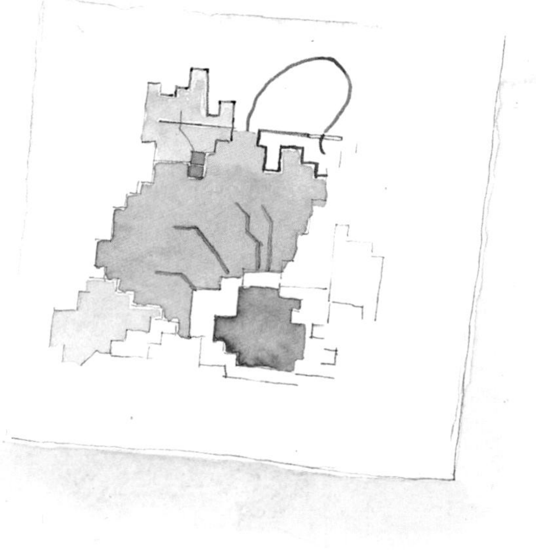

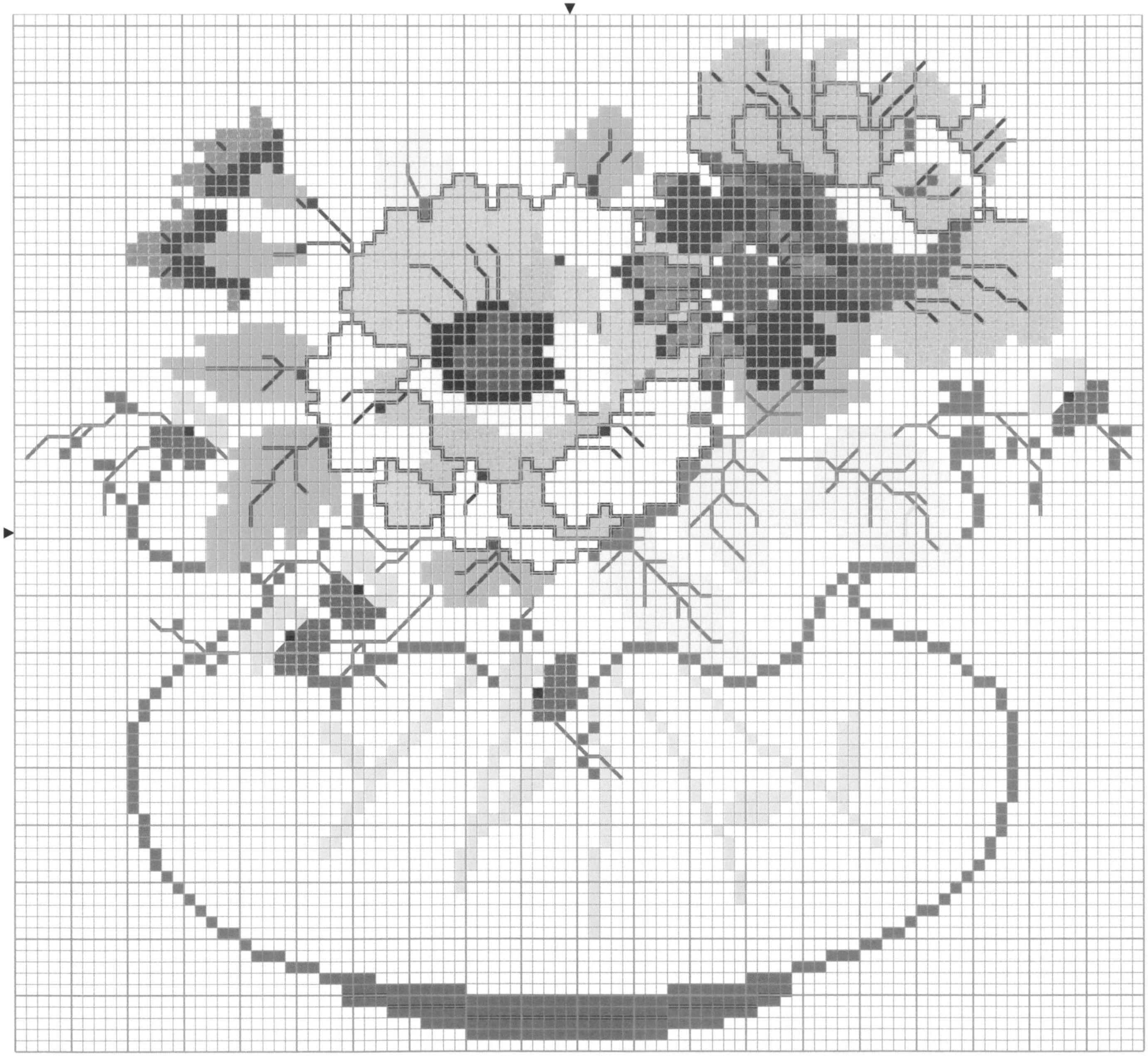

| | |
|---|---|
| ☐ | 445 |
| ☐ | 725 |
| ☐ | 977 |
| ☐ | 741 |
| ☐ | 951 |
| ☐ | 754 |
| ☐ | 605 |
| ☐ | 3731 |
| ☐ | 775 |
| ☐ | 799 |
| ☐ | 772 |
| ☐ | 3817 |
| ☐ | 913 |
| ☐ | 3012 |
| ☐ | 501 |

3 Trim the fabric so that it measures 25½ x 18½ inches, using the tacking stitches as a guide to cut all sides evenly. With wrong sides facing, make ⅜ inch double turnings on all sides and press the folds. Fold over the corners and trim across, as shown.

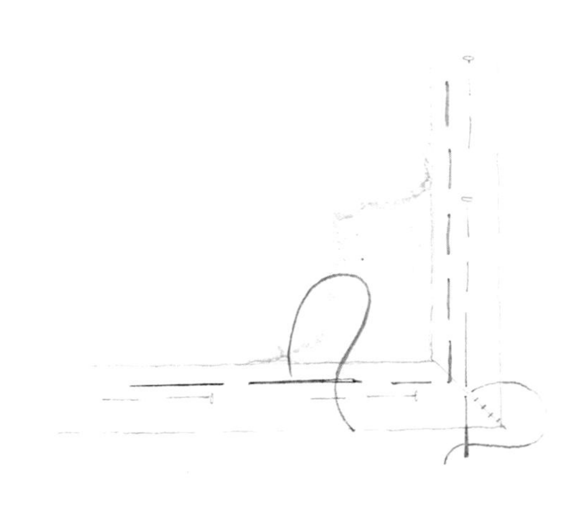

4 Refold the hem, mitring the corners, pin and tack to hold. Using matching thread, secure the mitred corners with slipstitch (see Techniques, page 97).

5 Using blues and greens at random and two strands of thread in the crewel needle, work herringbone stitch around the hem on the right side, holding down the hem at the same time. Working from left to right, make a small stitch through single fabric. Pull out the needle and, with the thread above, make a similar stitch below and to the right, through two layers of the hem only. Repeat the sequence to complete the hem.

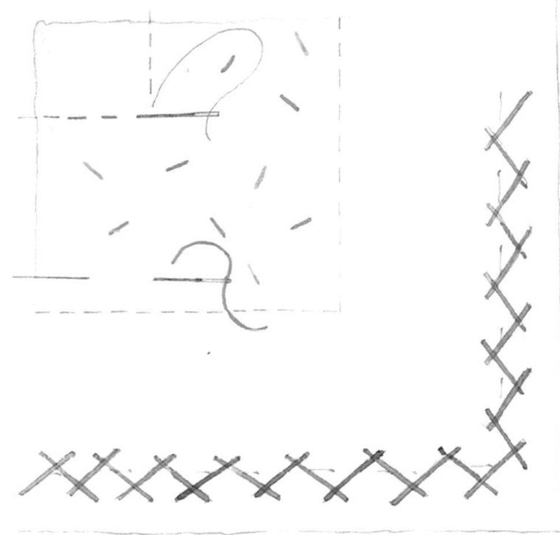

6 Work the 1¼ inch wide inner border in running stitches placed 1 inch inside the hem. Fill this with random straight stitches using the paler pinks and yellows.

# INITIALED BOOKMARK

*Finished size, including the tassel: 10 x 2 inches*

*This easy-to-make bookmark is worked in just one color on prepared evenweave band, prettily finished with a looped edging. Cross-stitch the background for your chosen initial (see page 136) in any color, and finish the pointed end with a handmade tassel.*

YOU WILL NEED

- 9 inches of 15 gauge white evenweave band, 2 inches
- tacking thread
- tapestry needle, size 24
- DMC stranded embroidery cotton: one skein of blue 3766
- matching sewing thread
- medium-sized sewing needle

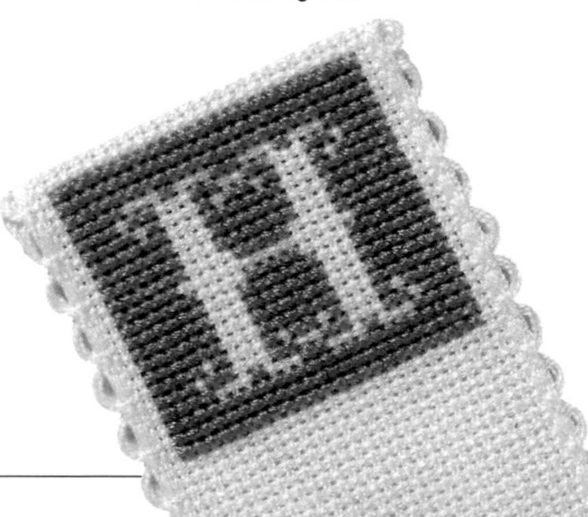

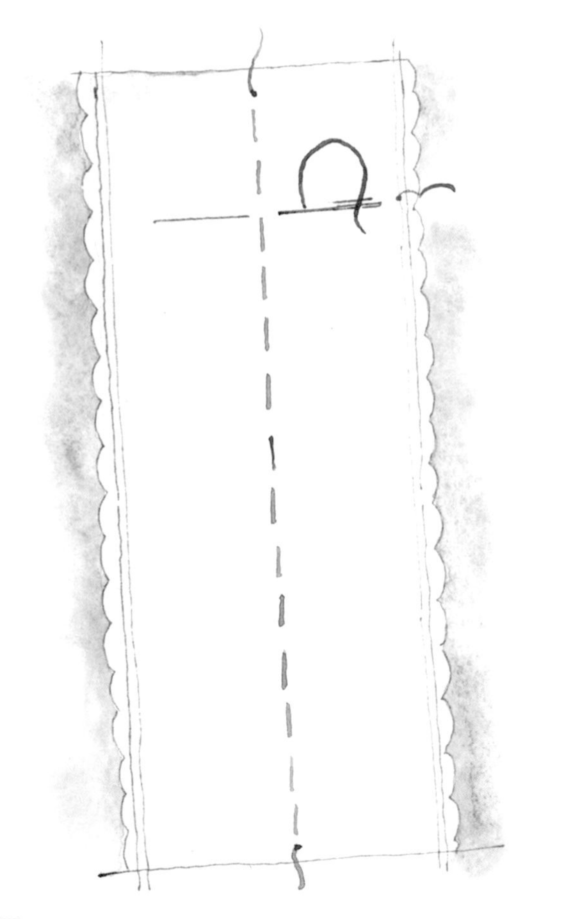

1 Mark the vertical center of the evenweave band with tacking stitches and, following the positioning lines on the chart opposite, mark the center of the initial 21 threads in from the top raw edge.

2 Following the color key and chart in which each square represents one cross-stitch worked over one thread intersection, use two strands of thread in the needle to work the embroidery, starting from the center.

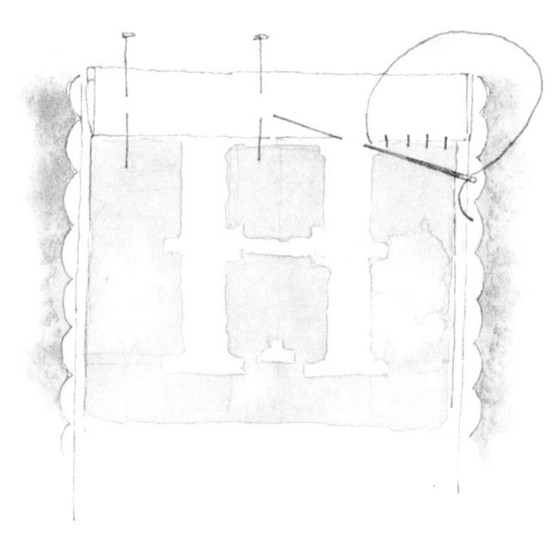

3 Lightly steam press the completed embroidery on the wrong side, if necessary. Make a small double turning on the top edge, leaving a border of two thread intersections, as shown. Using matching sewing thread, hem in place.

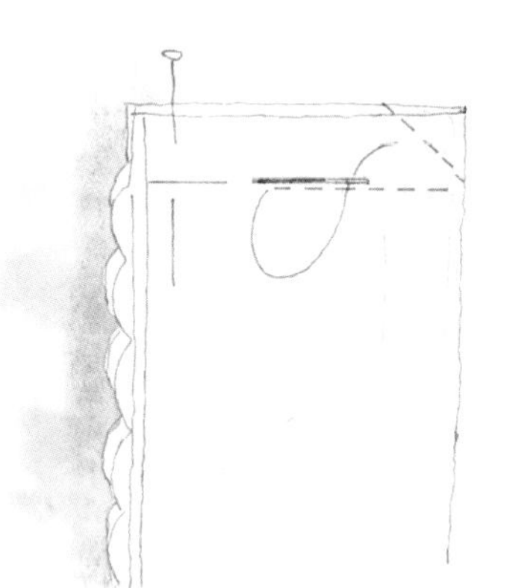

4 To make a point at the opposite end, fold the bookmark in half lengthwise, right sides together. Use backstitch to join the short edges, taking a ⅜ inch seam. Trim the corner, and press the seam open.

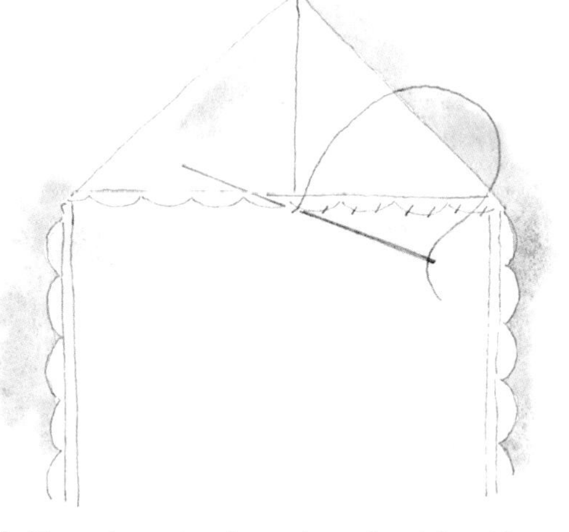

5 Turn the point through to the right side. Flatten out the bookmark, creating a neat point. Press on the wrong side and slipstitch the turning to secure.

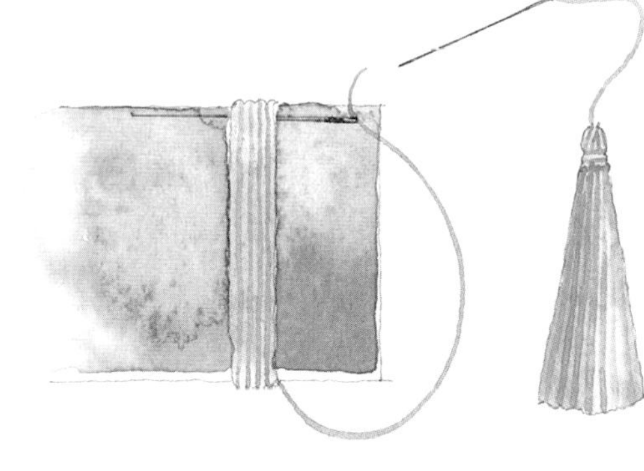

6 Make the tassel by winding white tacking thread around a small piece of card, 1¼ inches wide. Thread the loose end into a needle, slip the tassel threads off the card and wind the loose thread several times around them, close to the top. Pass the needle up through the bound threads and bring it out at the top of the tassel ready to be sewn to the point of the bookmark. Cut through the loops to finish.

3766

# MINIATURE PRIZE PIG PICTURE

*Finished unframed size: 8 x 7 inches*

*This tiny cross-stitched picture, worked on pale sky-blue linen, shows a prize pig eating flowers in a meadow, and is framed with a deep border of yellow and white gingham fabric. The grass may be quickly worked using a large cross-stitch.*

YOU WILL NEED

- 7 x 6 inches of 28 gauge pale blue linen
- tacking thread
- tapestry needle, size 26
- DMC stranded embroidery cotton in the following amounts and colors: one skein each of white, yellow 743, peaches 3774, 353, red 817, greens 704, 470, 501, and grays 3072, 3799
- embroidery hoop (optional)
- 16 x 9 inches of yellow and white gingham for the border
- matching sewing threads
- 8 x 7 inches synthetic wadding
- 8 x 7 inches of medium-weight mounting board
- masking tape
- picture frame of your choice

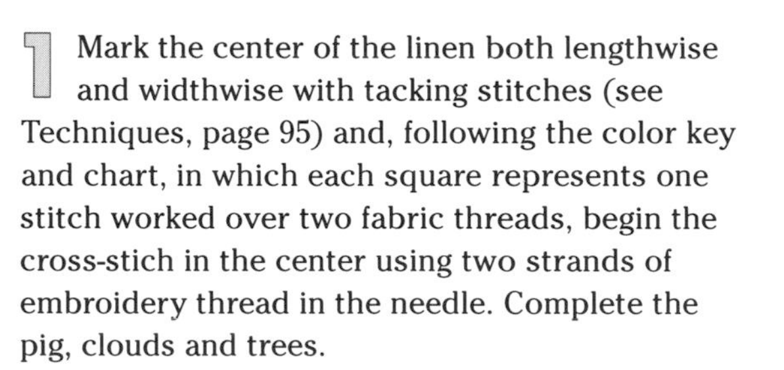

1 Mark the center of the linen both lengthwise and widthwise with tacking stitches (see Techniques, page 95) and, following the color key and chart, in which each square represents one stitch worked over two fabric threads, begin the cross-stich in the center using two strands of embroidery thread in the needle. Complete the pig, clouds and trees.

2 Using two strands of green 704 in the needle, embroider the grass, working the cross-stitch over two fabric threads across by four fabric threads down. Fill in around the pig and flowers with half and quarter stitches. Add the backstitch details (see Techniques, page 97) and the outer border to complete the picture.

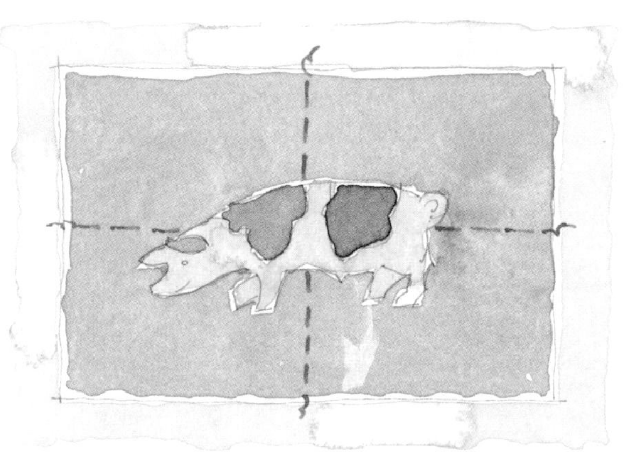

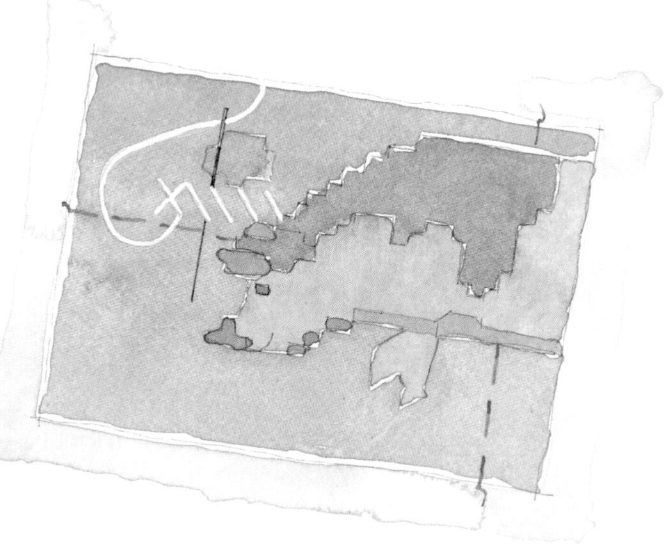

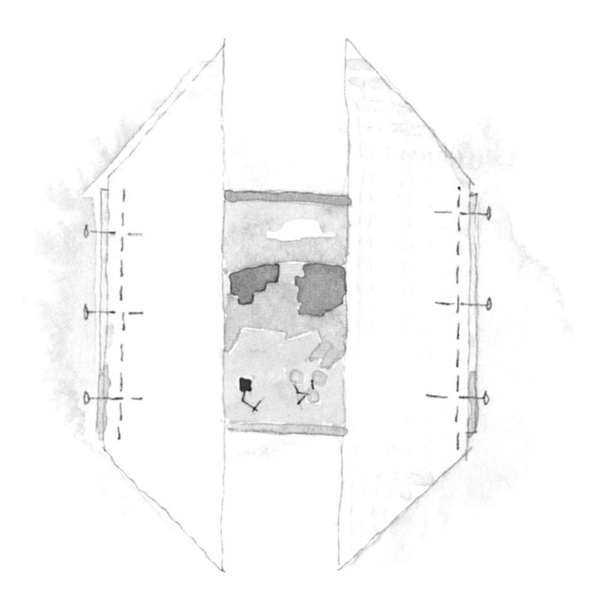

3 Lightly steam press the embroidery on the wrong side. From the gingham fabric cut two pieces 9 x 3 inches and two 8 x 3 inches for the border. With right sides together, pin and stitch the two shorter pieces to the short sides of the picture, taking a ½ inch seam.

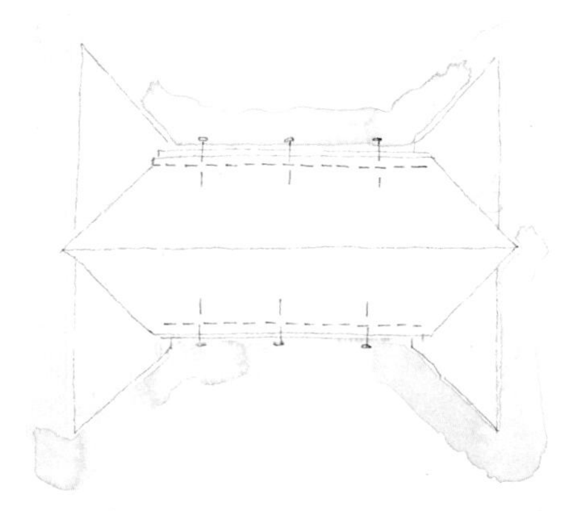

4 Press the seams open and repeat on the two long sides, stitching to within the seam allowance at each side.

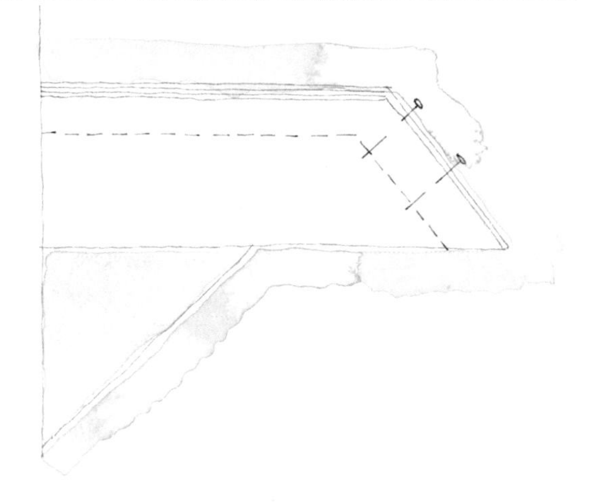

5 Working from the wrong side, place two adjacent borders together, and pin the two mitred edges to hold. Tack and stitch as shown. Repeat on each corner.

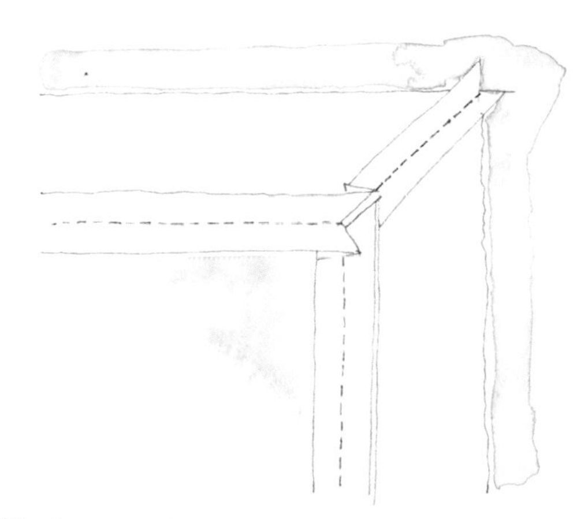

6 Remove the tacking stitches and trim the seams at the corners. Press the seam allowances open. Stretch the embroidery over mounting board with the wadding in between, securing with pieces of masking tape, ready to insert into the picture frame, following the instructions for the sampler on page 104.

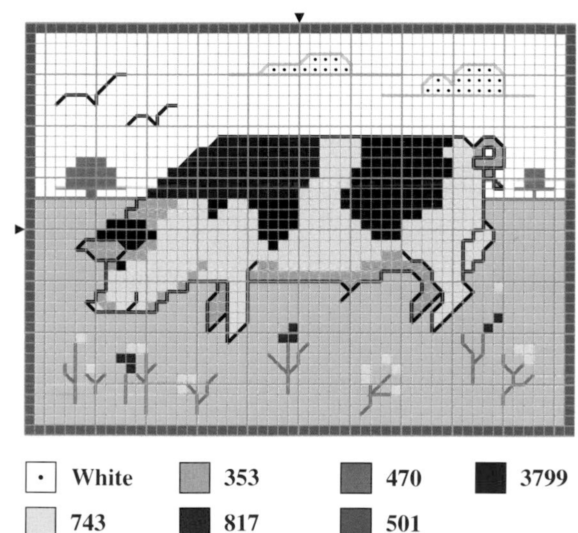

# GREETINGS CARDS

*Finished overall size: 8 x 5½ inches with a cut-out measuring 5½ x 3¾ inches*

YOU WILL NEED

BIRTHDAY CARD:

- 8 x 6 inches of pale blue 28 gauge evenweave fabric
- card mount with oval cut-out

NEW BABY CARD:

- 8 x 6 inches of white 18 gauge Aida fabric
- card mount with landscape cut-out
- small pearl beads
- 14 inches of turquoise blue satin ribbon, ¼ inch wide

GET WELL CARD:

- 8 x 6 inches of red 28 gauge evenweave fabric
- card mount with portrait cut-out
- tacking thread
- tapestry needle, size 26
- DMC stranded embroidery cotton in the following amounts and colors: birthday – one skein each of yellow 745, apricot 402, pinks 963, 3326, 962, red 3726, greens 907, 913, 905; new baby – one skein each of turquoise blue 3811, 3766, greens 472, 580, pinks 3727, 3688; get well – one skein each of yellow 743, red 917, greens 704, 993, 699, blue 792

*A birthday celebration, welcoming a new baby or sending a get well message are all important occasions which we like to mark with something special. And what better way to show you care than with your own hand-embroidered card?*

1 All three cards are embroidered in the same way. Overcast the raw edges of the fabric and mark the center both lengthwise and widthwise with tacking stitches (see Techniques, page 97). Following the appropriate color key and chart, in which each square represents one cross-stitch worked over two fabric threads – with the exception of the New Baby card which is over one fabric intersection – begin the embroidery in the middle using two strands of thread in the needle.

2 Complete the cross-stitching and then add the backstitch details (see Techniques, page 97). For the Birthday card, use one strand of green 905 for the leaf veins.

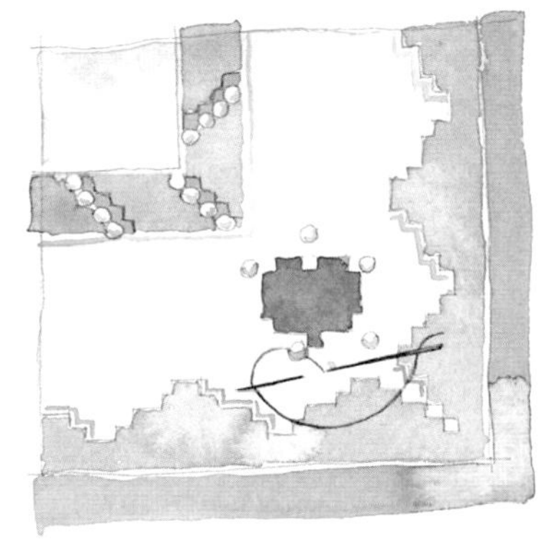

3 For the New Baby card, sew tiny pearl beads to the inner frame and around the hearts, as shown on the chart. Bring out the needle in the correct place, thread on a pearl and re-insert the needle into the same hole. Make a stitch the length of the pearl and bring it out with the thread below the needle. Take the needle through to the back, just beyond where it last emerged, and out again ready to sew on the next pearl.

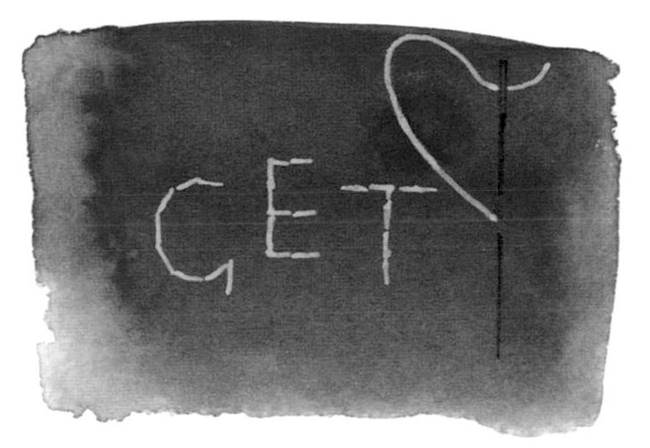


4 For the Get Well card, use two strands of green 699 to backstitch the message. Complete the embroidery and lightly steam press on the wrong side if necessary. Retain the tacking stitches – they will be useful for centering the design in the card mount.

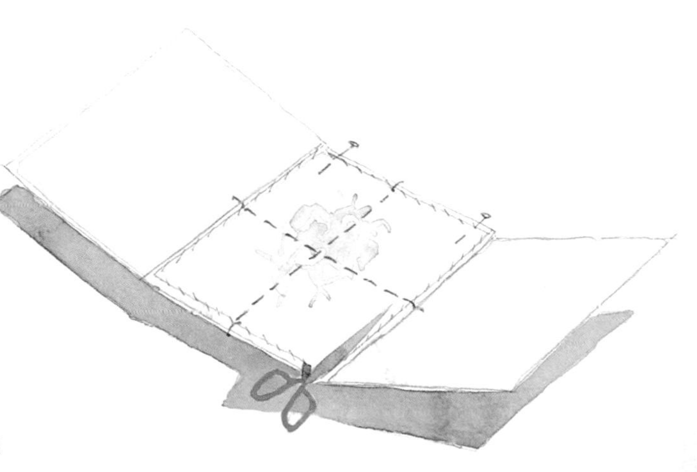

5 Open out the self-adhesive card mount and place the embroidery over the cut-out area, using the tacking stitches to center it. Trim the fabric so that it is ½ inch larger all round than the area marked on the card.

6 Remove the tacking stitches, re-position the embroidery and fold over the left-hand section of the card. Press firmly. For the New Baby card, fold the ribbon in half and attach it to the inner frame, as shown, then tie it in a bow to finish.

Receive this
infant as a trust
And treat it as
a Treasure
3811
3766
472
580
3727
3688
Pearl
Attach bow

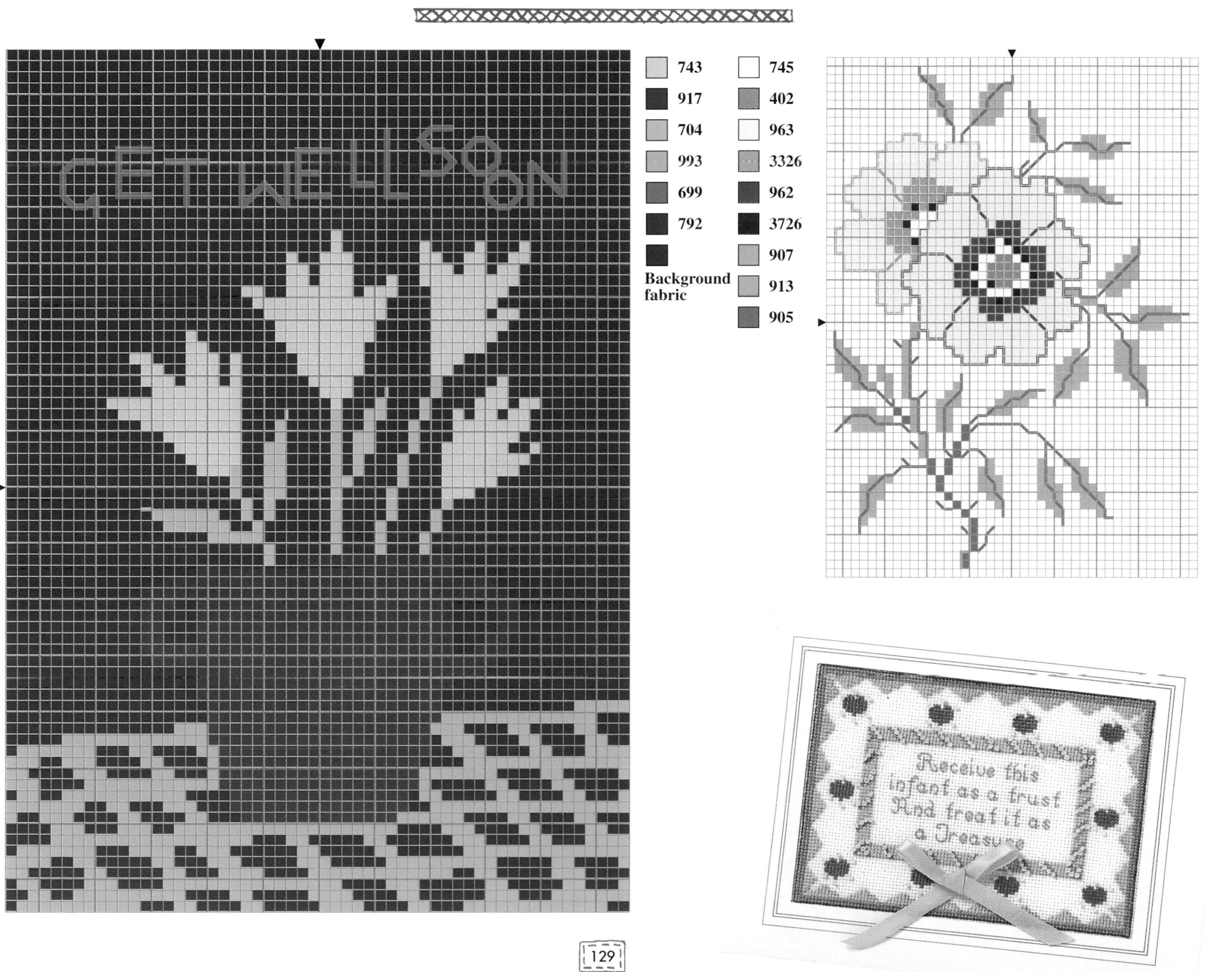
GET WELL SOON
743
917
704
993
699
792
Background fabric
745
402
963
3326
962
3726
907
913
905
Receive this
infant as a trust
And treat it as

# Christmas Tree Decorations

*Finished size of each decoration: 3½ x 3 inches*

YOU WILL NEED

- three 6 inch squares of 14 gauge red Aida fabric
- tacking thread
- tapestry needle, size 24
- DMC stranded embroidery cotton: one skein each of white and red 606
- embroidery hoop (optional)
- matching sewing thread
- tracing paper
- six 4 inch squares of thin cardboard
- six 4 inch squares of lightweight wadding
- masking tape
- three 6 inch squares of red and white checked gingham
- fabric adhesive

SNOWFLAKE A

- 24 inches white twisted silky cord
- two small silver bells

SNOWFLAKE B

- 30 inches green satin ribbon, ⅛ inch wide
- six silver sequins

SNOWFLAKE C

- 24 inches red and green twisted silky cord
- one large red bead

*In the past, the family Christmas tree was decorated with handmade toys and ornaments, and may have included sweetmeats, painted wooden toys and so on. You could start your own collection of cross-stitched decorations with these pretty white snowflakes decorated with tiny bells and sequins.*

1 All three snowflakes are embroidered in the same way. Mark the center of the Aida fabric both lengthwise and widthwise with tacking stitches (see Techniques, page 97). Following the appropriate chart, in which each square represents one stitch worked over one intersection of fabric, start the embroidery in the middle using two strands of white embroidery thread in the needle. Complete the cross-stitching, then add the backstitching in red (see Techniques, page 97).

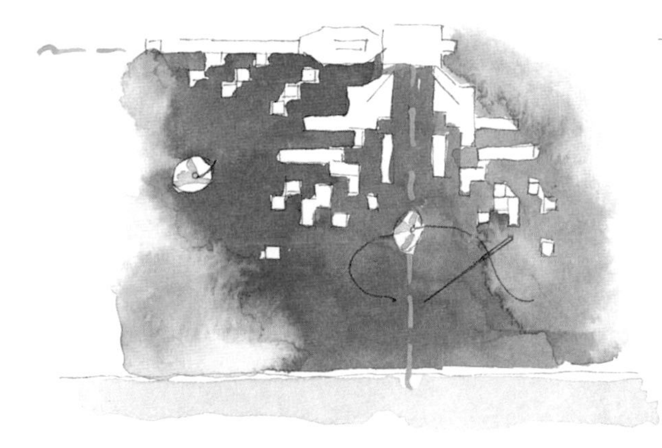

2 For snowflake B, attach the sequins as indicated on the chart before making up the ornament.

3 With tracing paper, trace around the hexagonal outline of the chart, add ¼ inch, and cut out the shape to use as a template. Place it on the cardboard, draw around it twice and cut out the two pieces.

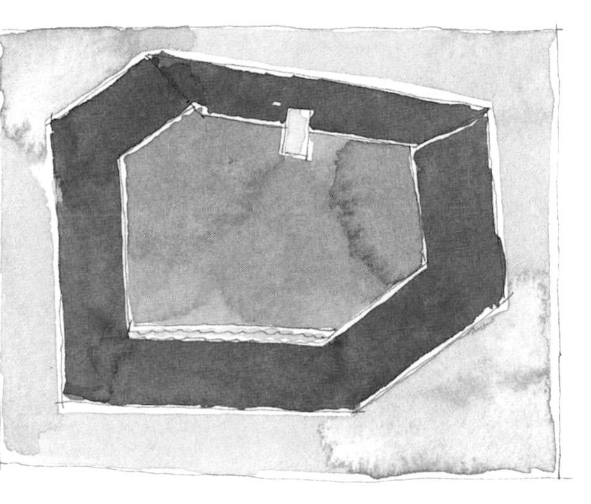

4 Cut out two layers of wadding in the same way. For the front of the ornament, assemble the three layers: place the wadding on the card with the embroidery on top, right side up. Fold the fabric to the underside and hold with pieces of masking tape. Cover the back section in the same way, with the gingham on top.

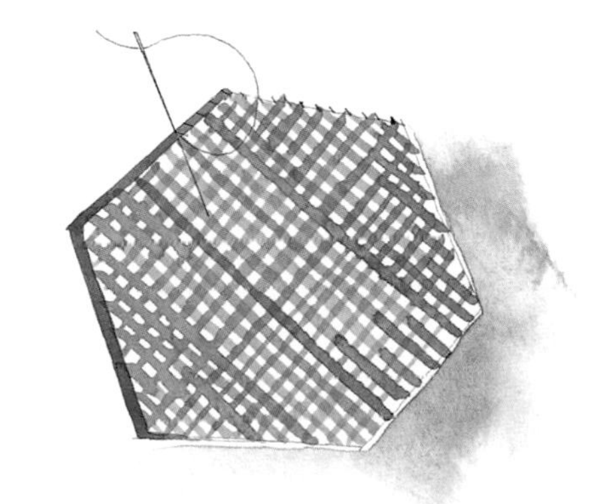

5 Place both front and back sections together and overcast the edges using matching thread.

6 For snowflake A, cover the edges with white cord, attaching it with a thin layer of fabric adhesive applied to the edge of the ornament with a thin piece of cardboard; press the cord in place and finish with a loop at the top. Tuck the loose ends just inside the seam. Attach the two bells to the bottom corners using matching sewing thread and one or two oversewing stitches.

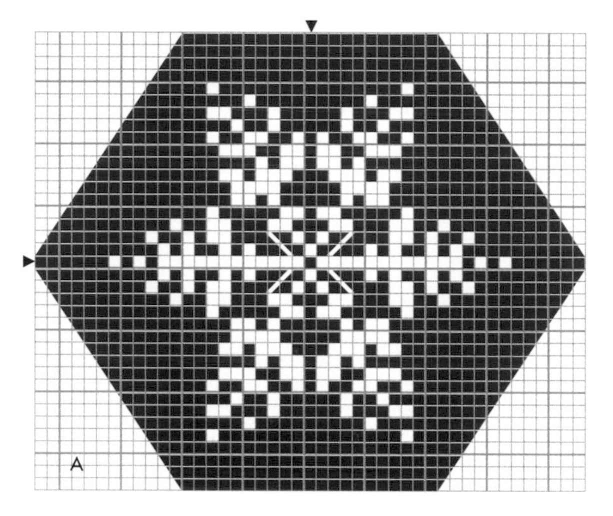


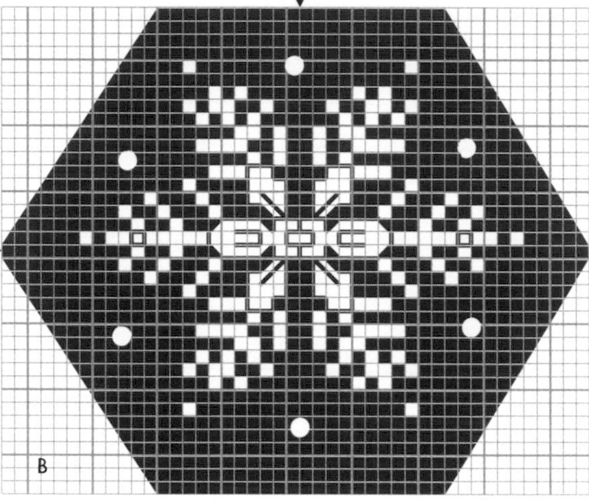


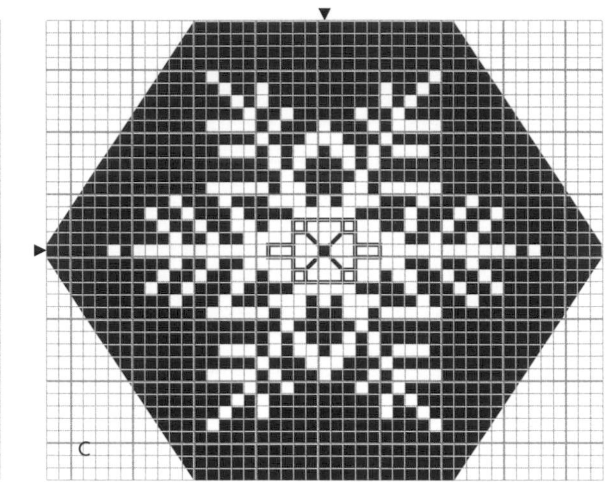


White

606

7 For snowflake B, attach the green ribbon to the outside edge as for A, first sticking the tails in position underneath the edging ribbon.

8 For snowflake C, attach the cord to the outside edge as for A. Knot the large bead at the bottom of the loop. Attach the small beads to the lower corners as mock tassels.

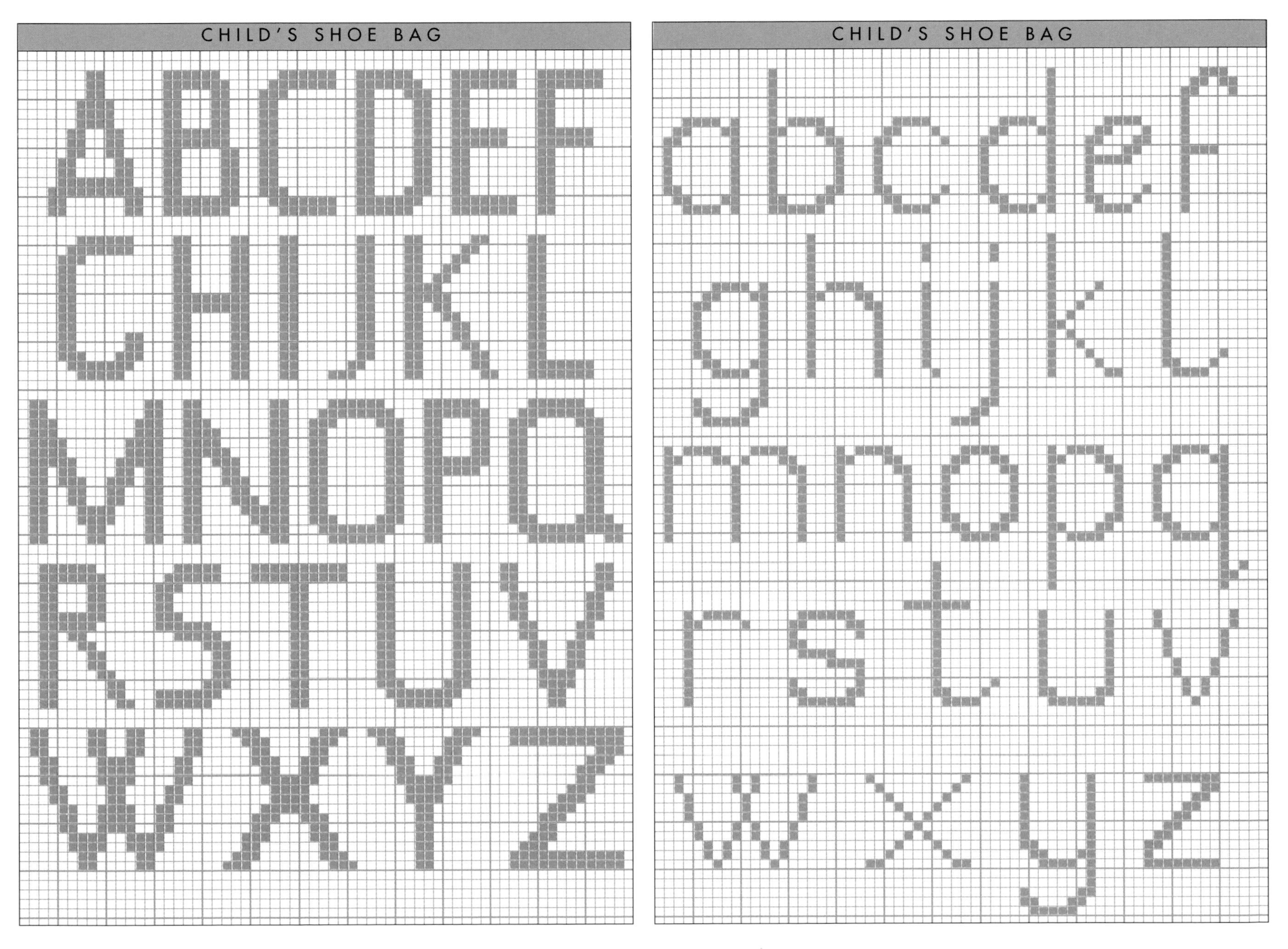
CHILD'S SHOE BAG
CHILD'S SHOE BAG

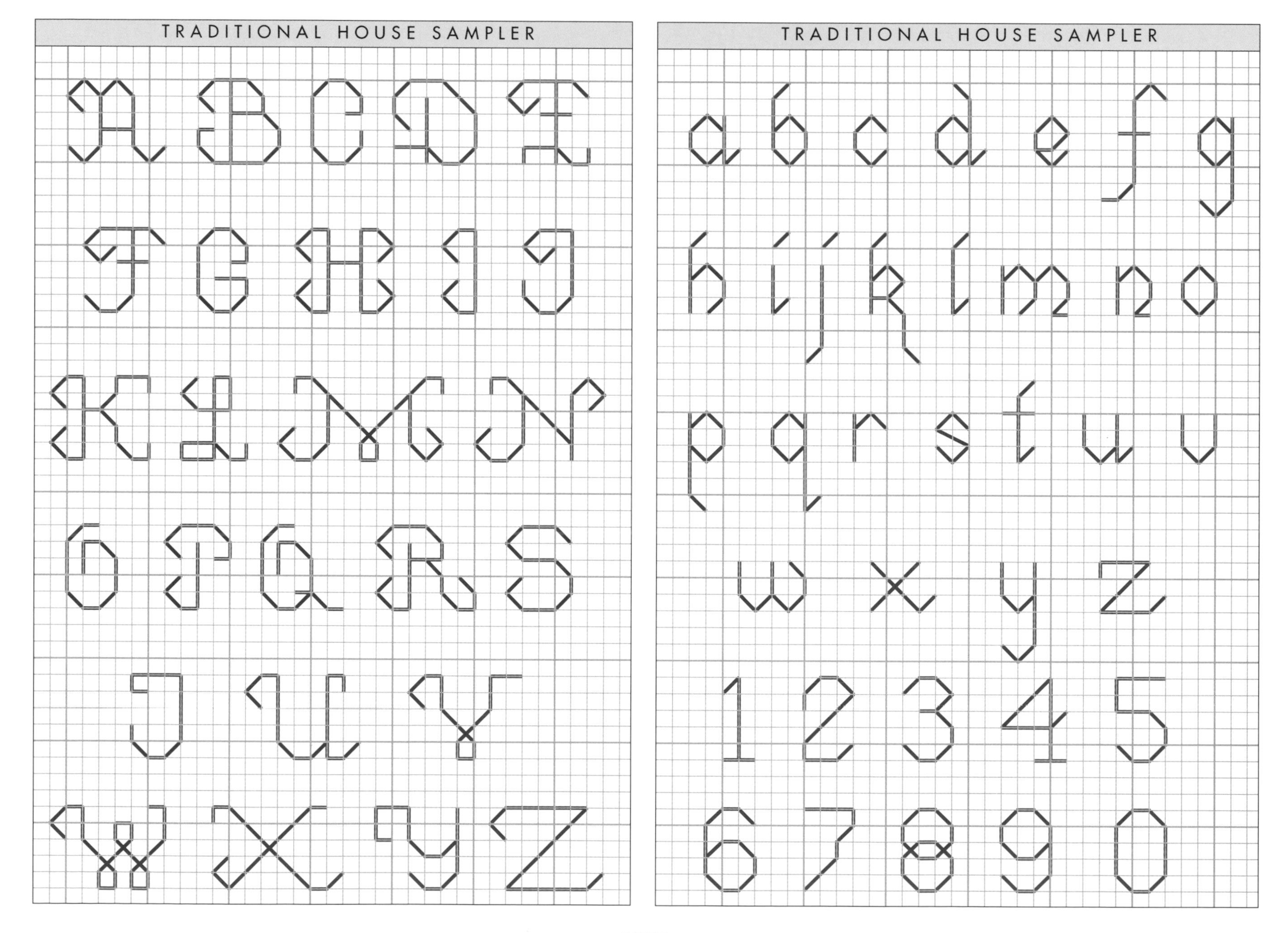
TRADITIONAL HOUSE SAMPLER
TRADITIONAL HOUSE SAMPLER

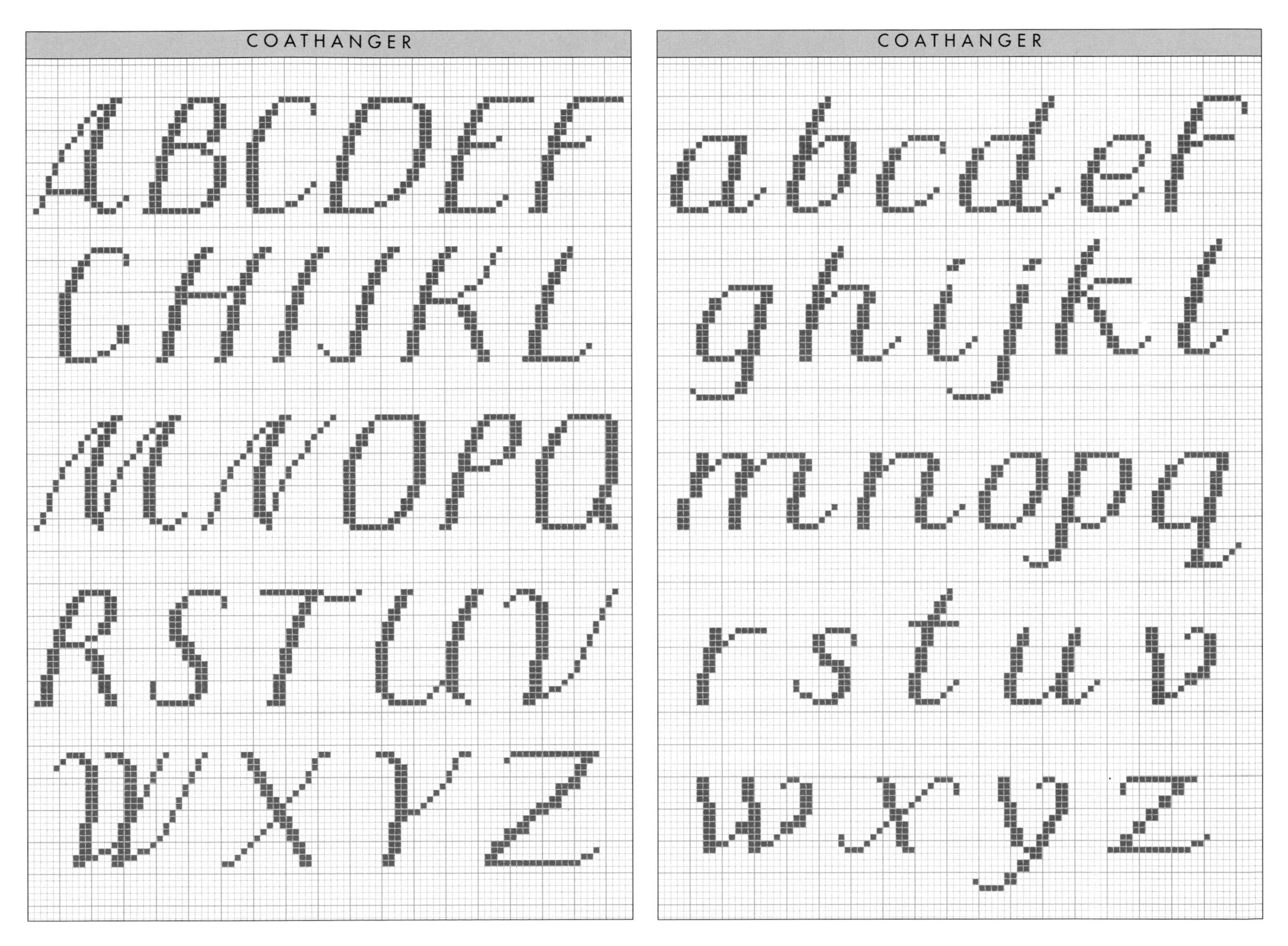
COATHANGER
COATHANGER

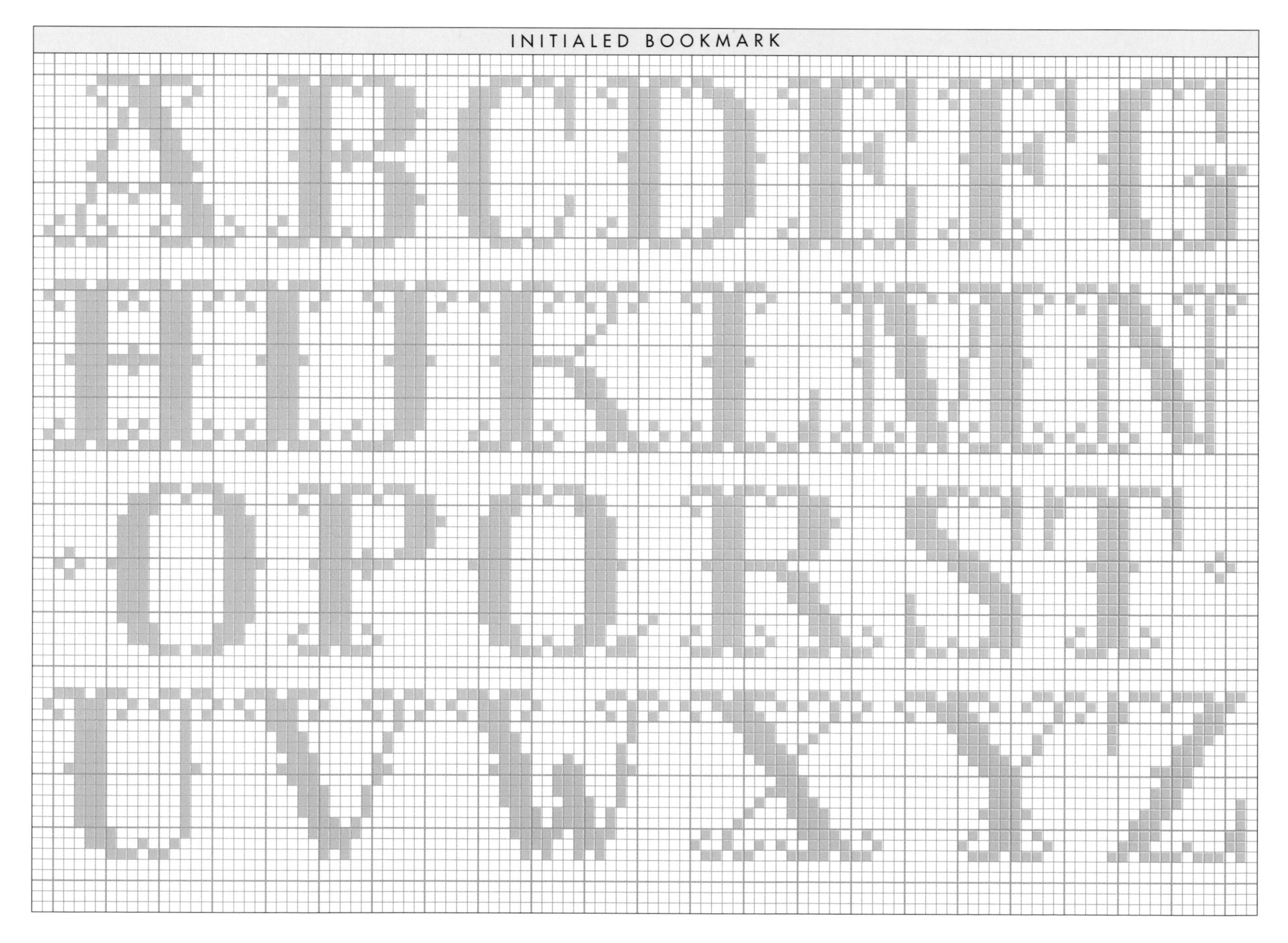
INITIALED BOOKMARK

# NEEDLEPOINT

*Beautiful items for the home and family to create using a collection of canvaswork styles and techniques*

# INTRODUCTION

Welcome to the wonderful world of needlepoint! Needlepoint is embroidery worked in a variety of different yarns over a canvas background. Often called tapestry or canvaswork, it appeals to all needleworkers because you can quickly create beautiful things for the home and family. Today this type of stitchery has broken away from its traditional past of complicated scenic designs worked in fine yarn to embrace a collection of styles and techniques using wool, embroidery floss, ribbon, and fabric, in fact almost any type of yarn which can be used over canvas.

Needlepoint is simple and fun to do, and once you have mastered a few simple stitches, you can create a host of patterns and designs. If you are a beginner, start with a simple project, such as the Country Scene picture on page 152 – it's a perfect first-time project. At the other end of the scale, the sumptuous floral tieback on page 17 will delight a more experienced stitcher.

Before you begin, read the following section on the materials and all the simple techniques you need to know. Then each of the projects comes complete with a chart, key, and step-by-step instructions to help you produce a stunning piece of needlepoint.

Happy stitching!

## MATERIALS AND EQUIPMENT

### *Canvas*

Canvas is specifically made as the base for needlepoint. It is woven from stiffened cotton or linen and is generally available in white, buff, or dark beige. Canvas is graded by the number of threads or holes to 1 inch. This is the mesh or gauge size – the smaller the number, the coarser the canvas. Choose the best quality canvas you can afford, because this will provide a firm foundation on which to build your stitches and give the needlepoint a long life.

To work out how much canvas you need for a project, add an extra 3 inches all around for standard and large pieces, and 2 inches for a small piece of work. This extra border of canvas allows for stretching and mounting. Canvas can be bought by the yard or by the piece. The two main types of canvas are plain or interlocking mono and penelope canvas.

**Mono canvas** is woven with single crossing threads – horizontally and vertically. The best variety is interlock canvas, in which the threads are twisted and bonded together, providing a very firm background. Mono canvas is easy to use, especially for a beginner, because any stitch can be worked over the even grid surface.

**Penelope canvas** has pairs of crossing threads interwoven horizontally and vertically. The double threads can be gently parted and used as a single canvas to gain smoother curved lines, and for areas of fine detailed work.

**Rug canvas** is a coarse interlock canvas which is available in a range of different widths.

**Plastic canvas** is bought in small sheets or pre-cut shapes, such as circles, and is generally used for three-dimensional pieces of canvaswork. It is easy to cut and will not fray. Plastic canvas is a good choice for children learning to stitch.

### *Yarns*

Choose a yarn appropriate to your needlepoint project, and then match the yarn to the type and gauge of canvas. It must be thick enough to completely cover the canvas, but the threaded needle must still be able to pass through the canvas mesh without pushing the threads apart and distorting the canvas. On large-gauge canvas, several strands can be used together to cover the canvas threads. Buy all the yarn at the beginning of a project since dye lots can change and even a slight variation will show up, especially in a large area of one color. Always work a test piece, using your chosen yarn on the chosen canvas, to see how the finished piece will look.

**Wool** is the traditional yarn for needlepoint. Choose from tapestry, crewel, and Persian yarns. Once you are more experienced at stitching, you can try a range of different fibers for experimental work, but use wool when you first begin to get the feel of needlepoint.

**Tapestry yarn** is a firm, tightly twisted single 100% wool strand which cannot be divided. It is available in 11-yard skeins in a huge range of colors. Tapestry yarn can also be bought in ¾ ounce hanks (grounding wool) in a smaller range of popular background colors.

**Crewel yarn** is a fine two-ply yarn used for delicate canvaswork. It can be used as a single strand, or two, three, four, or more strands can be used together on thicker canvases. Each color is available in a wide range of shades, making this yarn a good choice for detailed shading and ideal for blending different colors together to create muted shades.

**Persian yarn** is slightly thicker than crewel yarn. A loosely twisted three-strand yarn, it can be divided or added to for working on different size canvas and to blend different colors together.

**Cotton embroidery floss** is made up of multiple strands of mercerized cotton, loosely twisted together. It can be used as a single strand or in groups – nine strands of floss is equal to a single strand of tapestry yarn. Separate the strands before regrouping into the number of threads needed for the project.

**Matte embroidery cotton** is a soft, fairly thick twisted thread with a dull finish. It is a successful alternative to tapestry yarn for canvaswork.

**Metallic threads** are available in an extensive range of different thicknesses and shades, and small amounts can be mixed in or used over previously stitched sections.

### *Needles*

Tapestry needles have rounded, blunt tips which do not split the yarn or the canvas threads. Their large eyes can accommodate different threads and thicker yarns. Needles are graded into size by thickness – the higher the number, the finer the needle.

As a quick guide: use a size 18 for 10- and 12-gauge canvas; size 20 for 14-gauge canvas; size 22 for 16- and 18-gauge canvas, and size 24 for fine 22- and 24-gauge canvases.

### *Frames*

Mount the canvas in either a square or rectangular frame; there are two basic types:

**Simple stretcher frames** are made from two pairs of artists' stretchers. These are lengths of wood with mitered and slotted corners, which can be quickly put together. The canvas is held on the frame with thumbtacks.

**Rotating frames** are the most common of the frames. They come in a variety of sizes and are composed of two horizontal rods slotted into two side pieces. Each rod has a strip of webbing tape stapled along one edge. The rollers are set into two straight side pieces and held firmly with four butterfly screws, one in each corner. These frames can be mounted on floor-standing supports, leaving both hands free for stitching.

### *Other Equipment Required*

**Scissors** – use large dressmaker's scissors for cutting canvas, and a small, sharp-pointed pair for trimming and cutting yarn.

Floor-standing needlepoint frames allow both hands to be free for stitching.

**Thimble** – if you normally wear a thimble for sewing, you'll find it useful when stitching needlepoint to protect the middle (pushing) finger.

**Masking tape** – bind the raw canvas edges to protect the yarns and your hands.

**Buttonhole thread**, used in a sewing needle for lacing the canvas to a rotating frame and for holding the finished canvas over a backing board, ready for framing.

**Daylight bulb** – fit this special type of light bulb in a side lamp to help you see the exact yarn colors during dark or gloomy days.

**Tracing and graph paper** are needed for designing and transferring designs. A thick, black, waterproof felt-tip pen, ruler, and T-square are also useful for marking the canvas before stitching.

**Firm board and thumbtacks** – when the finished piece of needlepoint is complete, pin the canvas over blotting or tissue paper to block the canvas back into shape.

## Techniques

You don't need any special skills to work a piece of needlepoint. Once you have learned a couple of basic stitches, you can create a masterpiece! Just use the following techniques as a guide to help you gain the best results:

### *Preparing the canvas*

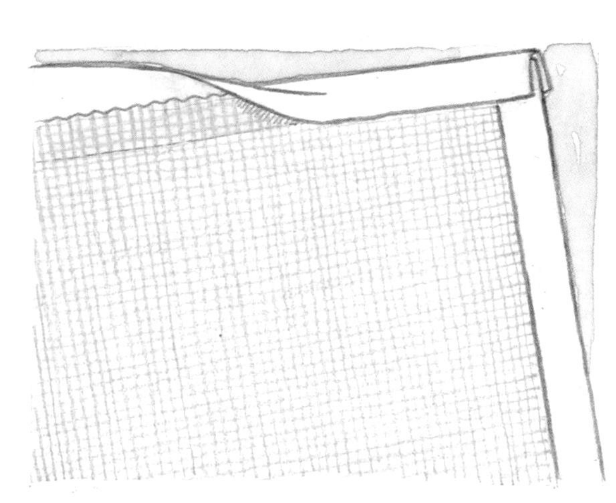

Cut canvas alongside a thread in both directions. To protect your hands and clothes from catching on the raw canvas, and to prevent the edges from unraveling, cover with masking tape. Cut a length of 1in wide tape for each side, and simply fold evenly in half over the canvas edges. Press the masking tape firmly in position.

### *Working in a frame*

Unless you are working with plastic canvas or on a very small piece of canvas, it is advisable to stitch your canvas in a needlepoint frame. It is a matter of preference, but if you learn to use a frame from the beginning, you will find it easier to work – both hands will be free – and you will gain an even result. A needlepoint frame keeps the canvas stretched taut, making it easier to stitch in two movements – the correct way to work a piece of needlepoint – up through the canvas and back down again. With more experience, you will find that you can stitch with a flowing rhythm, maintain an even tension, and effect the minimum distortion to the canvas.

### *Fitting the canvas into a frame*

1 Cut the canvas to the correct size for the project, at least 3 inches larger all around on standard and large projects, and 2 inches larger all around on smaller pieces. Bind all edges with masking tape, as shown.

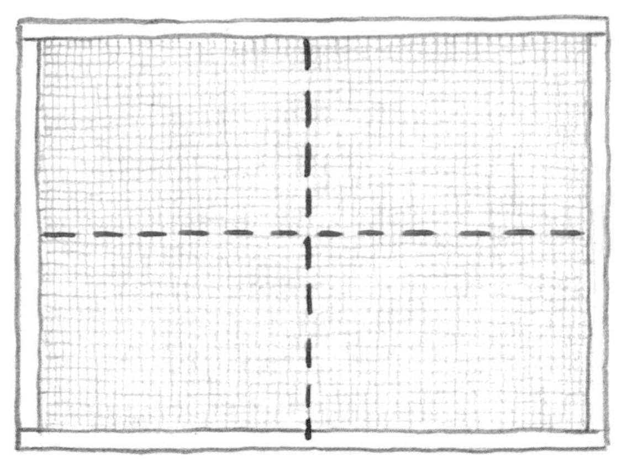

2 Use a doubled length of contrasting sewing thread to baste across the canvas both lengthwise and widthwise to mark the center of the canvas. Alternatively, use a permanent ink felt tip-pen to mark the center of the canvas on each side. Use a pencil to mark the center of the webbing tapes.

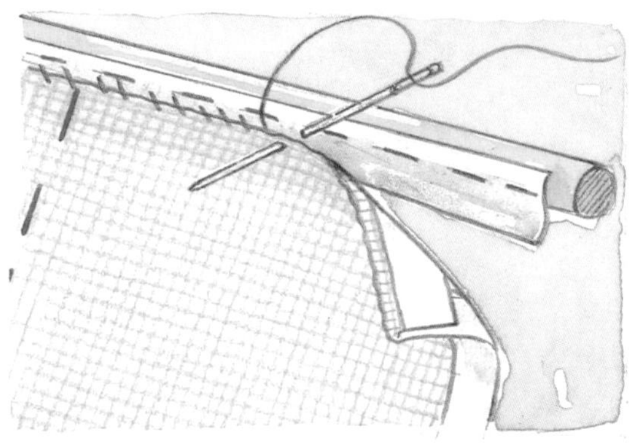

3 Turn under approximately ⅝ inch of canvas and, matching center marks, oversew the canvas to the tape along one rod. Repeat, to stitch the opposite edge of canvas to the row of webbing tape on the opposite rod. Begin stitching in the center and work outward to the edge on either side.

4 Assemble the frame. Wind any excess canvas around one of the rods, and tighten the screws to hold the canvas firm and taut.

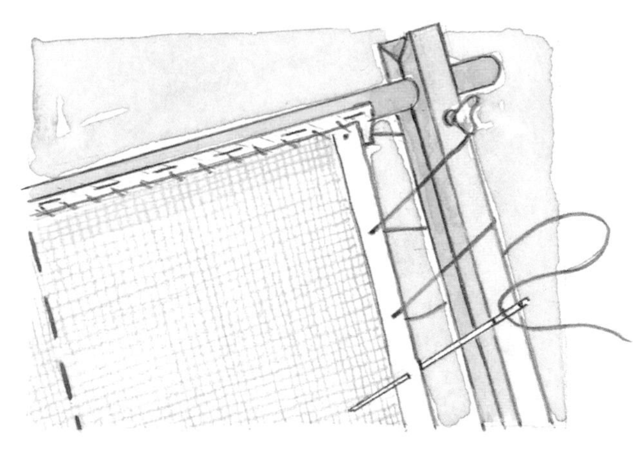

5 To help support the side edges of the canvas, use buttonhole thread or fine string to lace the side edges of the canvas around the side sections of the frame.

## Working from a chart

A needlepoint chart is made up of a grid of squares, with each square representing one stitch or one hole of canvas. Charts are not actual-size. In the materials list at the beginning of a project, you'll find the canvas gauge size stated – buy this size of canvas to achieve the finished size of the project. To enlarge or reduce the size of the project, simply work over a finer canvas or over a canvas with a larger gauge count.

1 Mark the center lines of the canvas – these will match up with the center lines marked on the chart. To make it even easier to follow the chart, you can subdivide the canvas into ten square sections to match up with the heavier guide lines found on most charts. Count out the squares, and mark across the canvas as before.
2 Each symbol or color on a chart represents the color and stitch with which that area is worked. Follow the key that goes with the chart, and match the symbol or color to the yarn color, then work the number of stitches shown on the chart. Use the marked lines as a guide, removing them as soon as you have stitched over them.

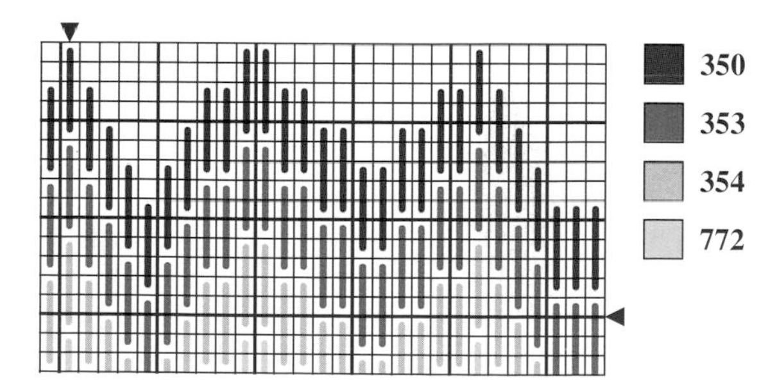


## Working from an actual-size design

Instead of using a chart, actual-size needlepoint designs can be marked on the canvas with a permanent ink felt-tip pen, or painted onto the canvas using waterproof paints. Mark out the outline before fitting the canvas into a needlepoint frame.

1 If necessary, enlarge the design on a photocopier to the desired finished size. Go over the outline with a black felt-tip pen, so you have a strong, clear outline. Mark the center of the design on each side.
2 Tape the design flat on a board. Matching center marks, tape the canvas over the design. You will see the design through the canvas threads. Mark the outline onto the canvas, following the outline of the design. Make sure that the outline goes around the canvas holes to make it easier to follow when stitching.
3 Alternatively, use waterproof paints to paint the design onto the canvas in your chosen colors. Then you can match the areas to the yarns when stitching.

## Beginning to stitch

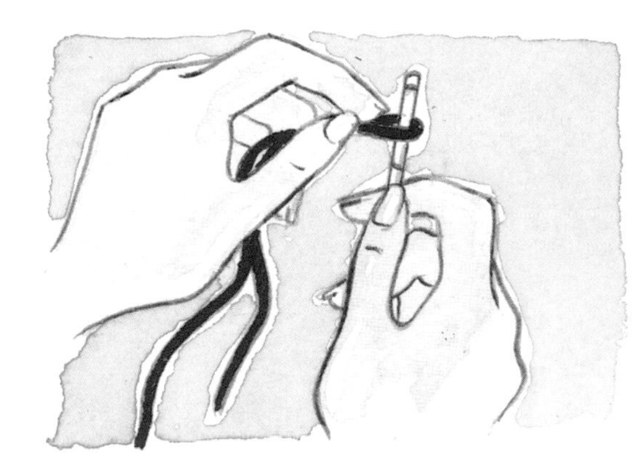

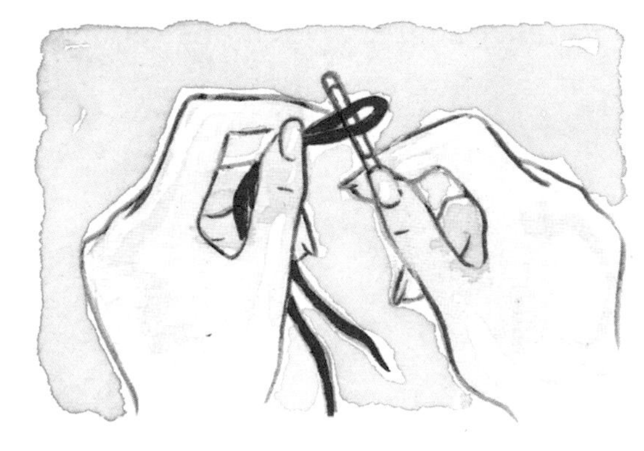

1 Cut approximately 18 inches of yarn. If the yarn is too long, the continuous rubbing against the canvas threads will make it fray and wear thin. Thread one end through a tapestry needle, wrapping the yarn tightly around the needle eye. Slide the yarn off the needle and thread through the eye. Knot the opposite end.
2 Take the threaded needle through the canvas, from the right side to the wrong side, leaving the knot ¾ inch in front of where the stitching will begin.

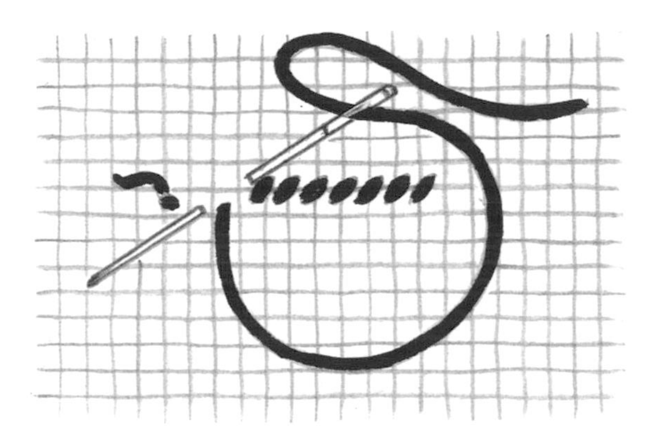

3 Bring the needle back to the right side of the canvas at the position for the first stitch. Work the first few stitches over the canvas and yarn end. When the knot is reached, cut it off and continue stitching.
4 Start new lengths of yarn by sliding the needle under the backs of a few worked stitches on the wrong side of the canvas, then bringing it through the correct hole to the right side, ready for stitching.

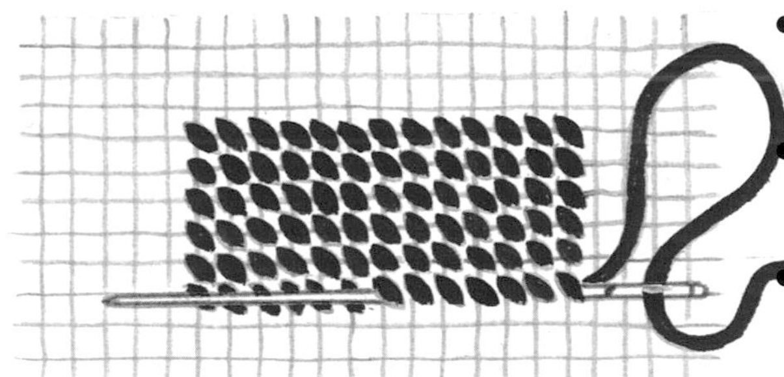

5 To end a length of yarn, slide the needle under a few stitches at the back of the canvas. Trim off the end close to the canvas.
6 Try to avoid beginning and ending yarn in the same place, row after row, because a ridge will form on the right side of the canvas.

### *Hints and tips for successful stitching*

- Work each stitch in two movements, with the left hand on top of the canvas and the right hand underneath. Feed the needle up through the canvas to the right side and back down to the wrong side. You can only work this two-step method when the canvas is stretched taut in a needlepoint frame. With practice, you will gain a flowing rhythm of stitching and maintain an even stitch tension with the minimum of canvas distortion.
- It is important to keep an even tension when stitching. Before you work any new stitch, practice on a spare piece of canvas to gauge the tension. If the stitches are too loose, they will not cover the canvas. If the stitches are too tight, the canvas will pucker and stretch out of shape.
- Try to come up through an empty hole of canvas and go down through the canvas in a partially filled hole. This will help to smooth down the yarn.
- The yarn will become twisted as you stitch – simply let the needle drop and the yarn will naturally untwist itself.
- Move the needle along the yarn as you stitch, to prevent the yarn from wearing thin where it is threaded through the needle eye.
- When stitching a tiny piece of canvas that can not fit into a needlepoint frame, place the canvas centrally on a spare piece of fabric and baste firmly together. Set the fabric in an embroidery hoop. Separate the rings; place the fabric over the smaller ring. Fit the larger ring over the top; press in place and tighten. Turn over and cut away the fabric from behind the canvas area – you can then stitch the canvas in the usual way.

### *Correcting mistakes*

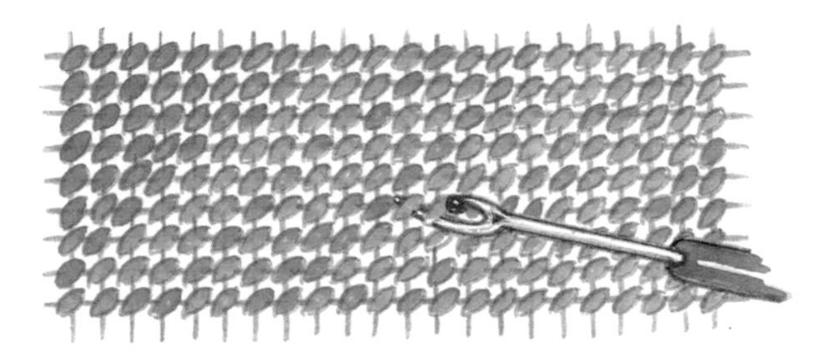

1 If you make a mistake, stitches can be quickly unpicked. Use a pair of small, sharply pointed scissors to snip through one stitch, then, using the blunt end of a tapestry needle, gently ease out the offending stitches. If you have a row of stitches to remove, use a seam ripper. Slide it just under the stitches on the wrong side to cut them. Re-stitch using a new length of yarn.

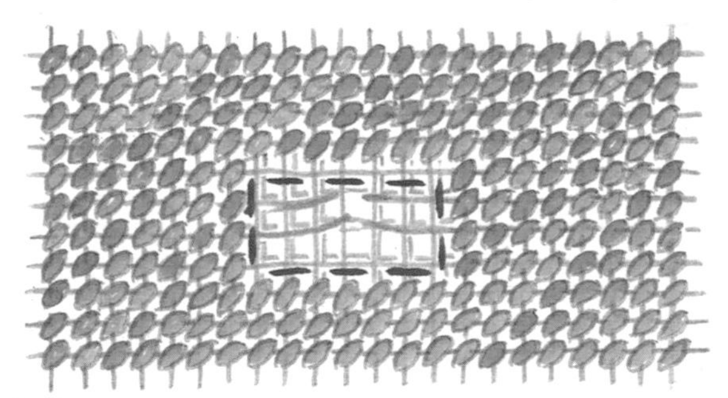

2 If you accidentally snip a canvas thread, a new piece of canvas can be grafted over the hole. Unpick the stitches surrounding the hole over a 1½ inch area. Cut a 1½ inch square of canvas with the same gauge count. Position the canvas square over the hole on the wrong side of the main canvas, match the canvas threads, and baste in place. Now stitch over the area again in the usual way, working through both layers of canvas.

*Blocking a piece of needlepoint*

When you have finished a piece of needlepoint, you may find it has been pulled out of shape. Generally this can be cured by a steam-press on the wrong side, while gently pulling the canvas back into shape. However, if the canvas is badly distorted, the best method is to stretch and block it back into shape.

1 Mark out the finished outline on a clean sheet of blotting or tissue paper, and pin this over a clean, flat wooden board.

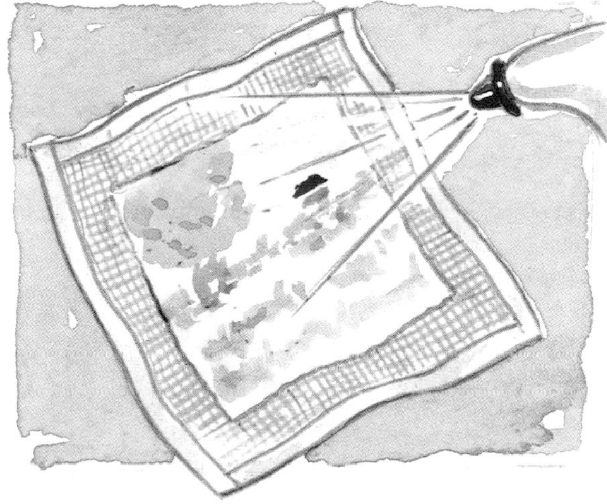

2 Dampen the back of the needlepoint using a wet sponge or plant mister. The water is used just to soften the canvas, so do not over-wet the canvas.

3 Lay the canvas, right side up, over the board. Gently pull the canvas to match the outline of the needlepoint to the marked outline on the paper. Pin in place with thumbtacks. Begin pinning at the center top and work outward, straighten the base edge to match, and, finally, stretch and pin the sides in the same way. Use a T-square to help check any right-angle corners. Space the thumbtacks approximately 1 inch apart.

4 Check that the canvas is straight, and leave to dry thoroughly for approximately 24 hours.

# WELCOME TO SPRING

*Finished size: 6 x 5 inches*

*This tiny springtime picture, complete with gamboling lambs, is worked entirely in half-cross stitch using soft embroidery cotton over a 14-gauge canvas, so it's a good project for a beginner.*

YOU WILL NEED

- 12 x 10 inch piece of white interlock mono canvas with 14 holes to 1 inch
- masking tape
- Anchor matte embroidery cotton in the following colors and amounts: two skeins of off-white 2, one skein each of geranium 11, cornflower 147, grass green 242, almond green 260, dark almond green 262, canary yellow 288, black 403, beige 679, dusty pink 892, and kingfisher 9159
- tapestry needle, size 20
- basting thread in contrasting color
- needlepoint frame
- picture frame and mount board

1 **To work** To prevent the canvas edges from unraveling, and to protect your hands and clothes, fold masking tape evenly in half over the raw canvas edges.

2 Using contrasting thread, baste across the canvas both lengthwise and widthwise to mark the center (see Techniques, page 142).

3 Mount the canvas into the frame (see Techniques, page 142).

4 The chart shows the complete design for the picture. The center is marked with black arrowheads – match these up with the lines of basting stitches on the canvas. Each square on the chart represents one half-cross stitch, worked over one canvas thread intersection.

5 Beginning in the center, work the whole design in half-cross stitch, following the chart and key.

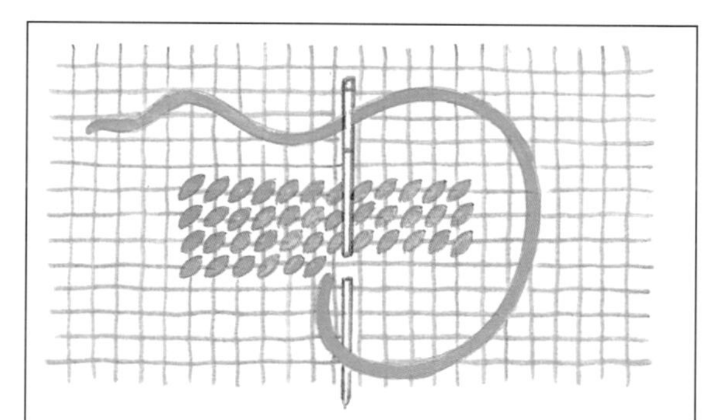

**Half-cross stitch.** Bring the needle out of the canvas and take a small diagonal stitch over one canvas thread intersection with the needle vertical, bringing it out of the canvas directly below. On the wrong side of the canvas the stitches will be vertical. Make sure that all the stitches slant in the same direction.

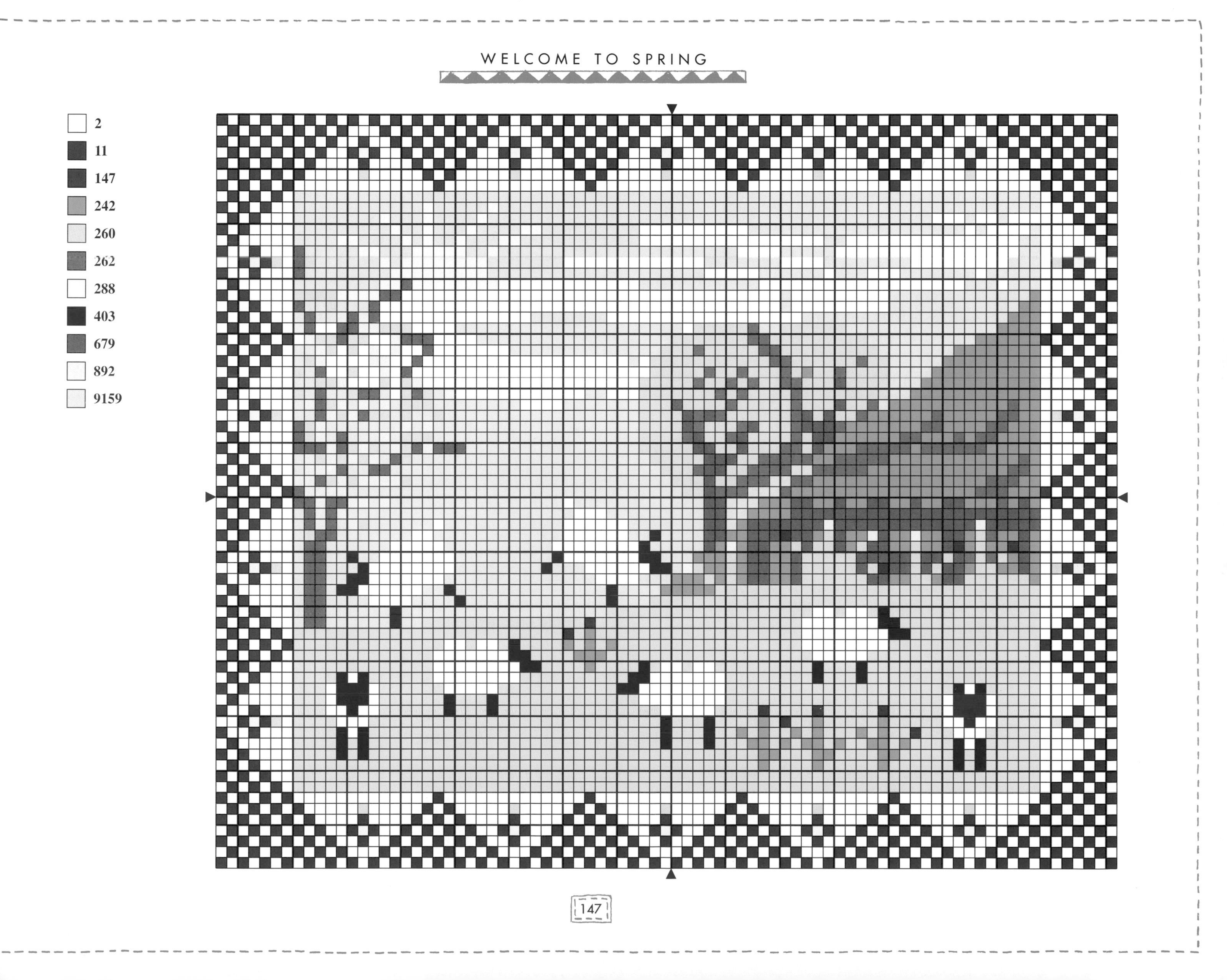
WELCOME TO SPRING
2
11
147
242
260
262
288
403
679
892
9159

6 **To finish** When the needlepoint is complete, remove it from the frame. Peel off the masking tape from the canvas edges. Press the needlepoint on the wrong side over a damp cloth, gently pulling the canvas back into shape (see Techniques, page 145).

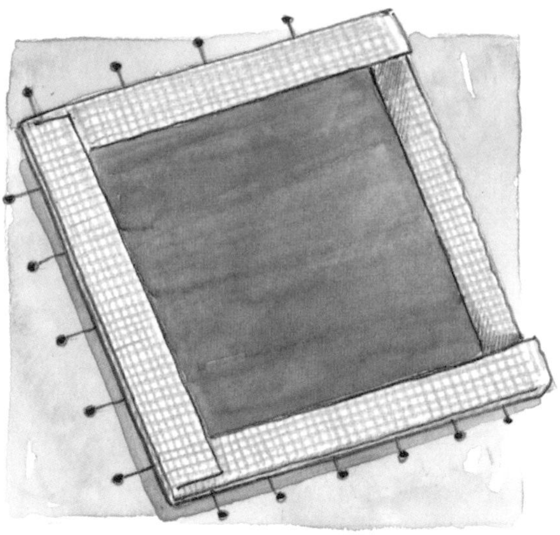

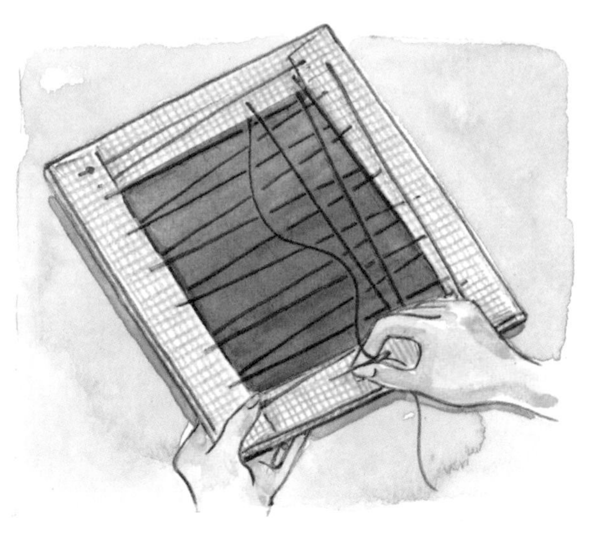

7 Remove the backing board from the frame and place the needlepoint centrally over it. Attach the needlepoint to the top edge of the board with a line of tacks. Pull the canvas over the bottom edge of the board and hold in place with tacks in the same way. Repeat on both sides.

8 Keep checking that the design is central and that the canvas is taut. Turn the board over to the wrong side and, using a doubled sewing thread, lace the two edges together from side to side and from top to bottom.

9 Remove the tacks and replace the board inside the frame. Add another piece of cardboard, and tape across frame back to secure.

# Decorative Address Book

*Finished size: to fit an address book 6⅛ x 4⅛ inches*

*This address book, with its delightful needlepoint cover, will inspire you to keep an up-to-date record of the addresses of your family and friends. Embroidered in tapestry yarn over a 14-gauge canvas, the whole design is worked in traditional tent stitch.*

YOU WILL NEED

- masking tape
- 16¼ x 12¼ inch piece of white mono canvas with 14 holes to 1 inch
- black, fine-point felt-tip pen with permanent ink
- basting thread in contrasting color
- needlepoint frame
- DMC tapestry yarn in the following colors and amounts: 10 skeins of blue 7820, one skein each of orange 7947, purple 7708, red 7666, turquoise 7996, yellow 7973, and green 7911
- tapestry needle, size 20
- address book with a front face 4⅛ x 6⅛ inches and ½ inch thick spine
- 1 yard of ⅝ inch wide blue binding tape
- sewing thread to match binding

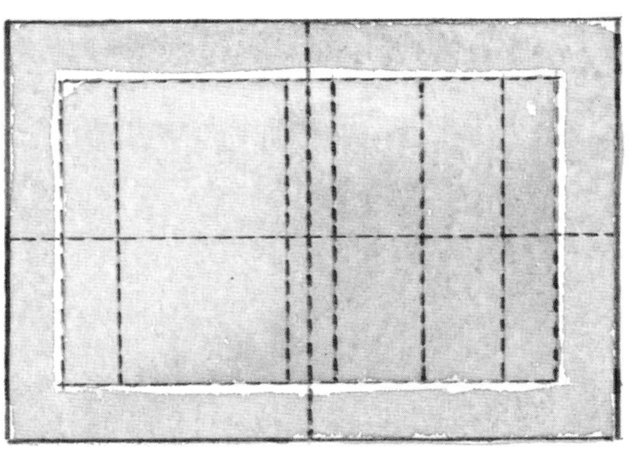

1 **To work** To protect your hands and clothes, and the yarn from catching on the canvas, fold masking tape evenly in half over the raw canvas edges.

2 Following the diagram and using the measurements of the address book, mark the outline of the cover centrally on the canvas with the felt-tip pen. Mark ¾ inch deep pockets on either end of the cover. With a line of basting stitches worked in a contrasting color thread, mark the center of the front cover section.

3 The chart shows the complete design for the front cover. The center of the design is marked by arrowheads – match these up with the marked lines on the canvas. Each square on the chart represents one tent stitch worked over one canvas thread intersection.

4 Mount the canvas into the frame (see Techniques, page 142).

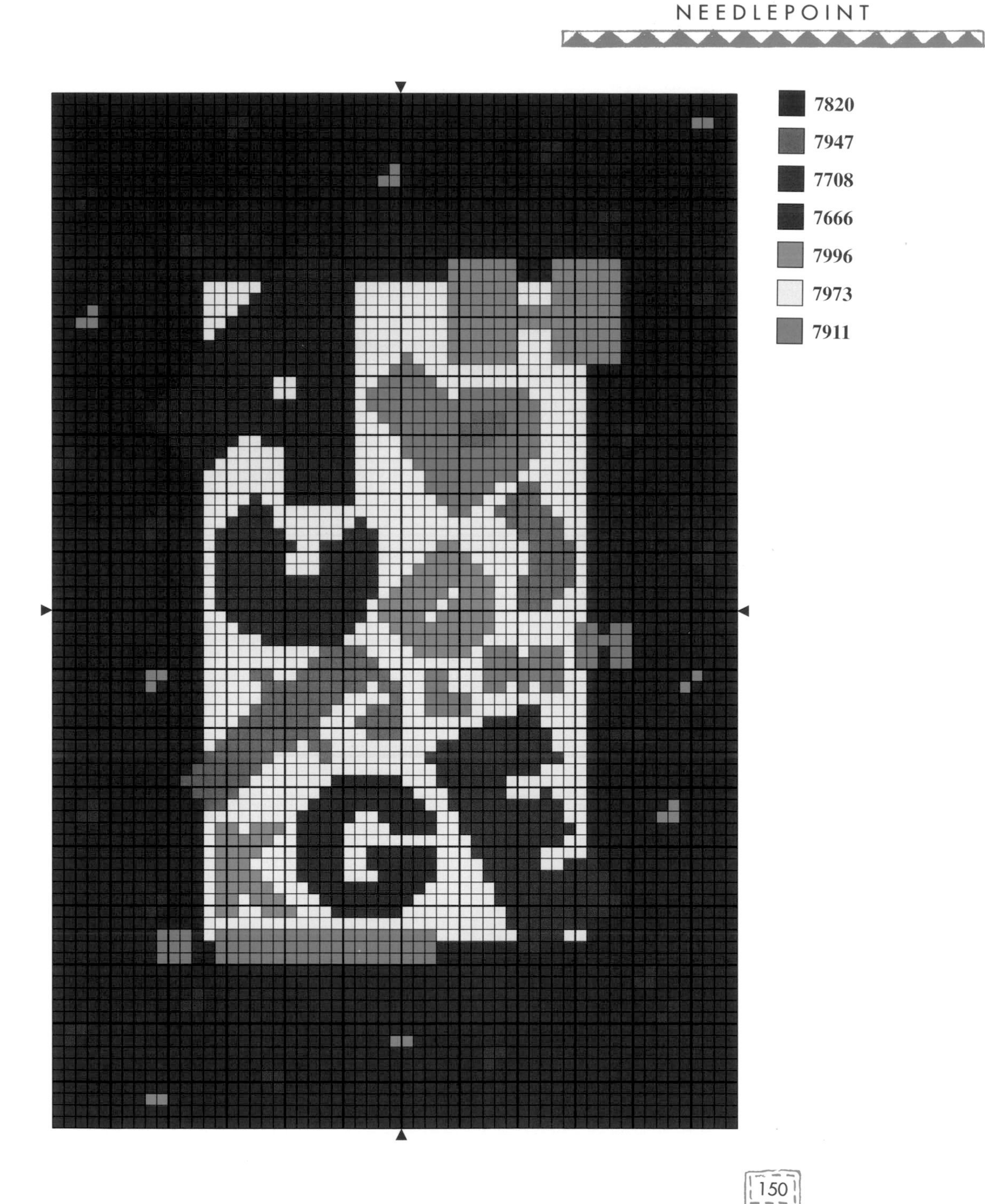


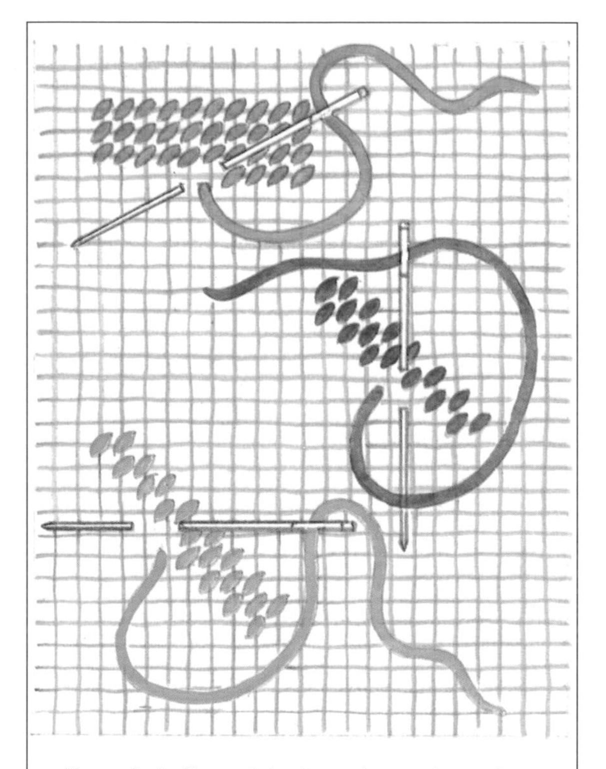

**Tent stitch.** To work horizontal rows, bring the needle out of the canvas and take a small diagonal stitch over one canvas thread intersection. Take the needle down diagonally behind one horizontal and two vertical threads, then bring it out ready for the next stitch. On the wrong side, the stitches will be slightly longer diagonal stitches.

To work diagonally down the canvas, take the needle diagonally up over one canvas thread intersection then pass it vertically down behind two horizontal canvas threads.

To work diagonally up the canvas, the needle is passed horizontally behind two vertical canvas threads.

5 The design is worked in tent stitch throughout. Stitch the front cover following the chart and key. Then work the spine and back cover section in blue 7820, with odd stitches worked in turquoise 7996 and purple 7708 scattered around, in a similar way to the background of the front cover.

6 **To finish** Remove the completed needlepoint from the frame. Peel off the masking tape from the canvas edges. Press the needlepoint on the wrong side over a damp cloth, gently pulling the canvas back into shape.

7 Trim the canvas to within ⅜ inch of the needlepoint. Pin and stitch the binding along the edges of the needlepoint all around the cover. Miter each corner, and join binding edges together to fit.

8 Turn the binding at top and bottom edges to the inside and press well. Catchstitch the edge of the binding down.

9 Turn in ¾ inch of needlepoint at each side to form pockets; press well. Catchstitch the pocket edges to the top and bottom of the cover to secure the pockets.

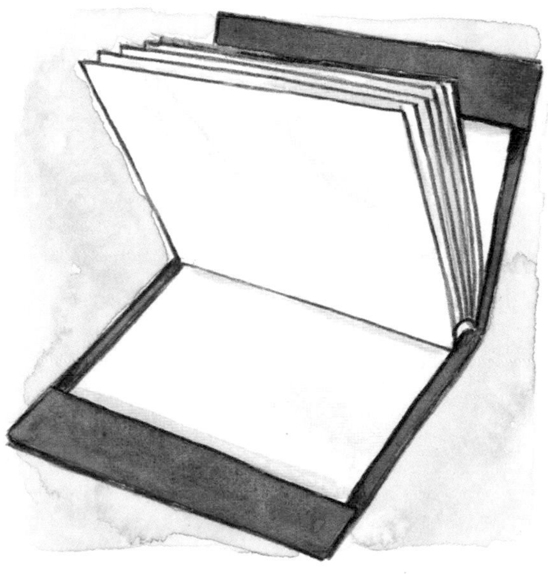

10 Insert the address book by slipping the cover ends inside the cover.

# A Country Scene

*Finished size: approximately 7 x 6½ inches*

*Quick to stitch, this charming country scene is worked in long stitch over a 14-gauge canvas. When the needlepoint stitches are completed, straight stitch, backstitch, and French knots are added to bring character to this little picture.*

YOU WILL NEED

- 11 x 10 inch piece of mono canvas with 14 holes to 1 inch
- masking tape
- Anchor Tapisserie yarn in the following shades: one skein each of white 8000, china blue 8624, laurel 9006, cornflower blue 8688, cathedral blue 8792, pale cornflower blue 8682, beige brown 9636, jade 8966, emerald 8988, spring green 9114, paprika 8240, and yellow/orange 8116
- Anchor embroidery floss: one skein of black 403
- tapestry needle, size 20
- crewel needle for embroidery details
- needlepoint frame
- picture frame and mount board

1 **To work** To protect your hands and clothes, and the yarn from catching on the canvas, fold masking tape evenly in half over the raw canvas edges.

2 The chart shows the complete picture actual-size. Trace the design and mark it on to a clean sheet of paper, going over it with black felt-tip pen. Tape the design flat, then tape the canvas centrally over the design. Use the felt-tip pen to draw the design onto the canvas (see Techniques, page 143). Remove the tape and mount the canvas into the frame.

3 Work the picture following the chart and key for colors of the tapestry yarns. The whole picture is worked in long satin stitch, working over a different number of canvas threads to completely fill each marked area.

4 When the needlepoint stitches are complete, embroider the smoke in backstitch using black embroidery floss. Work a French knot in black embroidery floss for each duck's eye, and use yellow/orange 8116 to work the flowers along the riverbank.

5 When the stitching is complete, remove the canvas from the frame. Press lightly on the wrong side over a damp cloth, gently pulling the canvas back into shape.

6 Frame the picture in the same way as for the Spring Picture (see page 148).

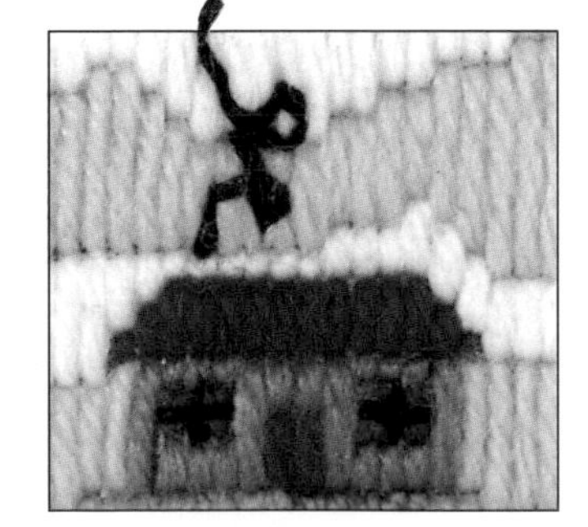

# A COUNTRY SCENE

| Key | Colour |
|---|---|
| 1 | 8000 |
| 2 | 8624 |
| 3 | 9006 |
| 4 | 8688 |
| 5 | 8792 |
| 6 | 8682 |
| 7 | 9636 |
| 8 | 8966 |
| 9 | 8988 |
| 10 | 9114 |
| 11 | 8240 |

403 Stranded cotton – Back stitch

8116 Tapisserie wool – Straight stitch

403 Stranded cotton – French knots

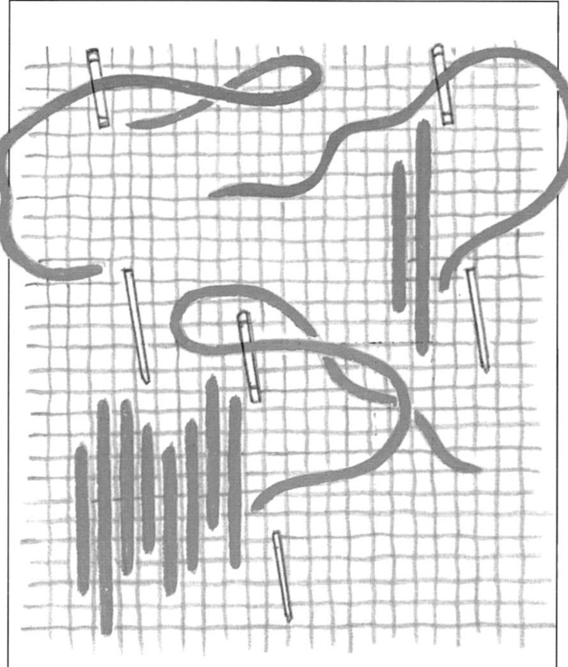

**Long stitch.** This stitch can be worked over a different number of canvas threads, depending on the area of the design. Always work in the same direction to keep an even tension.

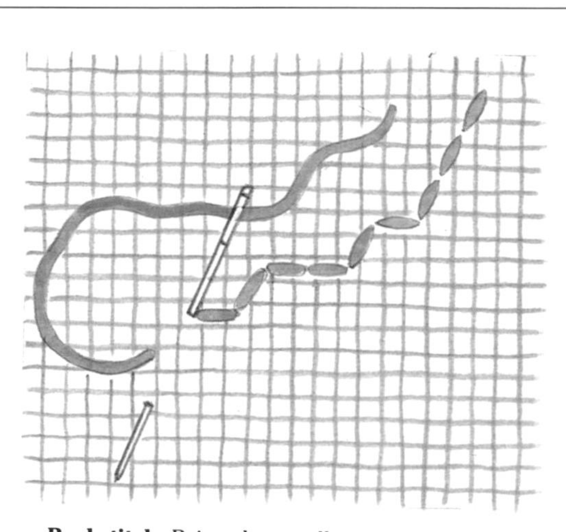

**Backstitch.** Bring the needle out of the canvas and take a backward stitch, bringing the needle out the same distance in front of the first stitch. Then go into the first hole, and out a stitch length in front. Keep repeating the same stitch.

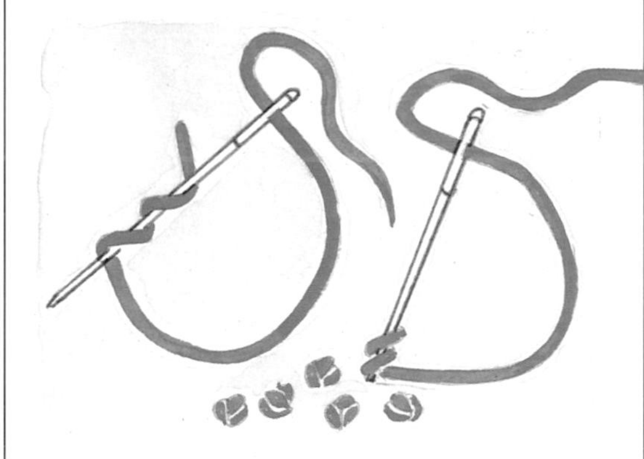

**French knots.** Bring the floss out of the canvas. Encircle the floss twice with the needle. Holding the floss firmly with the thumb twist the needle back into the canvas, close to where it first emerged.

# Ribbon Rings

*Finished size: approximately 6 inches*

*Brightly colored narrow ribbons are used to create napkin rings, being worked in Scotch stitch over a 7-gauge plastic canvas which provides a firm background.*

YOU WILL NEED
(for four rings)

- 14 x 6 inch piece of plastic canvas with 7 holes to 1 inch
- fine felt-tip pen with permanent ink
- 11 yards of ⅛ inch wide Offray Minidot ribbon in emerald
- 11 yards of ⅛ inch wide Offray Minidot ribbon in bright yellow
- tapestry needle, size 16
- 6 x 3 inch piece of felt in green and yellow
- fabric adhesive

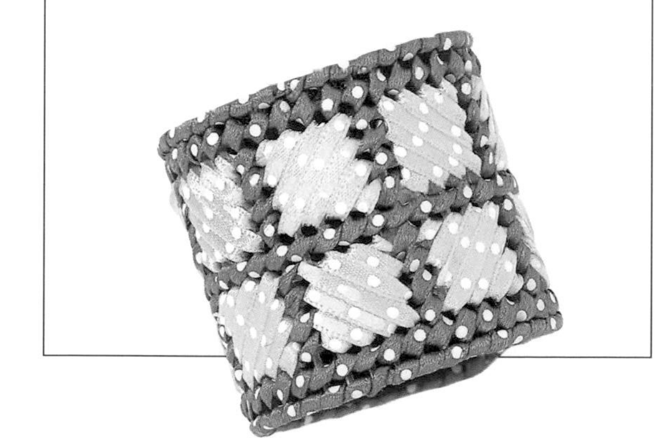

1 **To work** Each chart shows the complete design for one napkin ring. Each background square on the chart represents one hole of canvas. The design is worked throughout in Scotch stitch, but with the central straight stitches worked in opposite directions.

2 Following the chart, count out the number of holes for each ring. Use the felt-tip pen to mark out the outlines for the four rings, leaving at least two empty holes between each ring.

3 Work two rings using the green ribbon for the tent stitch (see page 150) and the yellow ribbon for the center slanted satin stitches; then work two rings in the reverse. Work each piece, following the chart and leaving the outer row of tent stitch unworked on each side edge.

4 When the needlepoint is complete, cut out each ring, leaving a margin of one unworked canvas thread all around each piece.

5 Make up each ring in the same way. Fold the canvas into a ring. Work tent stitch over the two edges to join them; fasten off the ribbon securely. Then overcast around the top and bottom of the ring in either yellow or green ribbon, being careful to cover the edges of the canvas.

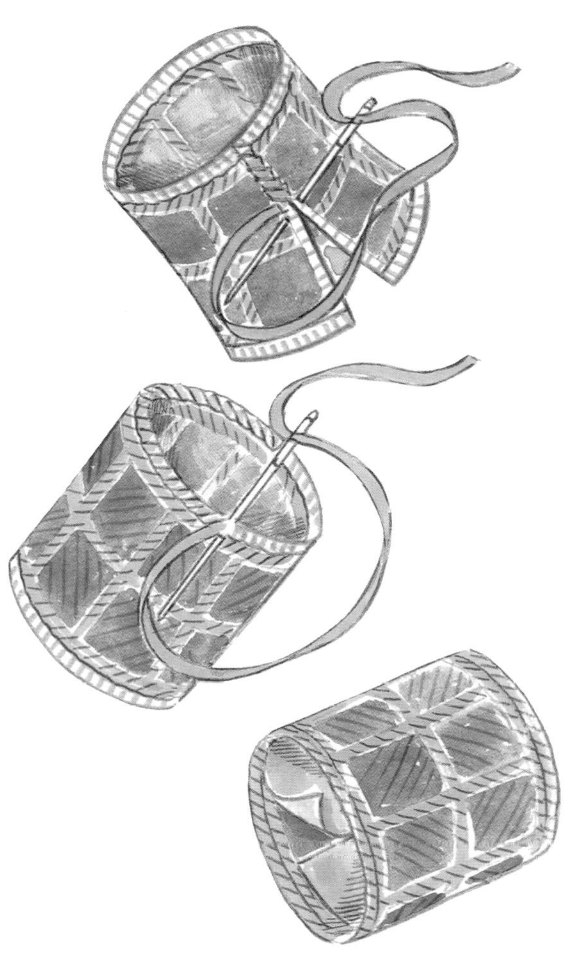

6 For each ring, cut a piece of felt 6 x 1½ inches. Using fabric adhesive, glue the felt centrally over the inside of each ring, butting edges together to neaten.

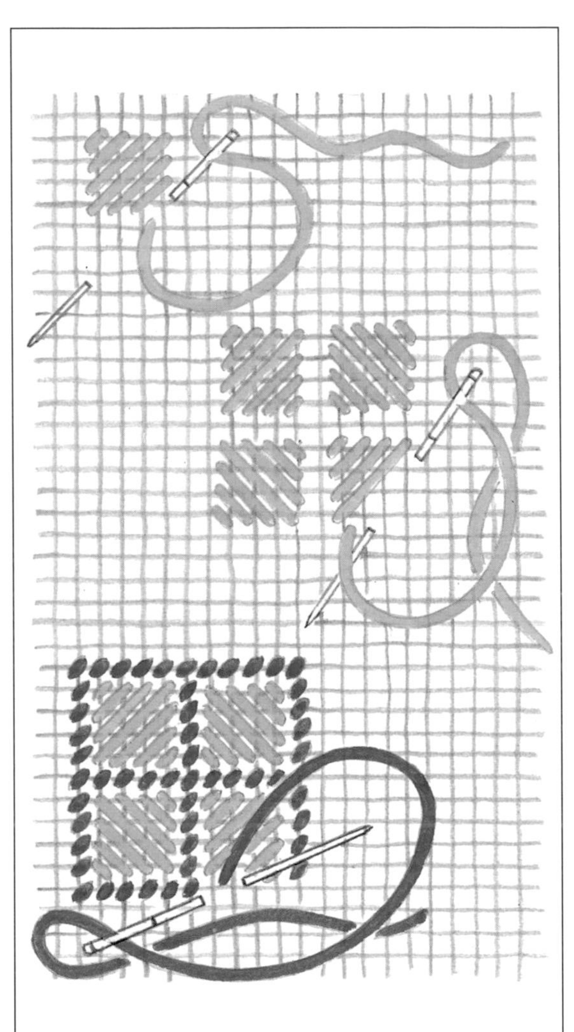

**Scotch stitch.** Work the slanted center stitches first, working over one, two, three, four, three, two, and one canvas thread. Work the next square of stitches in the opposite direction. Repeat, alternating the direction of the stitches. When the satin stitches are complete, outline the squares in tent stitch.

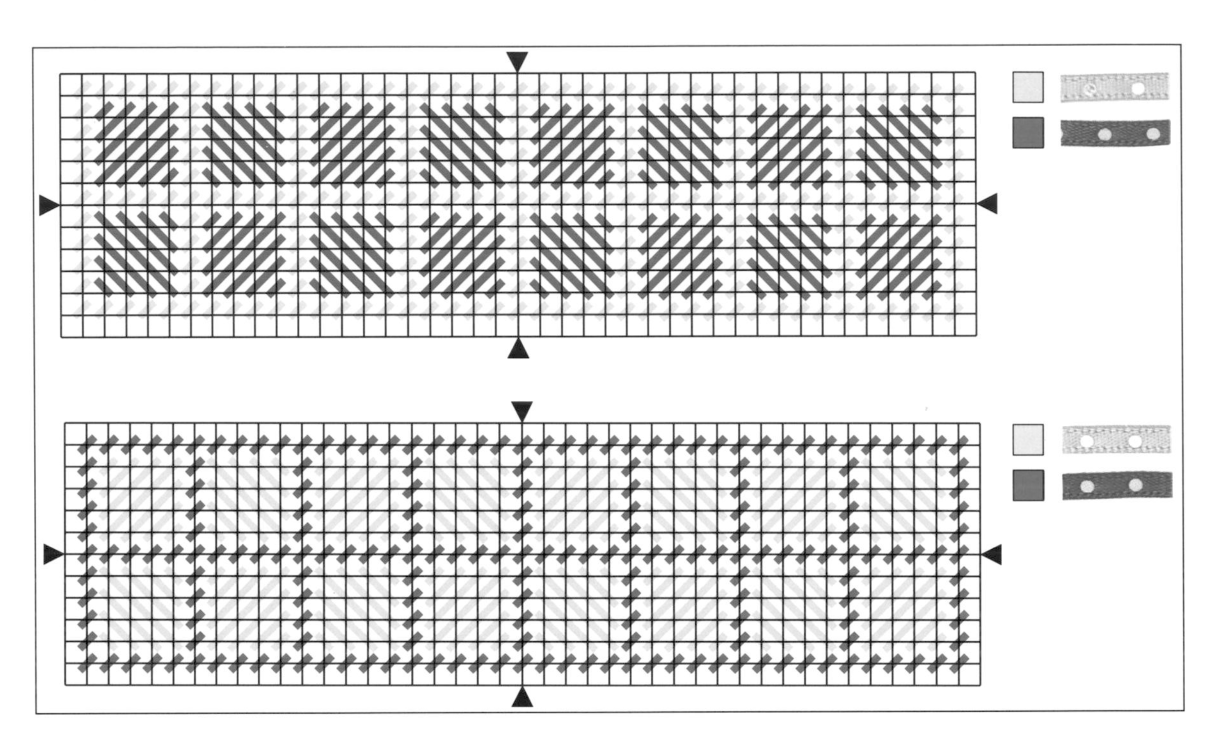

# Put Your Feet Up!

*Finished size: to fit a footstool pad 14 x 12 inches*

*Variegated yarn is used to great effect on this stool top cover – the design includes just three shades of yarn, but their changing hues provide a richness and variety of tone. The footstool cover is worked in straight Gobelin stitch over a 12-gauge canvas.*

YOU WILL NEED

- masking tape
- 21 x 19 inch piece of white mono interlock canvas with 12 holes to 1 inch
- needlepoint frame
- basting thread in contrasting color
- tapestry needle, size 18
- eight skeins of Brethyn Brith yarn in water
- six skeins of Brethyn Brith yarn in spring
- 12 skeins of Appletons yarn in mid blue 156
- footstool base with padded top 14 x 12 inches

1 **To work** To protect your hands and clothes, and prevent the yarn from catching on the canvas, fold masking tape evenly in half over the raw canvas edges.

2 Baste across the canvas both lengthwise and widthwise to mark the center.

3 Mount the canvas into the frame (see Techniques, page 142).

4 The chart shows just over one-quarter of the design. The center is marked with black arrowheads – match these up with the basting stitches on the canvas.

5 The design mirror-images vertically and horizontally along the center lines.

6 The design is worked in straight Gobelin stitch over four canvas threads, with a straight stitch to miter the blocks of stitches where they form a corner. Straight Gobelin stitch worked over two canvas threads is used to fill in, where necessary, around the edges.

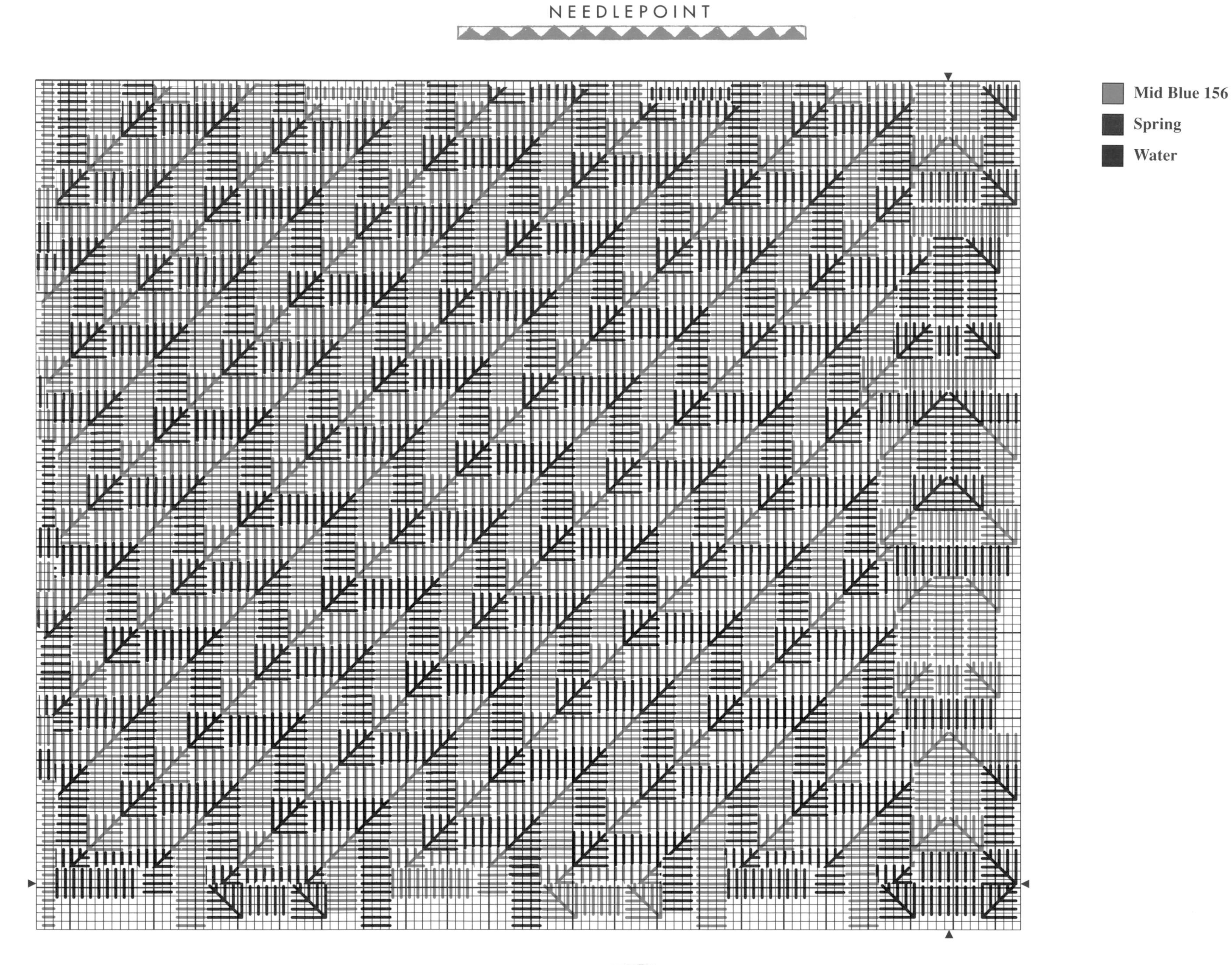
Mid Blue 156
Spring
Water

7 Work the first row out from the center, counting carefully. When this row is worked correctly, the whole pattern is set, and each row can be worked alongside the previous one. Work the rows, alternating the three yarn colors.

8 When the section shown is complete, work the remaining quarters in the same way.

9 **To finish** Remove the completed needlepoint from the frame. Peel off the masking tape and press on the wrong side over a damp cloth, gently pulling the canvas back into shape.

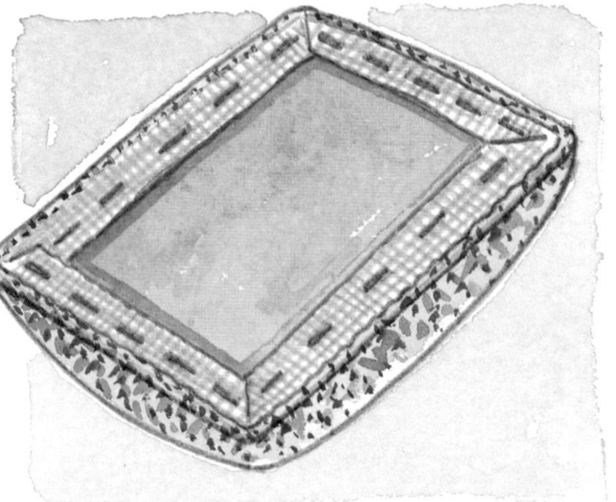

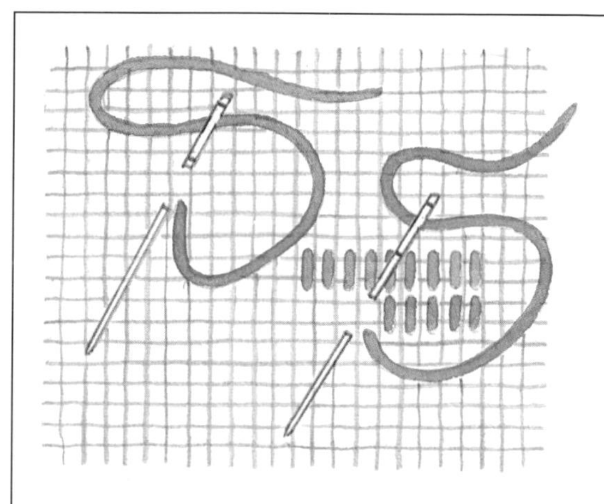

**Straight Gobelin stitch.** Bring the needle out of the canvas and insert four threads above. Bring the needle out to the left, ready for the second stitch. You can also work this stitch over two canvas threads to cover a smaller area.

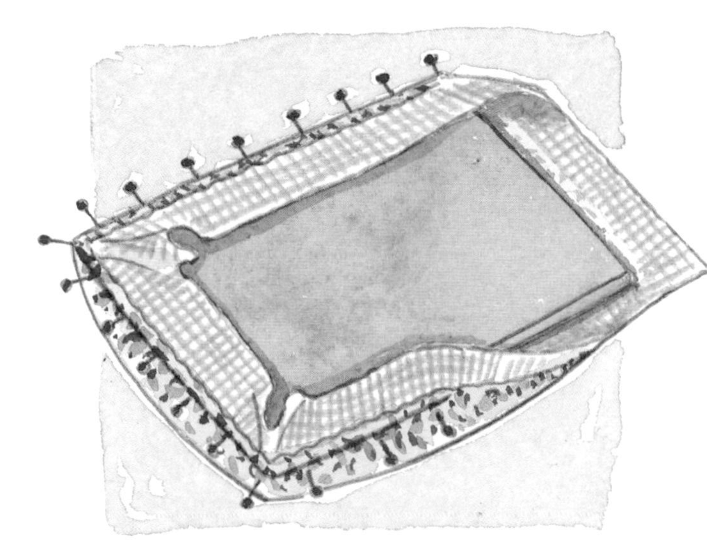

10 Remove the footstool pad from the base. Place the needlepoint centrally over the pad, and fold the surplus canvas to the back. Secure along the top edge with thumbtacks pushed into the pad. Pull the canvas taut over the opposite edge and secure with tacks in the same way. Repeat at both side edges.

11 Turn the pad over and, using a staple gun, staple the canvas firmly in place to the underside of the pad. Remove tacks and replace pad into the stool base.

# Box Clever

*Finished size: to fit a trinket box with a 3-inch lid*

*Keep all your trinkets and treasures in this pretty box, decorated with a tiny beaded pansy. Worked over a 14-gauge canvas, each stitch holds a bead offset by a stitched background of varigated embroidery floss.*

YOU WILL NEED

- 7 inch square of mono interlock canvas with 14 holes to 1 inch
- masking tape
- one packet of glass seed beads in the following colors: dark purple, mauve, crimson, dark red, and yellow
- Anchor embroidery floss in the following colors and amounts: one skein each of dark purple 102, mauve 100, dark red 45, crimson 59, yellow 291, variegated deep pink 1204
- circular wooden trinket box with 3 inch diameter lid
- tapestry needle, size 20
- crewel needle, size 10
- fine-point, black felt-tip pen with permanent ink
- needlepoint frame

1 **To work** To protect your hands and clothes, and the canvas from unraveling, fold the masking tape evenly in half over the raw canvas edges.

2 Trace the actual-size pansy onto a clean sheet of paper. Go over the outline with black felt-tip pen.

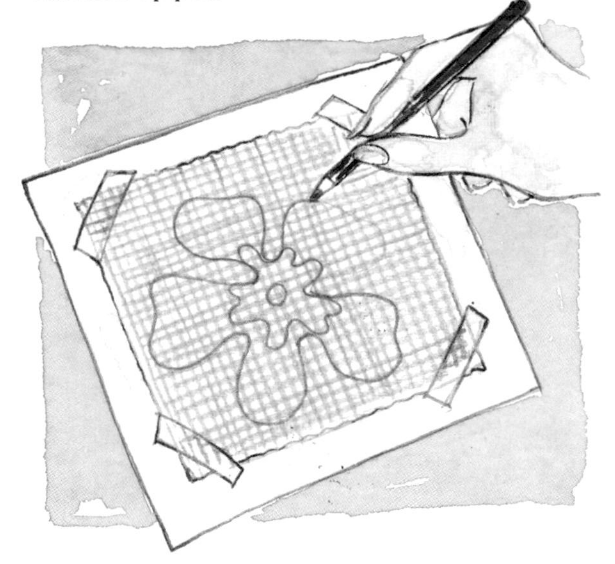

3 Tape the paper flat, then tape the canvas centrally over the design. Draw the design onto the canvas using the felt-tip pen.

4 Mount the canvas into the frame (see Techniques, page 142).

5 Work the pansy, following the actual-size motif and key. Work the beaded areas in tent stitch using two strands of embroidery floss in the crewel needle. Attach one bead with each stitch.

6 Stitch all the background in half cross stitch, using six strands of embroidery floss in the needle. Work the background up to the circular outline.

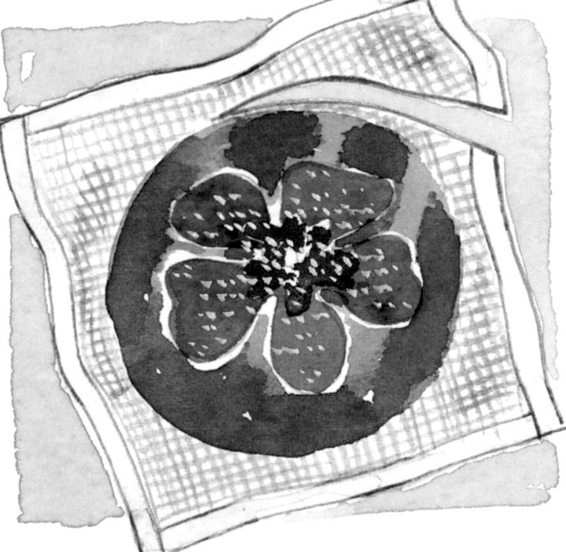

7 When the needlepoint is complete, carefully cut it out around the circular outline and fit inside the box lid, following the manufacturer's instructions.

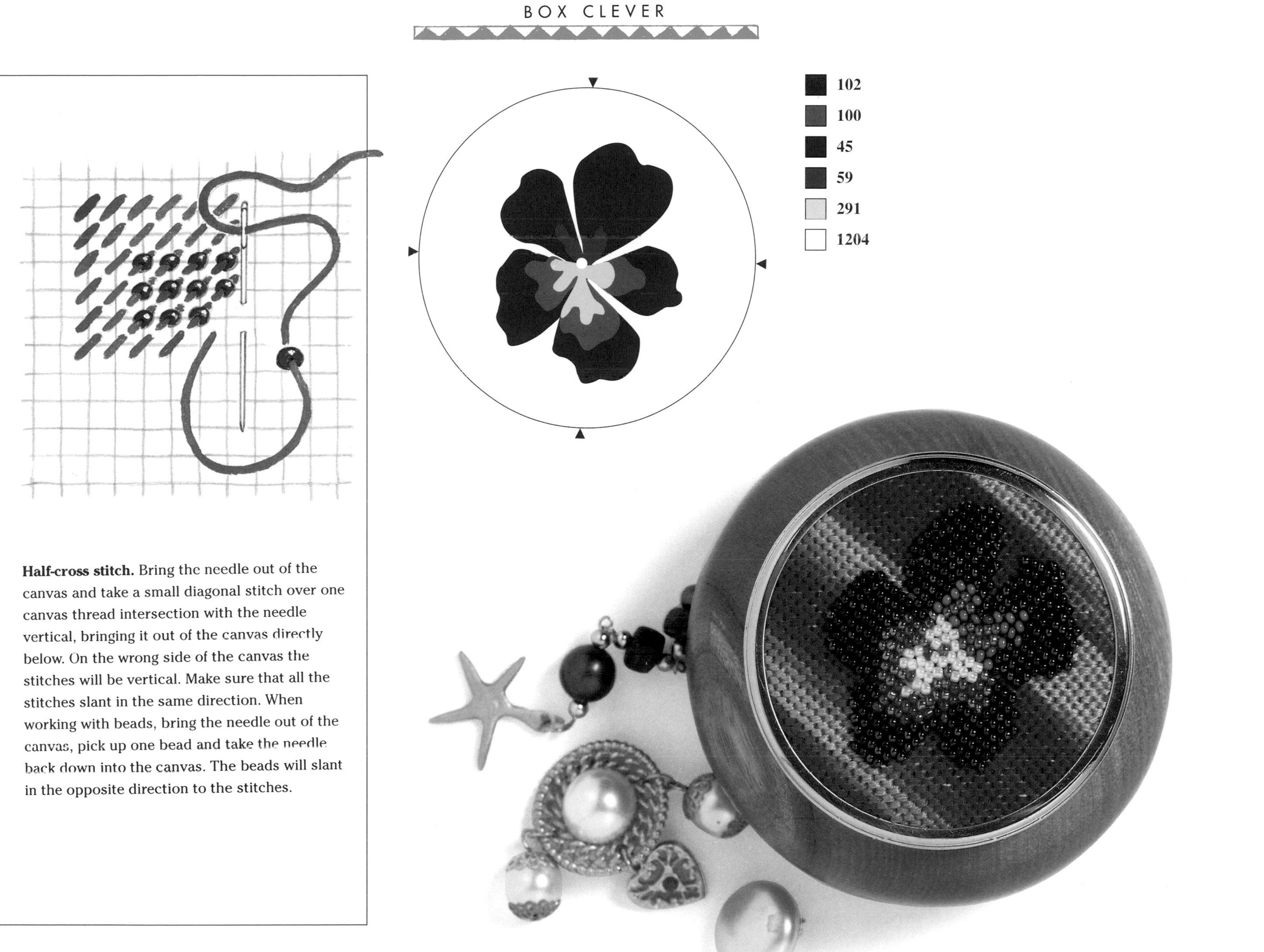


**Half-cross stitch.** Bring the needle out of the canvas and take a small diagonal stitch over one canvas thread intersection with the needle vertical, bringing it out of the canvas directly below. On the wrong side of the canvas the stitches will be vertical. Make sure that all the stitches slant in the same direction. When working with beads, bring the needle out of the canvas, pick up one bead and take the needle back down into the canvas. The beads will slant in the opposite direction to the stitches.

# Be Mine

*Finished size: approximately 14 inch square*

*This unusual pillow is worked in a variety of stitches over a 10-gauge canvas. Each square is worked in a different stitch and outlined in tent stitch, and tassels at each corner of the pillow are the perfect finish.*

YOU WILL NEED

- 18 inch square of white mono canvas with 10 threads to 1 inch
- masking tape
- basting thread in contrasting color
- tapestry needle, size 18
- needlepoint frame
- DMC tapestry yarns in the following colors and amounts: seven skeins of blue 7318, five skeins each of pink 7804 and blue 7319, four skeins each of blue 7314 and white, three skeins of pink 7708, two skeins of pink 7600, and one skein of yellow 7726
- 16 inch square of fabric for backing
- matching sewing thread
- 12 inch zipper
- 14 inch square pillow form
- 1¾ yard of cord
- four tassels, or four skeins of DMC tapestry yarn in blue 7318

1 **To work** To protect your hands and clothes, and the yarn from catching on the canvas edges, fold masking tape evenly in half over the raw canvas edges.

2 Baste lengthwise and widthwise across the canvas, using a contrasting sewing thread, to mark the center (see Techniques, page 142).

3 The chart shows the complete design for the pillow. The center is marked by black arrowheads, which must match up with the basting stitches on the canvas. Each background square on the chart represents one hole of canvas.

4 From the center, count out the holes and mark the squares that make up the design.

5 Fit the canvas into the frame (see Techniques, page 142).

6 The design is worked in a variety of needlepoint stitches. Work the design, following the chart for the stitches and the key for the yarn colors. Begin by working the central heart and square in velvet and diagonal mosaic stitch, then outline each of the remaining squares with a row of tent stitches (see page 150).

7 Fill in each square with the appropriate needlepoint stitch. In some cases, the stitch, then outline each of the remaining squares with a row of tent stitches (see page 150).

8 When the design is complete, remove the canvas from the frame. Peel off the masking tape. Press gently on the wrong side over a damp cloth, gently pulling the canvas back into shape (see Techniques, page 145).

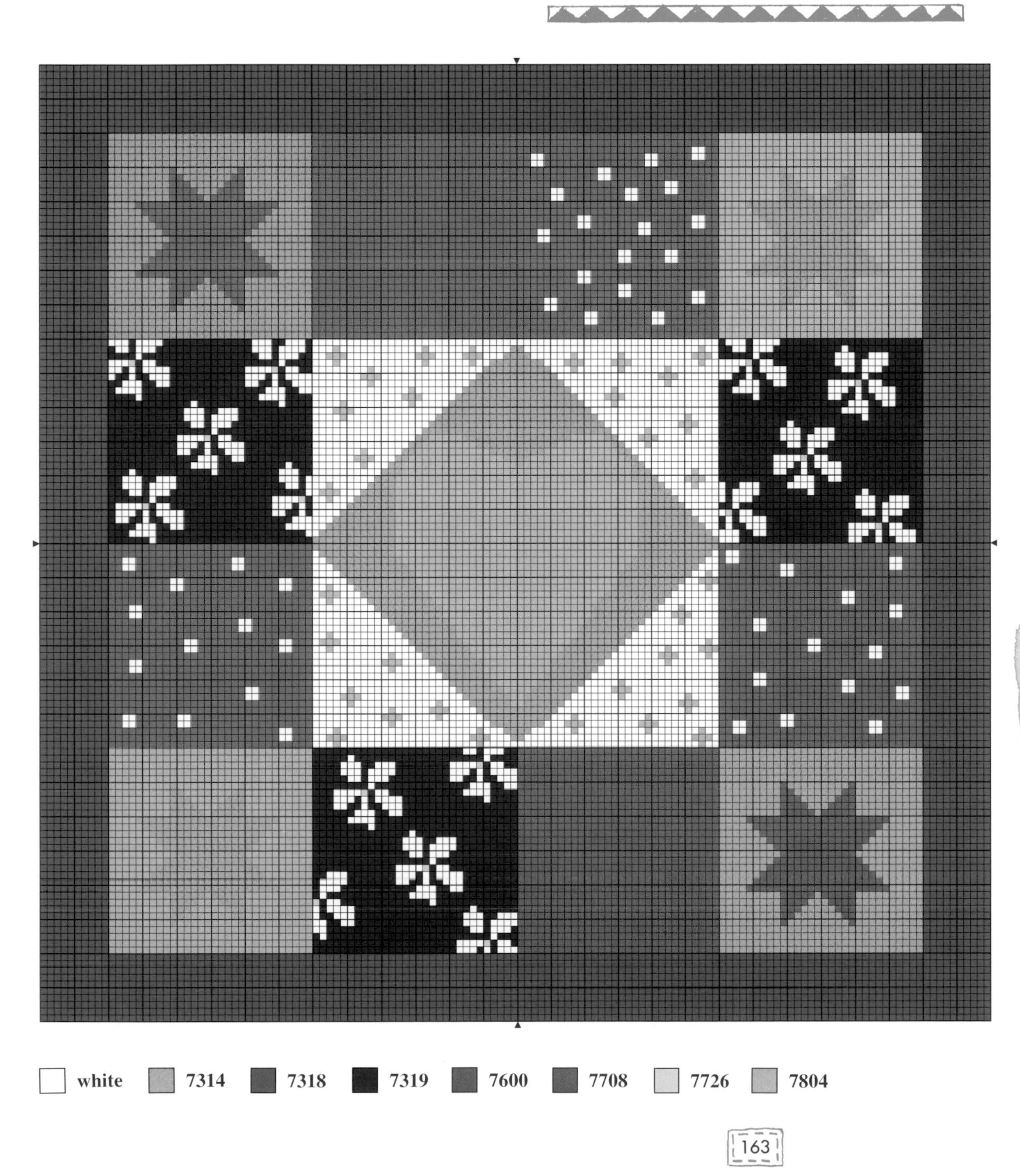


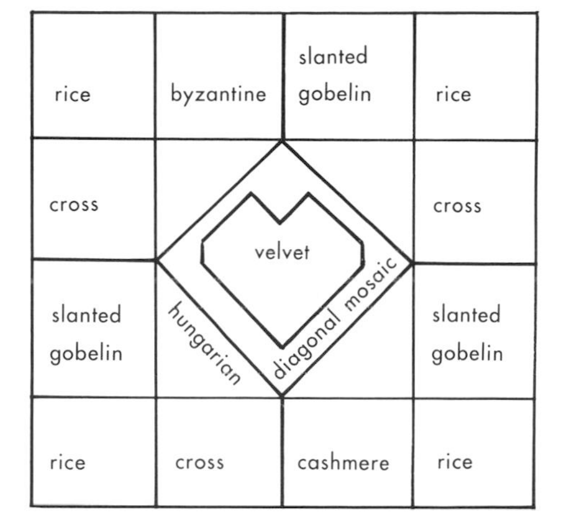


**9** For the back, cut two pieces of fabric, 15 x 8¼ inches. Place right sides together, and pin and baste across the center. Stitch in from each side, leaving a 12 inch central opening; press seam open.

**10** Place zipper, face down, over the basted seam; pin and baste. Turn fabric over and, with a zipper foot on the machine, stitch around zipper; partially open zipper.

**11** Place back and front right sides together; pin and stitch all around. Trim, and turn right side out through zipper. Insert pillow form and close zipper.

**12** Handsew cord around outer edge, slotting ends neatly into seam. Add tassels. To make tassels, cut two short lengths of yarn; tie one around a skein 1¼ inch from top. Slot second length through top loop and tie. Remove skein bands. Trim tassel to 5½ inches.

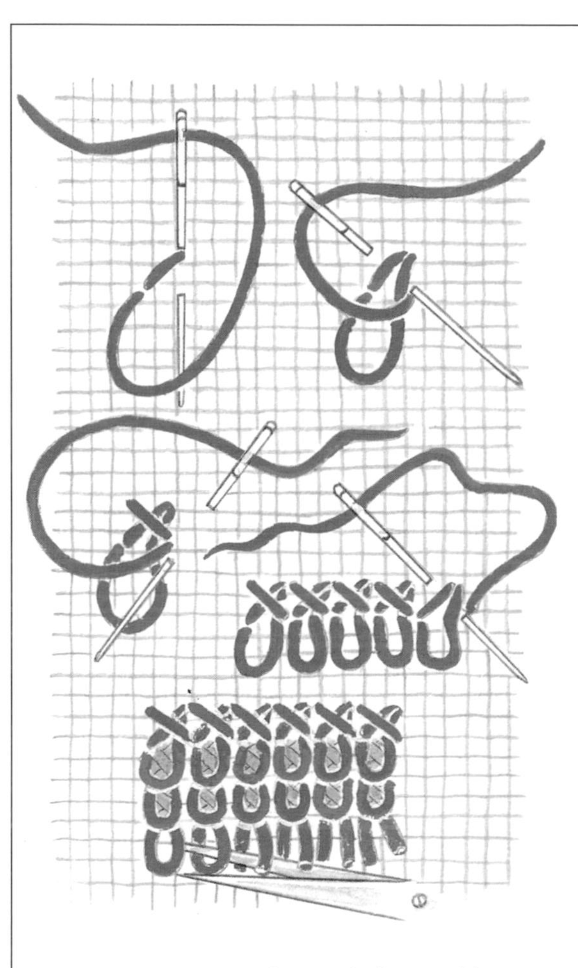

**Velvet stitch.** This stitch is worked upward from left to right. Bring the needle out of the canvas, and insert two threads up and two threads to the right. Bring the needle out again at the first hole and hold down a loop of yarn while taking a vertical stitch. Take the final stitch over the canvas, forming a cross with the first stitch. When the rows are complete, cut and trim the loops.

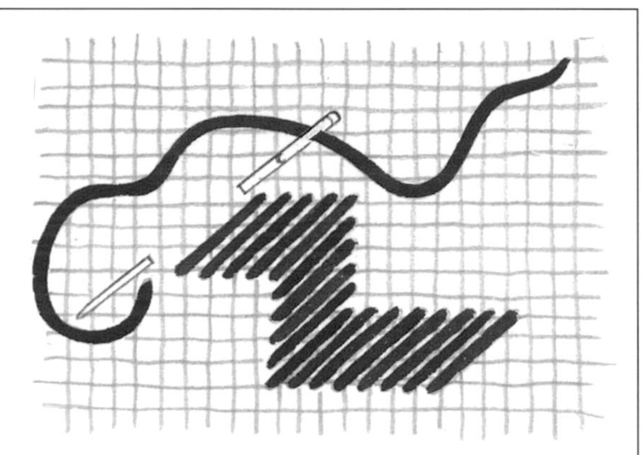

**Byzantine stitch.** Work satin stitches diagonally over four vertical and four horizontal canvas threads. This creates a woven, step effect.

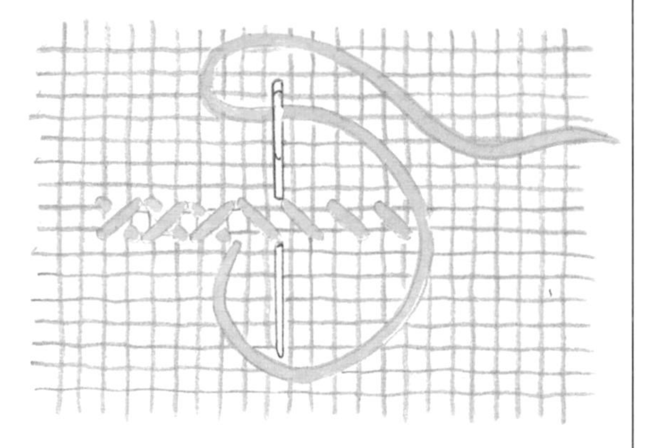

**Cross stitch.** Bring the needle out of the canvas and take a stitch two threads to the left and two threads up to form the half cross. Complete the crosses working in the opposite direction.

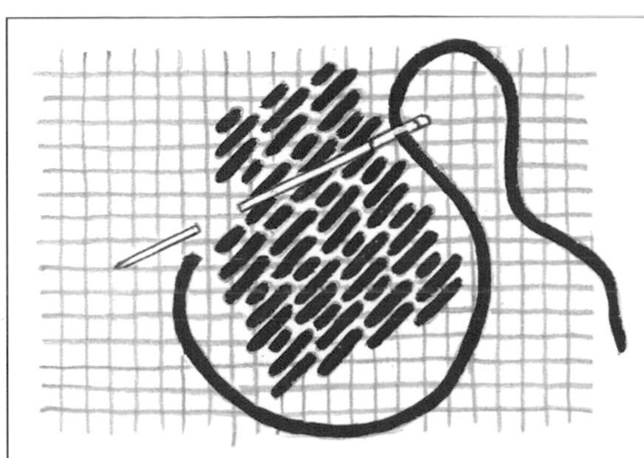

**Cashmere stitch.** Work diagonal stitches in sequence over one, two, and two canvas intersections, with the lower end of each stitch falling exactly beneath the other and with each set of three stitches moving one thread to the right each time when working diagonally downward. When working upward from right to left, move the three stitches one thread to the left.

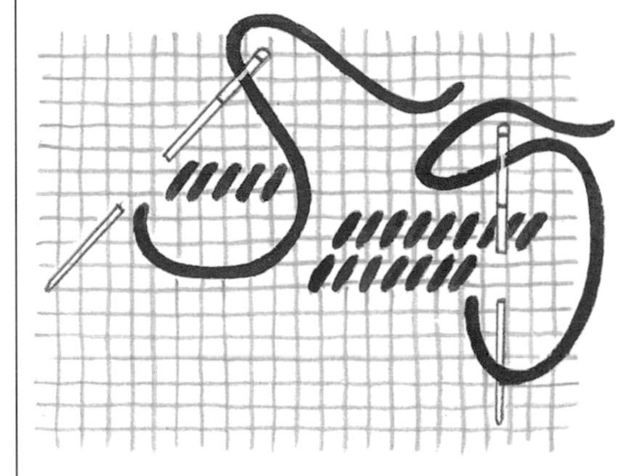

**Slanted Gobelin.** This stitch can be worked from right to left, or from left to right. Work each stitch over two horizontal and one vertical canvas threads.

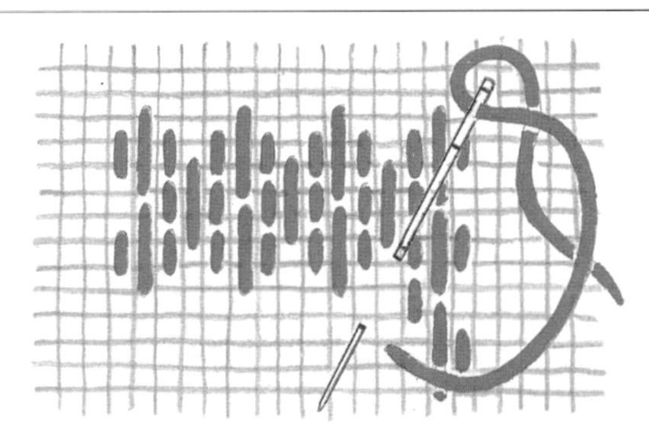

**Hungarian stitch.** This stitch can be worked in one or two different colors. Take vertical straight stitches over two, four, and two horizontal threads of canvas, leaving two vertical threads between each group of stitches. Fit each row alternately into the preceding row.

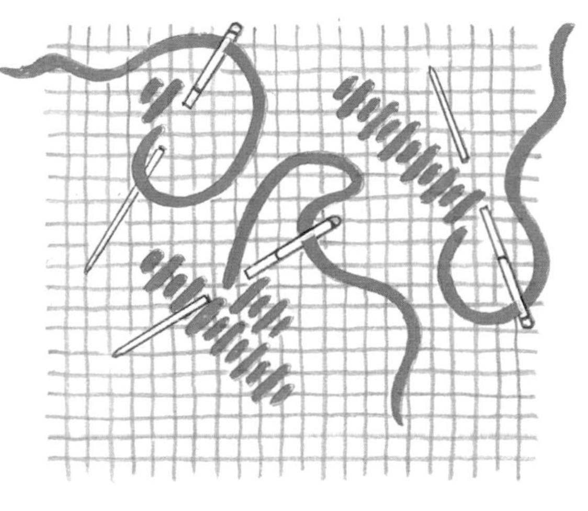

**Diagonal Mosaic stitch.** Work down the canvas from left to right, and then up again. Work over one, two, and one canvas thread. Fit the next row so the short stitches are next to the long stitches.

**Rice stitch.** First cover the area with cross stitch, worked over four canvas threads. Then work a small diagonal stitch over each corner of the cross stitch over two canvas threads.

# MAGIC CARPET

*Finished size: 39½ x 28 inches*

*Turn fabric strips into a woven carpet by working Parisian stitch over a rug canvas. The alternating rows of two cotton fabrics will create an attractive, hardwearing rug.*

YOU WILL NEED

- 4½ yards of 45 inch wide cotton fabric, such as Madras, in two different designs
- rotary cutter
- 46 x 28 inch piece of rug canvas with 3⅓ holes to 1 inch
- bodkin needle
- 3¾ yards of ¼ inch piping cord

1 **To work** To prepare the fabric strips, cut out 1⅜ inch wide strips from across the fabric.

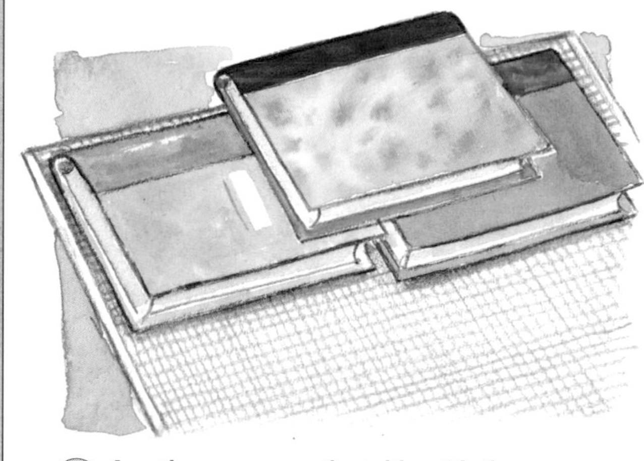

2 Lay the canvas on the table with the selvages on either side. Place a heavy object on the canvas end to prevent it slipping.

3 Count up the first eight rows; fold the canvas along the eighth row to the right side. Leaving two holes free, work the first few rows through both thicknesses of canvas.

4 Work each row in Parisian stitch, but take the long stitches over eight threads and the short stitches over four threads of canvas. Alternate the two fabrics, row by row.

5 Neaten all the fabric ends by running them through a few stitches on the wrong side when beginning a new length or ending a length of fabric.

6 Work across the canvas until you reach the last 16 rows, then turn the canvas up and work the final rows through double canvas, in the same way as before.

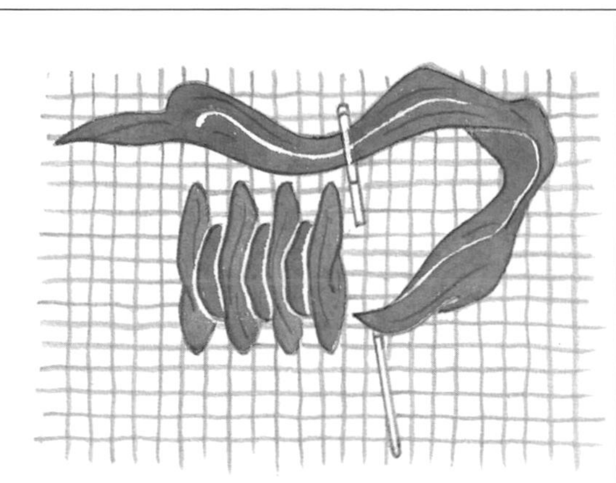

**Parisian stitch.** Working from left to right, bring the fabric through the canvas and insert the needle eight threads above, bringing the needle out six threads down and one thread to the right. To make the short stitches, insert the needle four threads up and come out six threads down and one thread to the right, ready for the next long stitch.

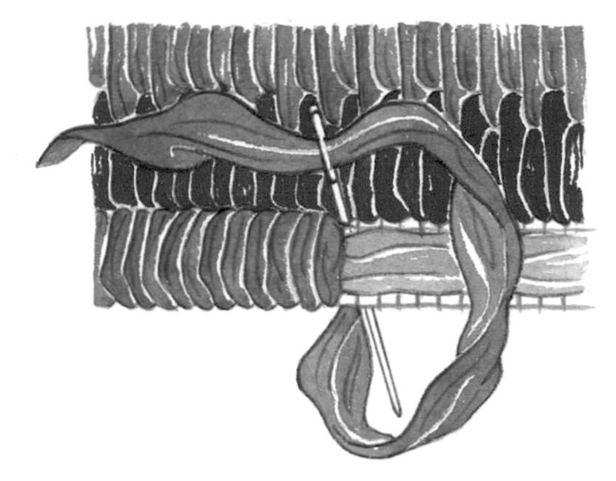

7 To neaten the edge, fold piping cord inside a fabric strip and lay along outer edge of rug. Overcast over the piping, turning under raw edge of strip and overlapping the stitches.

# FLORENTINE NEEDLECASE

*Finished size: 4¾ x 3½ inches*

*Worked in traditional Florentine stitch, this pretty needlecase will be a bonus for any sewing kit. Use stranded yarn and work over a 12-gauge canvas, then add felt leaves and complete with a twisted yarn edge.*

YOU WILL NEED

- 10 x 8½ inch piece of mono canvas with 12 holes to 1 inch
- masking tape
- basting thread in contrasting color
- tapestry needle, size 18
- needlepoint frame
- Paternayan Persian yarn in the following colors and amounts: one skein each of dark pink 350, medium pink 353, pale pink 354, and yellow 772
- 8 x 6 inch piece of cotton fabric for lining
- sewing thread to match lining fabric
- 5½ x 4¾ inch piece of pink felt
- 5 x 4¼ inch piece of yellow felt
- pinking shears

1 **To work** To protect your hands and clothes, and the yarn from catching on the canvas edges, fold masking tape evenly in half over the raw canvas edges.

2 Baste both lengthwise and widthwise across the canvas, using a contrasting sewing thread, to mark the center (see Techniques, page 142). Now mark the outline of the needlecase, 6½ x 4¾ inches, on to the canvas.

3 Mount the canvas into the frame (see Techniques, page 142).

4 The chart shows the rows of Florentine stitch that are worked in rows across the needlecase. The center is marked with black arrowheads, which must match the basting stitches on the canvas. Each background square on the chart represents one hole of canvas. Repeat the rows, working the colors in order.

5 Work the first row across the center of the canvas using dark pink 350 to set the pattern, working each stitch over four canvas threads. Then work each row in the same way above and below the first row, working the rows in color order, until the whole area is filled. At the side edges, some stitches will have to be shortened to fill the gaps.

6 When the needlepoint is complete, remove it from the frame. Peel off the masking tape and press lightly on the wrong side over a damp cloth, gently pulling the canvas back into shape.

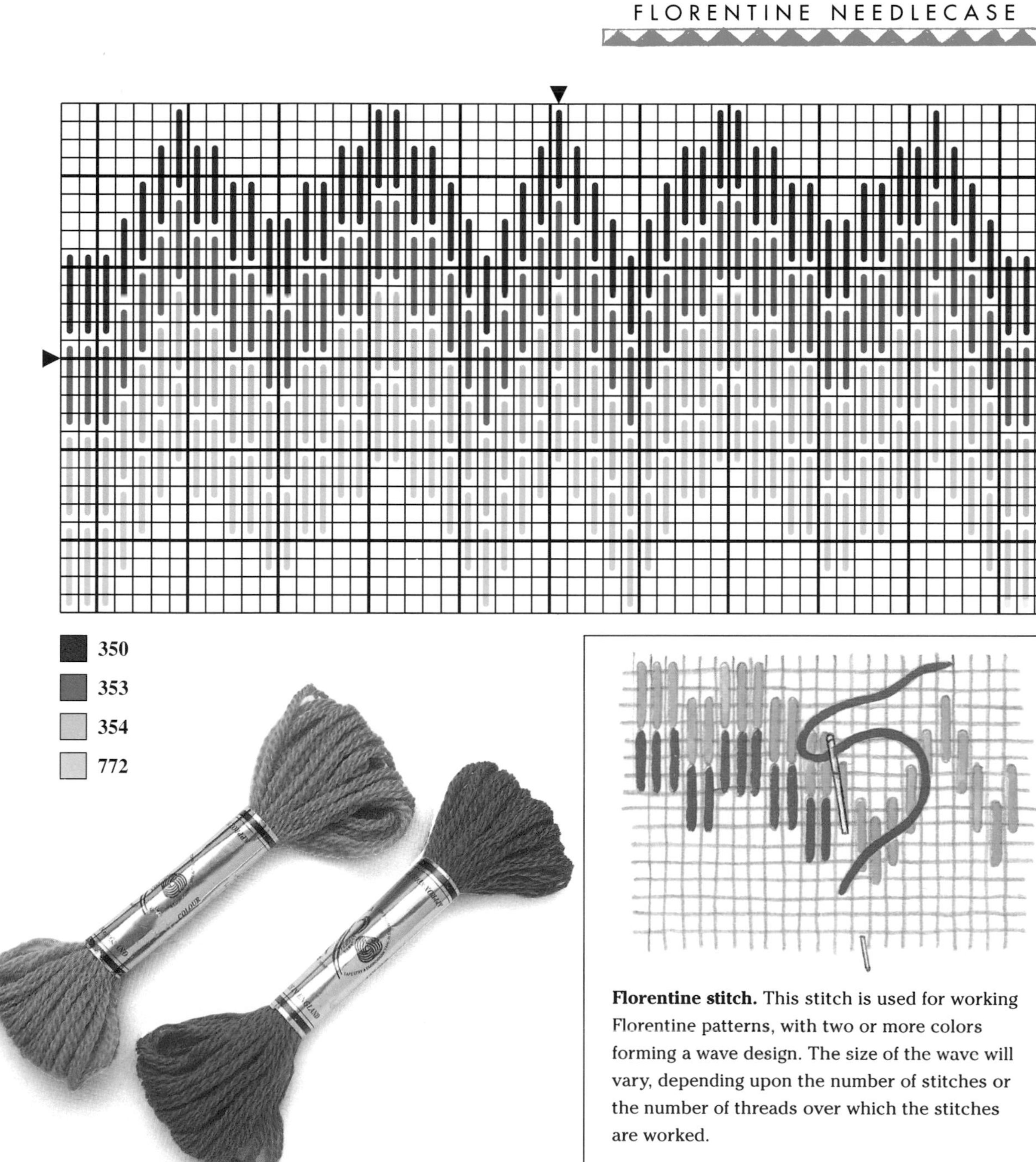


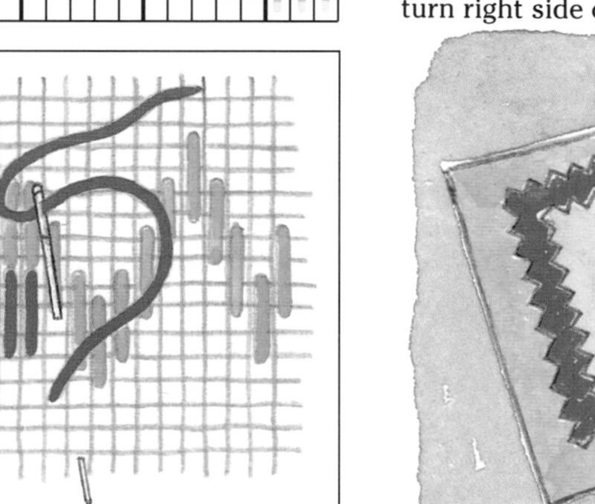

**Florentine stitch.** This stitch is used for working Florentine patterns, with two or more colors forming a wave design. The size of the wave will vary, depending upon the number of stitches or the number of threads over which the stitches are worked.

7 Place the canvas onto the lining with right sides facing; pin and stitch against the stitched area all around, leaving an opening in one side. Trim off corners and across seams, and turn right side out. Close opening; press again.

8 Using pinking shears, trim the two pieces of felt for the inner leaves. Lay the leaves centrally, one on top of the other, and position centrally onto the lining side of the needlecase. Handsew the leaves in place by stitching down the center.

**9** Measure around the outer edge of needlecase. Cut six strands each of pink 350 and yellow 772 to three times this length. Tie ends together. Slot one end over a door handle. Slide a pencil into opposite loop. Keep turning the pencil to twist the yarn. When tightly twisted, remove from handle and hold ends together while yarn twists together to form a cord. Handsew around case, neatening the ends.

# FABULOUS FLORALS

*Finished size: approximately 28½ x 4¾ inches*

YOU WILL NEED
(for one pair of tiebacks)

- 20 x 40 inch piece of white mono interlock canvas with 12 holes to 1 inch
- masking tape
- basting thread in contrasting color
- tapestry needle, size 20
- DMC tapestry yarn in the following colors: 22 skeins of ecru, four skeins each of dusky pink 7204, dark dusky pink 7205, pale rose 7132, medium rose 7760, dark rose 7759, pale green 7369, gray/green 7394, olive green 7396, dark olive green 7398, three skeins each of crimson 7212, deep rose 7758, yellow ochre 7504, two skeins each of mid crimson 7210, sea green 7326, dark sea green 7327, yellow/brown 7505, brown 7508, mauve 7896, deep purple 7228, one skein of gray/blue 7323, and deep mauve 7255
- needlepoint frame
- 32 x 16 inch piece of cotton fabric for lining
- 30 x 11 inch piece of interfacing
- 4½ yards of corded piping
- sewing thread to match lining fabric
- four ½ inch diameter curtain rings

*Hold back your curtains in style with this pretty flower-strewn tieback. Worked in tapestry yarn over a 12-gauge canvas, this beautiful addition to your home furnishings will last a lifetime.*

1 **To work** To protect your hands and clothes, and the yarn from catching on the edge, fold masking tape evenly in half over the raw canvas edges.

2 Baste both lengthwise and widthwise across the canvas, using a contrasting thread, to mark the center (see Techniques, page 142). Both tiebacks can be worked one above the other, with a gap of about 2¾ inches between them.

3 Mount the canvas into the frame (see Techniques, page 142).

4 The chart shows the right-hand side of one tieback with the center marked by black arrowheads, which must match up with the basting threads on the canvas. Each background square on the chart represents one tent stitch worked over one intersection of canvas. To complete the left-hand side of the tieback, reverse the section shown, and work from the center outward.

5 Work the design throughout in tent stitch, following the chart and key for colors. Begin by stitching the flowers, leaves, and other motifs across the whole tieback, then fill in the background in ecru.

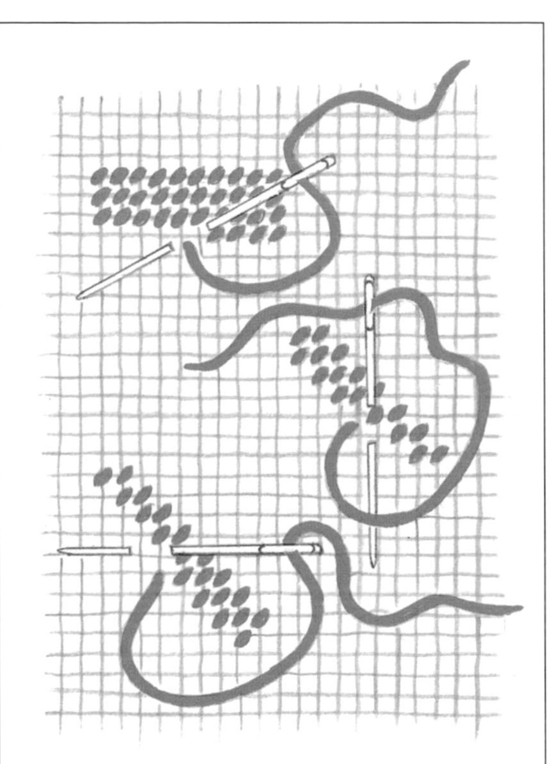

**Tent stitch.** To work horizontal rows, bring the needle out of the canvas and take a small diagonal stitch over one canvas thread intersection. Take the needle down diagonally, behind one horizontal and two vertical threads, then bring it out, ready for the next stitch. On the wrong side, the stitches will be slightly longer diagonal stitches.

To work diagonally down the canvas, take the needle diagonally up over one canvas thread intersection, then pass it vertically down behind two horizontal canvas threads.

To work diagonally up the canvas, the stitches are worked in the same way, but the needle is passed horizontally behind two vertical threads.

6 When the needlepoint is complete, remove it from the frame. Peel off the masking tape and press on the wrong side over a damp cloth, gently pulling the canvas back into shape.

7 Cut out each needlepoint piece, leaving a ⅝ inch border all around. Use the needlepoint as a pattern to cut one piece from the lining and one piece from the interfacing to the same size.

8 Place the interfacing onto the wrong side of needlepoint, catchstitching together around the outside edge. Pin the piping around needlepoint, on the right side, with the piping facing inward and edges matching. Join ends together to fit.

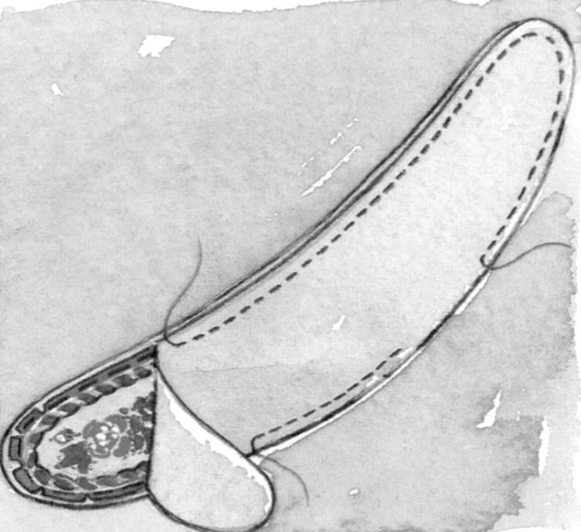

9 Place lining fabric onto the needlepoint with right sides facing; pin and stitch against the needlepoint all around, leaving an opening in one side. Trim, and turn right side out. Turn in opening edges and slipstitch to close.

10 Handsew a curtain ring to both ends of the tieback.

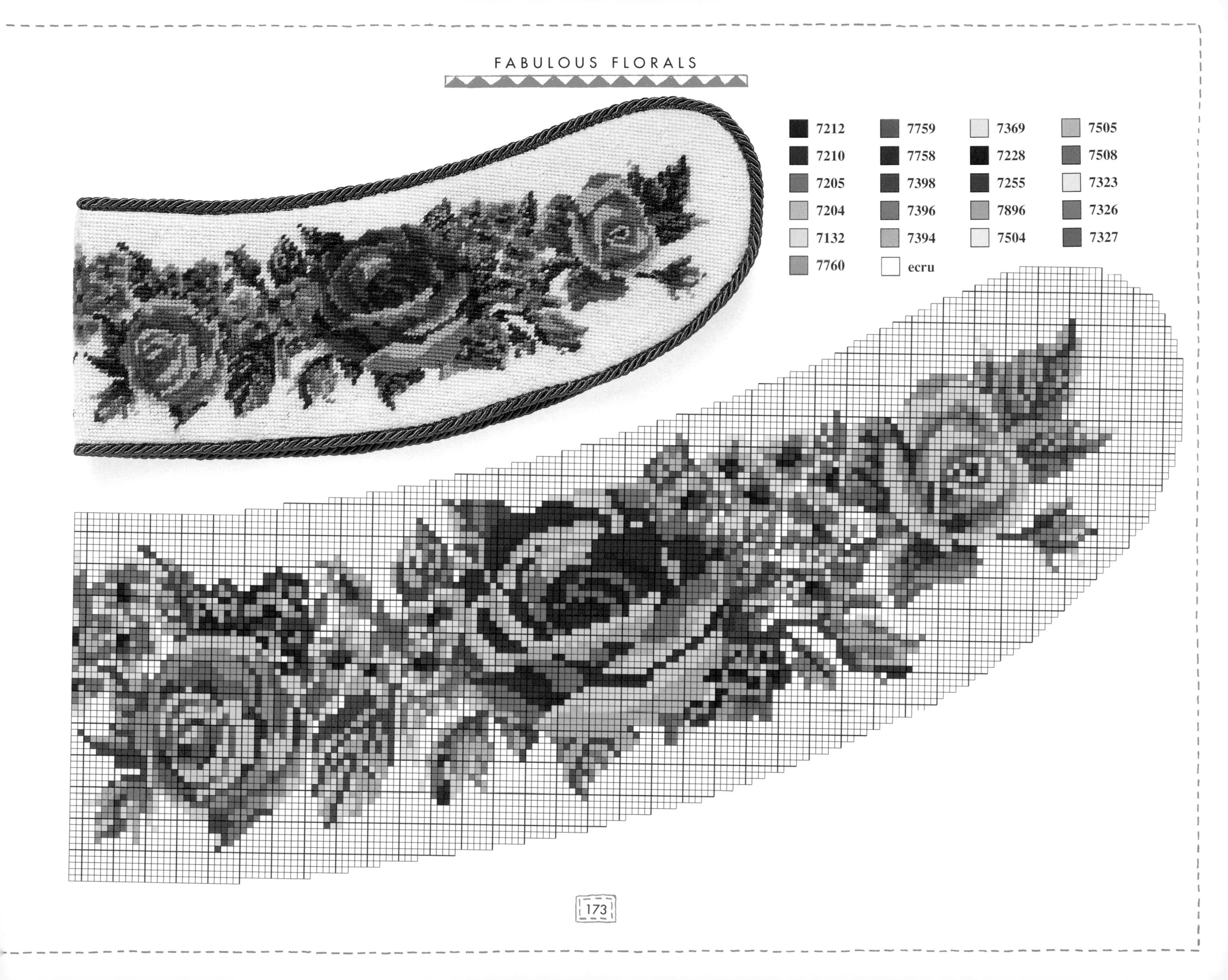
7212
7210
7205
7204
7132
7760
7759
7758
7398
7396
7394
ecru
7369
7228
7255
7896
7504
7505
7508
7323
7326
7327

# Belt and Buttons

*Finished size: Belt: 25 x 1½ inches Buttons: 1¼ inch diameter*

*Stitch a matching pair of stylish self-covered buttons and belt for a child. Worked in pearl cotton in cross-cornered cushion stitch, choose colors to suit the outfit.*

YOU WILL NEED

- belt: 29 x 5½ inch piece of white mono interlock canvas with 14 holes to 1 inch
- buttons: 8½ inch square of white mono interlock canvas with 14 holes to 1 inch
- masking tape
- DMC pearl cotton no 5 in the following colors and amounts: two skeins of navy 939, one skein each of green 502, orange 742, mauve 208, red 321, pink 893, and blue 792
- tapestry needle, size 20
- needlepoint frame
- 26 x 2¾ inch piece of navy blue cotton fabric
- 25 x 1½ inch piece of medium-weight fusible interfacing
- basting thread
- three hook and eye fasteners
- Self-covering buttons, 1¼ inch in diameter

1 **To work the belt** To prevent the canvas edges from unraveling, and to protect your hands and clothes, fold masking tape evenly in half over the raw canvas edges.

2 Mount the canvas into the frame (see Techniques, page 142).

3 The chart shows a section of the design, which is repeated across the canvas. Each square on the chart represents one hole of canvas.

4 Beginning 2 inches in from one short edge, work an outline of tent stitch (see page 150) centrally across the canvas in navy 939, following the chart.

5 Fill in the spaces with cross-cornered cushion stitch, using the remaining six colored embroidery threads randomly.

6 To complete the belt, work a row of plaited stitch all around the outer edge in navy 939.

7 **To finish** Remove the completed needlepoint from the frame. Peel off the masking tape from the canvas edges. Press the needlepoint on the wrong side over a damp cloth, gently pulling the canvas back into shape.

8 Turn in all edges along the line of the needlepoint, and press. Trim raw canvas edges, as necessary.

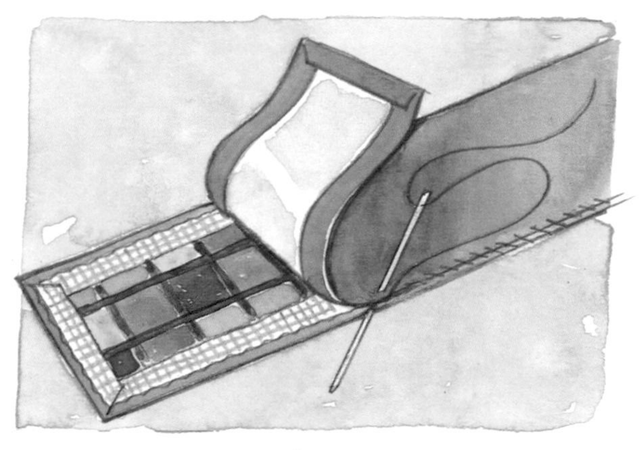

9 Fuse the interfacing centrally to wrong side of fabric strip. Turn in raw edges of fabric strip for ⅜ inch. Place strip to needlepoint belt with wrong sides facing. Slipstitch the fabric to the needlepoint all around the outer edge.

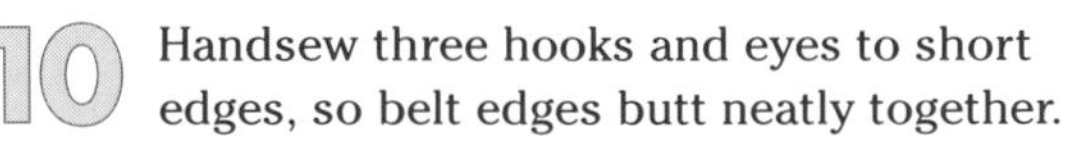

10 Handsew three hooks and eyes to short edges, so belt edges butt neatly together.

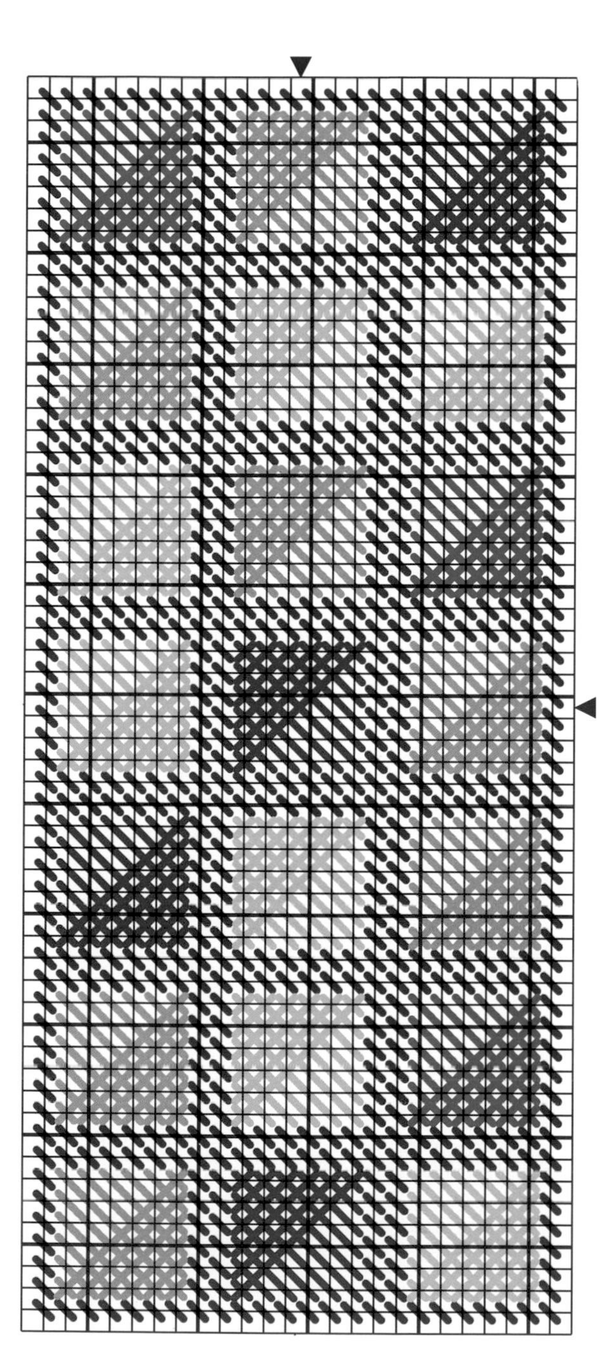

| | | | | | | | |
|---|---|---|---|---|---|---|---|
| | 792 | | 742 | | 321 | | 939 |
| | 502 | | 208 | | 893 | | |

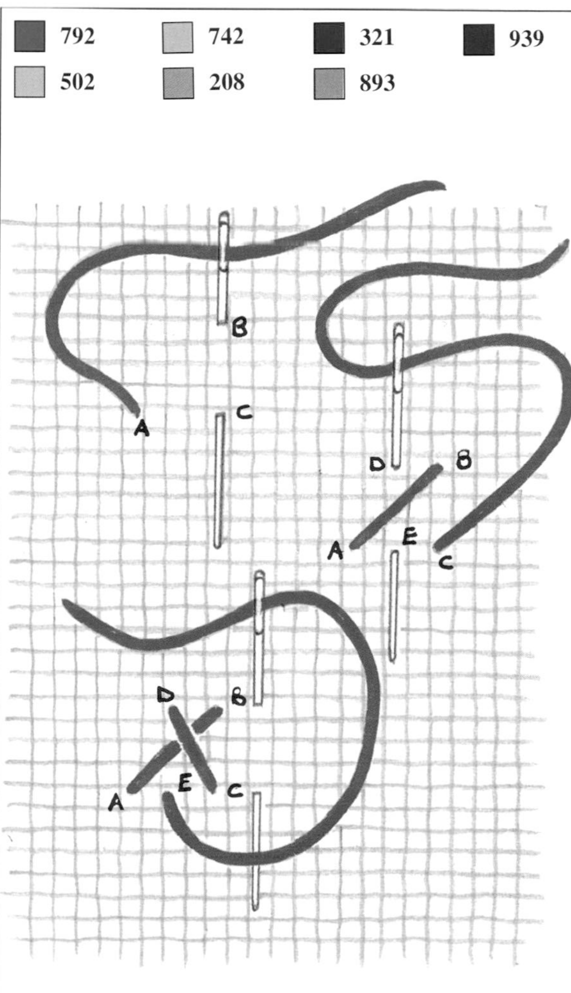


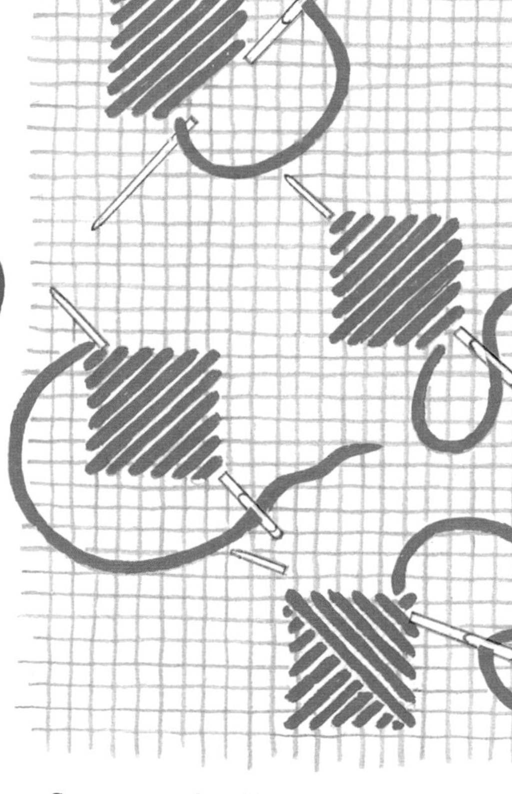

**Plaited stitch.** Bring the needle out of the canvas (A) and insert four threads to the right and four threads up (B), coming out of the canvas directly below (C), forming a diagonal stitch. Insert the needle at (D), four threads up and two threads left, bringing the needle out directly below (E). Keep working in the same way across the canvas.

**Cross-cornered cushion stitch.** The stitch is worked over six vertical and six horizontal canvas threads. Begin at one corner of the square, and work over one, two, three, four, five, six, five, four, three, two, and one canvas thread intersections to cover the square. Then bring the needle up at the opposite corner, and work diagonal stitches across half the square again, working in the opposite direction. The squares can be arranged together in different ways to form a further pattern.

**11** **Buttons** Divide the canvas equally into four with contrasting thread. Work one four-square pattern in the center of each canvas section, working with random colors, in the same way as for the belt.

**12** Cut out and fit the canvas into a button mold, following the manufacturers' instructions.